MULTICULTURAL NEEDS ASSESSMENT FOR COLLEGE AND UNIVERSITY STUDENT POPULATIONS

MULTICULTURAL NEEDS ASSESSMENT FOR COLLEGE AND UNIVERSITY STUDENT POPULATIONS

Edited by

SALLY D. STABB, PH.D.

Texas Woman's University

SHANETTE M. HARRIS, PH.D.

University of Tennessee—Knoxville

JOSEPH E. TALLEY, PH.D., ABPP

Duke University

With a Foreword by

Harold E. Cheatham, Ph.D.

The Pennsylvania State University

With

Robin A. Buhrke, Ph.D., Edward F. Etzel, Ed.D.
J. Scott Hinkle, Ph.D., James W. Pinkey, Ph.D.
and Susan L. Prieto, Ph.D.

CHARLES C THOMAS · PUBLISHER
Springfield • Illinois • U.S.A.

Published and Distributed Throughout the World by

CHARLES C THOMAS • PUBLISHER
2600 South First Street
Springfield, Illinois 62794-9265

© *1995 by* CHARLES C THOMAS • PUBLISHER

ISBN 0-398-05933-0

Library of Congress Catalog Card Number: 94-33052

With **THOMAS BOOKS** *careful attention is given to all details of manufacturing
and design. It is the Publisher's desire to present books that are satisfactory as to their
physical qualities and artistic possibilities and appropriate for their particular use.*
THOMAS BOOKS *will be true to those laws of quality that assure a good name
and good will.*

Printed in the United States of America
SC-R-3

Library of Congress Cataloging-in-Publication Data

Multicultural needs assessment for college and university student
  populations / edited by Sally D. Stabb, Shanette M. Harris, Joseph
  E. Talley ; with a foreword by Harold E. Cheatham ; with Robin A.
  Buhrke . . . [et al.].
     p.   cm.
  Includes bibliographical references and index.
  ISBN 0-398-05933-0
  1. Counseling in higher education—United States.
2. Multicultural education—United States.   3. Minority college
students—United States—Attitudes.   4. Needs assessment—United
States.   I. Stabb, Sally D.   II. Harris, Shanette M.   III. Talley,
Joseph E.
LB2343.M85   1995
378.1′94′0973—dc20   94-33052
                                                                    CIP

CONTRIBUTORS

Robin A. Buhrke, Ph.D., Coordinator of Gay, Lesbian and Bisexual Services and Sexuality Programming, and Staff Psychologist, Counseling and Psychological Services, Duke University, Durham, North Carolina.

Edward F. Etzel, Ed.D., Staff Psychologist, Carruth Center for Counseling and Psychological Services and Assistant Professor, Sport Behavior Program, West Virginia University, Morgantown, West Virginia.

Shanette M. Harris, Ph.D., Assistant Professor, Department of Psychology, The University of Rhode Island, Kingston, Rhode Island.

J. Scott Hinkle, Ph.D., Assistant Professor, School of Education, The University of North Carolina at Greensboro, Greensboro, North Carolina.

James W. Pinkney, Ph.D., Professor, Department of Counseling and Adult Education, East Carolina University, Greenville, North Carolina.

Susan L. Prieto, Ph.D., Coordinator of Clinical Services and Staff Psychologist, Counseling and Psychological Services, Purdue University, West Lafayette, Indiana.

Sally D. Stabb, Ph.D., Assistant Professor, Department of Psychology and Philosophy, Texas Woman's University, Denton, Texas.

Joseph E. Talley, Ph.D., ABPP, Coordinator of Research, Program Evaluation and Testing Services and Staff Psychologist, Counseling and Psychological Services, Duke University. Assistant Clinical Professor, Division of Medical Psychology, Depart-

v

ment of Psychiatry, Duke University Medical Center, Durham, North Carolina. President-Elect of The Academy of Counseling Psychology of The American Board of Professional Psychology.

FOREWORD

In the late 1960s the nation's embattled collegiate institutions were called upon to move dramatically toward fulfilling a "citizen's obligation" to educate students who then were variously referred to as "new," "nontraditional" and even "disadvantaged"—a descriptor that lingers still. Those responsive to the call quickly realized that new programs and offices or, at minimum, extensions and adaptations of existing service delivery units on campus would be required to serve these students. Ultimately, what would be required was a transformation of the nation's "Eurocentric" campuses. Some would agree that the transformation which was begun in the 1960s continues apace today under the beleaguered banner of *multiculturalism.*

The intervening history which gave us the terms Eurocentric and multiculturalism, among many related others, is checkered with the successes and failures that attended institutional efforts to accommodate the needs of "newcomers" to higher education. Some program administrators, themselves educationally deprived of solid know-how or what now might be termed culturally sensitive methodologies, but assigned—and often inspired—to serve "disadvantaged" students, actually invented and perpetuated "disadvantaged programs." The disadvantage was that these programs often were based on cultural "deficit" or "deficient" models derived from assumptions and stereotypes regarding who the consumers were and what were these consumers' needs.

Many collegiate institutions either assigned or brought newly into their employ ethnic minority staff and faculty for the specific purpose of providing or assisting in the design of "ethnic-oriented educational service delivery"—usually as extensions of existing student support services. Numerous research studies and scholarly critiques have been addressed to these program efforts and their effects and particularly so regarding the commonplace, if not universal, commitment among higher education institutions to create culturally diverse living-learning environments on campus. All collegiate institutions intend to affect positively students' well-being and academic growth and development. This mission objective does not seem likely to be accomplished short of curriculum and co-curriculum revisions that recognize and graciously incorporate the essentials of diverse students' cultural values, practices and needs.

Even while graduate education programs continue the contemporaneous practice of training researchers and practitioners for cross and multicultural competence, thanks to the scholarship of Stabb, Harris and Talley and their distinguished associates, a critical foray has been launched simultaneously against culturally insensitive methodologies and "culturally disadvantaged programs." Collectively, these authors provide critical insights that contribute to broadened understanding of the developmental issues and needs of a diverse student clientele and, more important, to the reader's ability to design, administer and interpret culturally sensitive needs assessments.

The volume is based on the premise that student affairs professionals armed with sound and culturally sensitive theory and research methodologies are better prepared to provide appropriate and contemporary student services on campus. This is an elegant collection, well researched and written. It is, as Joe Talley notes in the Introduction, a meta-methodology book in which the authors explore problems, means, methods and the method selection process. One of the central themes of the volume is that when properly derived and employed, multicultural assessment is a potent instrument in the transformation process—that, in the place of informed speculation, data derived from multicultural needs assessment are useful in constructing the persuasive case for program modifications that improve service to traditionally underserved populations. Provided in the appendices are exemplary needs assessment instruments, one useful for assessing a general student population followed by complementary versions one might use for needs assessments intended for several select, specific populations. A related theme is that benefits are not limited to a targeted group but that as services are improved for a specific cohort or in a specific student affairs function area the benefits extend potentially to all student cohorts. Another theme of note is that the respective and respected target group's members should be co-participants in the entire needs assessment process from issue definition through instrument construction, results interpretation and utilization.

The tone set by Joe Talley in the Introduction is continued in Shanette

Harris' conceptualization (Chapter Two) of cultural concerns in needs assessment and particularly in her proposition that problem analysis conducted from a cultural perspective can lead to more effective program services. Harris also provides an heuristic model of factors influencing nonwhite students' needs. Those left unsure or otherwise discomfited by the academy's point-counterpoint debate that often values quantitative over qualitative methodologies should find relief in Sally Stabb's (Chapter Three) expansive treatment of the matter complete with informative discussion and examples of the what, why, when and how (and even some of the political considerations!) relevant to the use of qualitative and mixed models. Harris and Talley then team up to present in Chapter Four a critique of the preponderant single-domain (i.e., academic performance OR social characteristics), cross-sectional research that exists as profiles of African American college students. They present findings from their study employing concurrent techniques to complete needs assessments with this student cohort.

The remaining chapters of this volume are addressed to needs assessments with selected, specific student populations. Susan Prieto (Chapter Five) acknowledges the growing trend in collegiate institutions toward providing culturally sensitive services to Hispanic students and offers historically grounded, cogent discussion of important continuing considerations relative to Hispanic cultural values and level of acculturation. As well, Prieto addresses some problems and potential pitfalls and provides helpful suggestions about how to conduct culturally sensitive needs assessment with Hispanic students. Edward Etzel, James Pinkney and Scott Hinkle weigh-in next (Chapter Six) with a most informative discussion of the developmental issues and stereotypes that can impede sensitive service being provided to student-athletes. These writers note the relatively thin research literature that assesses student-athletes' specific psychosocial needs and treatment issues and advance some "culture-sensitive" formal and informal assessment techniques ranging from individual counseling to modified Delphi approaches that would prove useful with this population and its members.

In Chapter Seven, Robin Burkhe and Sally Stabb provide an exposition of homophobia and heterosexism as these are implicated in minority group status as experienced by many lesbian, gay and bisexual college students. They note that many of the issues, attitudes and behaviors that these students face create stresses that are analogous to those experienced by women and students of color and further how this status is perpetuated through research and language bias and in institutional policy and practice. They address the specific needs of each of these three groups and suggest some procedures and important considerations for collecting needs assessment data with lesbian, gay and bisexual college students.

A considerable literature exists regarding international students, but it is unusual and refreshing to find this population included in a volume addressing special students. In Chapter Eight, Susan Prieto notes the increasing incidence of international students on U.S. campuses and provides some insights into the specific issue of adjustment, cultural values and beliefs regarding physical and mental health and related utilization of health professionals and services. Underutilization of student services on campus, it is noted, might be owed to the students' unawareness or to the unawareness of these students' needs by those providing the services.

There likely are other "special" student groups that readers would like to have included in this collection. Alas, no volume can treat every population, but these writers have joined their scholarship in such a way as to point the way for others' scholarly inquiries. For me, they have provided new and intriguing insights into a matter of pressing importance. The challenge to advance our theory and practice continues!

We owe praise to these colleagues for helping to make plain the matter of needs assessment with diverse student clientele. Their efforts place us in a greatly improved position for inspired and triumphant service to our students and to our collegiate institutions. None committed to the critical task of promoting the institutional mission of creating "welcoming environments" can ignore this important collection. Committed as I am to understanding and contributing to our knowledge of student development and institutional culture, I am indebted to Sally, Shanette, and Joe and their associates for allowing me the privilege to review their scholarship and commend it to you.

HAROLD E. CHEATHAM, PH.D.
Professor of Education and Head
Department of Counseling and Rehabilitation Education
Pennsylvania State University

ACKNOWLEDGMENTS

The editors would like to acknowledge the contributions of Duke University Counseling and Psychological Services, which supported the foundational research in this endeavor and was the link that brought the three editor-contributors together. Additionally, Dr. Sally Stabb would like to acknowledge the help of her doctoral research assistants, Trina Davis, John Hoper, Carol Montgomery, Diane Myers, and Janice Melester, as well as the staff at Texas Woman's University Center for Academic Computing, and the colleagues, friends, and family who gave support throughout the process. Dr. Shanette Harris wishes to express appreciation to Dr. Richard Winett for his introduction to the topic of needs assessment. She also wishes to express appreciation for the support of colleagues and students at the University of Tennessee, Knoxville.

CONTENTS

Appendices

MULTICULTURAL NEEDS ASSESSMENT FOR COLLEGE AND UNIVERSITY STUDENT POPULATIONS

Chapter 1

INTRODUCTION: PURPOSE, RATIONALE, CONTENTS AND BACKGROUND

Joseph E. Talley

PURPOSE

This book is written to serve as the first and primary resource for anyone planning to conduct a multicultural needs assessment, particularly in the college or university setting. Yet much of the material is relevant for conducting a multicultural needs assessment in any setting. This volume familiarizes the reader with the issues to consider in selecting the methodology of a multicultural needs assessment and weighs advantages and disadvantages of the different approaches. Other resources are suggested that will be helpful with regard to implementing a particular type of strategy.

This work raises the issues relevant for particular *special populations* (i.e. international students, African-American students, gay/lesbian/bisexual students, Hispanic American students and student athletes). However, the process by which the relevant factors for these particular special populations are approached is applicable for the assessment of most if not all special populations. Problems and concerns that are significant at every stage of the needs assessment process will be addressed. We began our work evaluating needs primarily with regard to counseling and psychological services related needs. Nevertheless, this writing is applicable for the assessment of needs in any area (particularly of student life) as it is a methodology book. In fact, this is a pre-methodology or a *meta-methodology* book as we explore problems, means and methods as well as the method selection process.

RATIONALE

Issues of ethnic and cultural diversity are at the forefront of our society today and university counseling services and other student services are no exception. This book demonstrates how student service professionals might assess the needs of various student populations in an accurate, timely and culturally sensitive manner in order to provide better services for traditionally underserved populations. All of the editors and contributors to this volume have experience in multicultural needs assessments and as a group we have worked in a variety of settings. This book is aimed primarily at professionals in student life and student services with particular emphasis on college and university mental health services. Yet, academic psychologists and counselors as well as those in a variety of settings such as the community mental health center setting will be particularly interested in the proposed methodologies and their multicultural considerations. Thus, the rationale of our writing is to provide comprehensive models with a sound research base and a solid theoretical base for persons who wish to provide contemporary, multicultural mental health (or other) services on college and university campuses.

CONTENTS

In Chapter Two particular cultural issues as they pertain to needs assessments will be discussed including the following:

1) History and rationale for a cultural perspective:
   This section will present a brief history of the needs assessment literature in addition to the historical notes offered in the introduction. There will be a description of early methods, attempts and assumptions as well as the earlier conceptualizations of needs assessments. The current social context will be discussed in more depth including issues of world views, cultural relativism as well as pluralism and diversity as givens for the immediate future and thus for systemic thinking pertaining to the immediate future. The relationship of multicultural needs assessments to demographic shifts and current ethical guidelines in the mental health professions will also be addressed.
2) In-depth discussion of the concept of culture:
   The concept of culture will be described in detail, including definitions and relationship to worldviews and values. Student cultures, institutional cultures, college/university cultures, and community cultures will be addressed. Basic research in such

areas as minority identity development will be noted as guides to planning and implementing needs assessments.

3) Integration of cultural concepts with general needs assessment strategies:

A conceptual model of non-white student's needs will be presented that integrates chapter material. Additionally, culture-specific considerations in needs assessment will be delineated.

Chapter Three addresses needs assessment methodology including the following:

1) Basic definitions and models of needs assessment will be presented and clarification will be made between this and other types of evaluation in related areas.

2) Identification of needs and data collection:

This chapter covers both quantitative and qualitative approaches. Survey methods including those of direct interview, mail and telephone survey techniques are reviewed. Issues surrounding the development of assessment instruments and their validation are discussed.

3) Appropriate analysis:

Appropriate techniques of analysis, again both quantitative and qualitative are presented. Issues with regard to the interpretation of the data are also discussed.

4) Follow-up responsibilities:

The method of presenting the data to various groups including upper-level administration, student life staff, counseling center personnel, the students themselves and the wider professional community are addressed. It is underscored that how the needs assessment data are used is of critical importance. The discussion focuses on issues such as the availability of the data and the interpretation of the data as well as its possible social, educational and policy uses.

Chapter Four will address the assessment of African-American student needs. This chapter provides a perspective for using assessment procedures and principles to identify the unique needs of African-American students who attend predominantly Euro-American colleges. A perspective is also provided as to how the results from such an assessment may be applied in ways that positively influence the students' well-being and academic performance. Previous research in the area will be summarized, including issues of retention, graduation, academic/ social/personal adjustment, use of services, and methodological critiques.

A description of two needs assessment approaches utilized at a private medium-sized Southeastern university campus is also presented. These studies examine the methodological issues of anonymity versus confidentiality, and the effects of cover letters either signed or unsigned by prominent African-American administrators on campus. The results of the needs assessment study and recommendations for similar and dissimilar approaches are discussed in relation to university and student characteristics. The framework presented is a student oriented one that discusses the definition of such a project, the conceptualization and operationalization of the objectives as well as the specific techniques involved in the process.

Chapter Five examines the area of needs assessment with Hispanic American students and considers the history and social context relevant to this topic. A review of the current literature available on needs assessments conducted with Hispanic populations will be included. A description of different techniques employed and a comparison of their advantages and disadvantages as well as a brief presentation of relevant results will be included. An area of primary consideration will be concerns with regard to how the results from such an assessment are used and disseminated with the Hispanic American population.

Noteworthy points include: issues of commitment on the part of the group or organization conducting the needs assessment, the usefulness of the results in the short-run and in the long-run for the population studied, the political repercussions possible with such surveys and the implications of these for the Hispanic American population as well as for the researchers. Issues regarding the inclusion of the target population in the process of a needs assessment as an active participant from the beginning in order to address concerns of relevance and validity are discussed. Models of minority identity development are reviewed and applied to Hispanic American populations to the degree possible. Implications of these models for the development of the content and the format of a needs assessment instrument are explored.

Special concerns for the Hispanic American population in the area of developing the needs assessment instruments will be addressed including: issues pertaining to language and the relative importance of language to different Hispanic American groups depending on such matters as the person's country of origin, length of time in the United States, socioeconomic status and degree of acculturation. Further, issues with regard to world view (i.e. the importance of the individual versus the group, the acceptability of seeking help and the sense of locus of control) will be discussed. Finally, recommendations for future needs assessment efforts with Hispanic American college and university populations will be presented in the summary and conclusions.

Chapter Six discusses the assessment of and psychological needs of student athletes in the college or university environment. Highlights include a discussion of how little is known about the often misunderstood student athlete special population considering the large number of female and male student athletes that participate in intercollegiate athletics in America's junior and community colleges as well as four-year colleges and universities. The authors discuss issues associated with the assessment of student athletes' needs by the presentation of reasons for helping professionals to be concerned about such needs, some of what is currently known about student athletes as a special population, and methods for assessing these needs as well as the likely barriers to this assessment.

Chapter Seven provides a review of the current literature on gay, lesbian and bisexual student needs. Considering lesbian women, gay men, and bisexuals as distinct populations with unique needs is recognized as important. For example, AIDS is likely to be of greater concern to gay males than to lesbian women. Additionally, the presenting concerns of these groups often vary in other ways. Issues common to gay, lesbian and bisexual students are included such as the disclosure of sexual orientation.

Special concerns with regard to data collection and data use are also addressed. It is noted that access to these students is often difficult for data collection purposes as they may comprise somewhat of a hidden community. Thus, to study their needs and assess them, not only are innovative techniques necessary but also particularly special care must be taken in the protection of the students' confidentiality or anonymity. Special guidelines for avoiding heterosexist bias in research are included as Appendix H. Recommendations for the study of gay, lesbian, and bisexual students are discussed.

Chapter Eight examines needs assessment issues as they relate to international student populations. A review of the current literature available on needs assessments with international student populations is presented. Methods utilized in previous assessment efforts are described, and the advantages and disadvantages associated with them are evaluated. Models of acculturation and assimilation are reviewed and the pertinence of their implications for the international population are discussed. Specific concerns in the study of international students are addressed. These include the following:

1) Issues concerning studying students from different cultural backgrounds and variables affecting the acculturation process.
2) Concerns with regard to the use of language such as the degree of mastery of the English language, familiarity with terminology and the social meaning associated with asking about areas that may be considered personal and/or private.
3) Various cultures' attitudes towards seeking help and the implications of these for the format and/or content areas included in the needs assessment.
4) Issues with regard to how the results are to be shared and utilized as well as how they might affect the international students surveyed.

In the summary and the conclusions the salient matters with regard to conducting needs assessments with international students are noted as are the methods that have been employed with their pros and cons and the recommendations for future needs assessment endeavors with this population.

The last chapter offers conclusions that set the philosophical and ideological tone for future work. General conclusions are also presented. The reader may also want to examine Appendices A through G, which contain samples of needs assessment instruments for general populations and special populations, as well as examples of cover letters and follow-up letters.

BACKGROUND

What is a needs assessment? McKillip (1987) makes an important contribution as he writes, "Recognizing need involves values. People with different values will recognize different needs" (p. 10). I would add that the diverse social, political and environmental circumstances as well as diversity with regard to biological, cultural, racial, gender, ethnic and psychological (etc.) characteristics foster diverse values in persons based in part on their experiencing the world very differently such that we might even say that at some point we truly live in different worlds. Thus, it is not strange that one product of a diverse population is diversity concerning needs.

To further delineate the term *need,* it is a value of some relative weight among other values. It is not always a necessity of life in the sense that living existence cannot continue without it. Rather, as used in this area of study, it more often than not pertains to quality of life or bettering the circumstances of the life generally of a "target population". Moreover, a need as used here is not simply a want, something one will pay for, in terms of economics. A need in the sense of a problem may well exist, yet it may also be that no one is willing to buy the solution. Needs such as these have to do with problems for which there are solutions as perceived by a target population (McKillip, 1987). Bringing into focus the issue of solutions, a given agency would ordinarily be interested in assessing only the needs for which they might provide solutions or work in the process of providing the solutions unless the agency or group was doing a study for another group or groups who would then facilitate or provide the solutions.

An *assessment* here is used to mean a gathering of information or data of some type for review, analysis and/or description in some manner. (See Chapter Three for detail as to the varieties utilized). Considering alternative approaches in needs assessment is not a new matter and writing that is still relevant goes back at least twenty years (Warheit, Bell & Schwab, 1974; Milford, 1976). Some earlier studies have investigated particular subsets or types of students such as seniors (Carney & Barak, 1976) or married students (Flores, 1978). Other earlier investigations concluded that what you find depends on who you ask, such as the study by Henggeler, Sallis and Cooper (1980) which contrasted the needs of students as perceived by students versus professionals. They found great differences between the groups regarding perceived needs.

Earlier investigations found vocational identity and career choice as well as academic concerns to be areas of the greatest perceived need (Carney & Barak, 1976; Weissberg, Berentsen, Cote, Cravey & Heath, 1982; Kramer, Berger & Miller, 1974). This was particularly true for students surveyed but not seeking services (Indrisano & Auerback, 1979). Further, earlier work often revealed little difference by sex and class in school (Kramer, Berger & Miller, 1974). However, ten years later it was reported (Talley, 1985) that the number of needs rated as "of some importance" or more decreased as the mean age of the group increased and that younger, female minority undergraduate students who were single had the greatest likelihood of experiencing at least one of the items to be "of some importance" at the time surveyed while older, married, male, Caucasian graduate students were the least likely to experience (or report) one of the items to be "of some importance" at the time surveyed.

Other more recent studies (Bertocci, Hirsch, Sommer & Williams, 1989; Stabb, Talley, Barrow, Prieto & Etzel, 1989) have still found academic and vocational needs to be the greatest or among the greatest concerns with regard to mental health and counseling related needs for all special populations within the general student population surveyed. However, differences by group have been noted also with regard to other items that were less directly related to academic life (Bertocci, Hirsch, Sommer & Williams, 1989). Likewise, earlier work has shown that the accurate assessment of student needs leads to better student services (Lenning, 1989; Kuh, 1982).

If a paper and pencil survey is to be used, as is often the case, then Fowler (1984) and Dillman (1978) offer valuable insights with regard to the particulars of the methodology and instruments employed. Included in the appendices of this volume are sample forms that we have used (see Appendices A–E). Revision of item content should be considered as it may be desirable to do so. Likewise, we have included sample cover letters (see Appendices F and G). The general methodology of our studies included the use of a computer generated stratified (by sex, age, race, school/program of enrollment and marital status) random sample of ten percent of the entire student body. (Given a stratified random sample a smaller percentage would have been acceptable).

To ensure large enough samples of special populations much larger percentages of the enrolled international students, athletes playing varsity sports and African-American students were randomly sampled while attempts to get gay, lesbian and bisexual students to complete inventories were made through campus organizations and informal networking. For the special populations, additional questions were generated (see Appendices) from the literature and from meeting with representative members of the special populations. Follow-up questionnaires were sent to all non-respondents three weeks from the first mailing.

For the results to be meaningful with regard to solutions, it is important to also assess the relative likelihood that proposed solutions will be utilized by members of the target population. Earlier studies have suggested that assessing this likelihood is not as easy as it may appear. With regard to counseling and psychological services for students, the results from needs assessments may be quite different than what the utilization statistics indicate students actually seek services for (Barrow, Cox, Sepich & Spivak, 1989).

Since the focus of this book is methodology, the chapters that are not population specific should apply to all populations and special populations. Every special population has not been included due to the vast number. Conceivably we might study populations by every descriptive characteristic imaginable as a separate group and then also combination populations by race and gender and orientation, etc. The particular populations addressed here are included because they arose as most significant in the course of our applied work and in the field. There are many noteworthy omissions as groups but the process of studying them can to some extent be taken from the process of studying other special populations and considerations for one group often apply to another.

Another critical point is that while we would want to assess as many special populations as possible, such groups are also artificial as *Asian-Americans* includes people from many diverse and very different cultures. Likewise, the grouping *Hispanic American* implies one unit when in fact the cultural heritages of Spanish speaking peoples vary markedly. Often one part of the grouping has been at odds historically with another part of the grouping (e.g. Northern Koreans and the Japanese). This is all to say that grouping may make an error in the assumption of greater uniformity than is the case. Each assessment project must decide what the most meaningful and helpful groupings are for that particular place (campus) and time.

Further, race, gender, ethnicity, athletic status and sexual orientation are obviously not the only important variables to consider groupings by in the student population. Among other things such factors as the type of training program the student is enrolled in will affect the student's needs. The perceived needs of students in an engineering school may be very different from those in a school of education. Different types of people are, of course, drawn to a given field which contributes to the environment of that school or program within the college or university. Whether or not one has a spouse affects responses to needs assessments (Talley, 1985). We might expect that physical differences and handicaps would also affect perceived needs as might a students values including religious, political or other ideological beliefs (Bergin, 1991). For example, religiously concerned clients may conceptualize their sense of self in different ways than most and therefore they may have different feelings with regard to boundaries between self and others. They often have intensely affective subjective experiences and have thoughts or use terms that may make a therapist suspect more psychopathology (Agosin, 1992) than is warranted given their *culture.* These beliefs, whether Buddhist, New Age, or Christian fundamentalist, are a significant part of and often the primary context in which such clients need to be understood.

The cardinal rule here is—you will hear about what you ask about. So we need to initially ask in each group, one way or another—"what do we need to ask you about?" Our prior investigations have shown few statistically significant differences between special populations within the general student population when all people are asked the same questions (Stabb, Talley, Barrow, Prieto & Etzel, 1989). This is perhaps due to the fact that in a student population there is much common to all in the area of academic and vocational concerns. However, whenever the question is asked of any special population within the student body—"what most concerns you about your life here and now and what are your present needs?" the answers vary widely from group to group. Thus, if we are to look at responses to the same questions by all special populations, it is certainly also warranted if not essential to ask the open question of—"what are your greatest needs now?"—to these groups, too. The assessor may wish to restrict the area of inquiry, however, to matters the assessor can address with solutions.

The present work has grown out of a line of inquiry in the process of applied, on campus work that has looked at the differences resulting from particular survey techniques such as telephone versus mail (Talley, Barrow, Fulkerson & Moore, 1983), anonymous versus confidential (Harris & Talley, 1991a) and co-signed (by a known group member) and non-cosigned cover letters with African-American students (Harris & Talley, 1991b) and the needs assessment survey results as they compare to service utilization (Talley, 1985; Barrow, Cox, Sepich & Spivak, 1989). Technique differences yielded no significant differences in results although one may be more efficient than another depending on whether the investigators have more money for postage than person power for interviews. This, in turn, has led to multicultural needs assessments and the assessment of special populations within the student bodies of higher education.

The studies initially focused on counseling and psychological service related needs as most of the contributors to this volume either did their predoctoral psychology internships at Counseling and Psychological Services of Duke University or are on the senior staff of this agency where our projects began. The area of study has gone with these former interns to their new university homes and has now broadened to issues of general methodology. The results of this line of research have also noted little change over the years with regard to the academic and career-related concerns as the primary areas of need. Again, this is in all likelihood an artifact of the common denominators of the total population and the fact that its members are in this population because they want an education and a career related to this education. However, questions related to extracurricular matters and phenomenologically generated items do show the different needs of special populations. Studies done at universities with a more diverse student body (Bertocci, Hirsch, Sommer & Williams, 1989) have shown noteworthy differences by groupings on items of general concern. Thus results from one student body have only limited generalizability to another. Each college or university needs to do its own study looking at groups as is most relevant for that setting, but the decision as to which groups should be studied must not be made a priori by the researchers in isolation.

Pilot studies will indicate possible needs of diverse groups. The need for multicultural counseling in an increasingly pluralistic society (which appears to be becoming ever more pluralistic) and the need for multicultural interventions has been stated well recently by Lee and Richardson (1991). Dana (1993), who has concentrated primarily on multicultural psychological assessment, has also discussed training for "ethnorelativistic thinking". It is my hope and belief that our volume will assist you in the task of conducting a helpful and thus a meaningful series of studies in your setting to identify the needs of the many different students on your campus and to then begin the task of meeting those needs.

REFERENCES

Agosin, T. (1992). Psychosis, dreams and mysticism in the clinical domain. In F. Halligan and J. Shea (Eds). *The fires of desire: Erotic energies and the spiritual quest.* New York: Crossroad Publishing Company.

Barrow, J., Cox, P., Sepich, R. & Spivak, R. (1989). Student needs assessment surveys: Do they predict student use of services? *Journal of College Student Development, 66,* 164–167.

Bertocci, D., Hirsch, E., Sommer, W. & Williams, A. (1989). *Columbia University mental health survey: Summary of results.* Unpublished manuscript, Columbia University, Columbia University Health Services, New York.

Bergin, A.E. (1991). Values and religious issues in psychotherapy and mental health. *The American Psychologist, 46*(4), 394–403.

Carney, C.G. & Barak, A. (1976). A survey of student needs and student personnel services. *Journal of College Student Personnel, 17*(4), 280–284.

Dana, R.H. (1993). *Multicultural assessment: Perspectives for professional psychology.* Needham Heights, MA: Allyn and Bacon.

Dillman, D. A. (1978). *Mail and telephone surveys: The total design method.* New York: Wiley.

Flores, T. R. (1978). Student personnel programs for married students: A needs assessment. *Journal of College Student Personnel, 16*(2), 154–159.

Fowler, F. J. (1984). *Survey research methods.* Beverly Hills, California: Sage Publications.

Henggeler, S. W., Sallis, J. F. & Cooper, P. F. (1980). Comparison of university mental health priorities identified by professionals and students. *Journal of Counseling Psychology, 27*(2), 217–219.

Harris, S. & Talley, J. (1991a). The effect of anonymity and confidentiality on African-American students' response rates. Presented at the American Psychological Association National Convention, San Francisco, August, 1991.

Harris, S. & Talley, J. (1991 b). Minority students' response rates. Presented at the Southeastern Psychological Association Convention, New Orleans, March, 1991.

Indrisano, V. E. & Auerbach, S. M. (1979). Mental health needs assessment of a major urban university. *Journal of the American College Health Association, 27*(4), 389–393.

Kramer, H. C., Berger, F., & Miller, G. (1974). Student concerns and sources of assistance. *Journal of College Student Personnel, 15*(5), 389–393.

Kuh, G. D. (1982). Purposes and principles for needs assessment in student affairs. *Journal of College Student Personnel, 23,* 202–209.

Lee, C. & Richardson, B. (1991). *Multicultural issues in counseling: New approaches to diversity.* Alexandria, VA: American Association for Counseling and Development.

Lenning, O. T. (1980). Assessing student program needs. In P. Jedamus and M. W. Peterson (Eds.) *Improving academic management* (pp. 263–288) San Francisco: Jossey-Bass.

McKillip, J. (1987). *Need analysis: Tools for the human services and education.* Newburg Park, California: Sage Publications.

Milford, J. T. (1976). Human service needs assessment: Three non-epidemiological approaches. *Canadian Psychological Review, 4,* 260–269.

Stabb, S., Talley, J., Barrow, J., Prieto, S., & Etzel, E. (1989). *A comparative needs assessment: Four special populations.* Unpublished manuscript, Duke University, Counseling and Psychological Services, Durham, N.C.

Talley, J. (1985). Psychological needs reported by students not seeking services. In J. E. Talley and W. J. K. Rockwell (Eds.) *Counseling and psychotherapy services for university students.* (pp. 18–30). Springfield, Illinois: Charles C Thomas.

Talley, J., Barrow, J., Fulkerson, K. & Moore, C. (1983). Mail vs. telephone as a means of conducting a needs assessment. *Journal of American College Health, 32*(3), 101–103.

Warheit, G. J., Bell, R. A., & Schwab, J. J. (1974). *Planning for change in needs assessment approaches.* Washington, D. C.: National Institute of Mental Health.

Weissberg, M., Berentsen, M., Cote, A., Cravey, B., & Heath, K. (1982). An assessment of the personal, career, and academic needs of undergraduate students. *Journal of College Student Personnel, 23*(2), 115–122.

Chapter 2

CULTURAL CONCERNS IN THE ASSESSMENT OF NONWHITE STUDENTS' NEEDS

SHANETTE M. HARRIS

Over the last several years, university personnel and administrators have debated concerns associated with increasing numbers of African-American, Asian American, Native American, and Hispanic American students who will constitute a significant proportion of the university population by the year 2000. In particular, factors related to the recruitment, retention and graduation of these populations have become significant areas of attention in higher education.

This chapter focuses on specific cultural concerns that must be addressed in order to generate information that is relevant for the development, implementation and operation of programs and services for heterogeneous student populations. The following examines the needs assessment concept in relation to the future social context of institutions of higher education and discusses issues that become relevant when assessment is targeted at culturally diverse student groups. It is proposed that problem analyses conducted from a cultural perspective can lead to more effective program services. Approaches and strategies are offered to guide university administrators, program personnel and advisors in the conceptualization of the assessment process.

RATIONALE FOR A CULTURAL PERSPECTIVE

Access to and attainment of an education have historically been desired American objectives. The attainment of a college degree has been a gatekeeper to sociocultural, economic and personal rewards. A college education has also served to promote employment, acceptance and status within an ever-evolving society of scarce resources. At the same time, educational advancement has contributed to social class differences and maintenance of the existing status quo.

17

Recognition that education can have dual social effects has led to closer scrutiny of educational processes and outcomes. Results of these investigations reveal that American students perform less well than students in other industrialized nations. A major attempt to alter this situation is reflected in the current emphasis on educational reform. During a time of few government resources and substantial social problems, the need to establish standards in higher education has contributed to a demand for greater institutional responsibility. Central to reform efforts are concerns that pertain to the access, progress and status of nonwhite students. Rapid growth in the diversity of the American population make these issues pertinent for students throughout the educational pipeline.

Ethnic and racial minorities currently represent 24 percent of the U.S. population and will comprise a majority of the U.S. population in the near-by future. Data indicate that more than one-third of the U.S. population will consist of nonwhite group members by the early to mid twenty-first century (American Council on Education, 1988; Levine & Associates, 1989; U.S. Department of Commerce, 1991). Sue (1991) projects, however, that ethnic and racial minorities will comprise about 52 percent of the total population by 2010. Changes in the nonwhite population between 1980 and 1990 provide evidence of these trends. Compared to an 11% increase in the Euro-American population, African-Americans, Asian Americans, Native Americans, and Latino groups experienced population increases at rates of 13%, 38%, 108%, and 53%, respectively (Andersen, 1991).

In addition to predicted demographic changes, nonwhite group members experience negative social conditions at a significantly higher rate than Euro-Americans. Unemployment and underemployment, poor health outcomes, frequent exposure to criminal acts, poor housing conditions, and high incarceration rates disproportionately affect Latino, Native American and African-American populations (U.S. Department of Commerce, 1988; National Center for Educational Statistics [NCES], 1990). Although Asian Americans fare better than do most nonwhites in these areas, they are still less often employed than Euro-Americans in executive and administrative positions (Sue, Sue, & Wong, 1985). Asian Americans are also less likely to receive salary and rank commensurate with their qualifications (Nagasawa & Espinosa, 1992; Suzuki, 1990). As the demographics change more negative responses are also emitted. Increased visibility of these populations give rise to racial and ethnic intolerance on college campuses and hate crimes in general (Magner, 1989; Marable, 1988; National Institute Against Prejudice and Violence [NIAPV], 1987).

There is some consensus that college matriculation can improve socio-economic concerns of nonwhite Americans. However, only a small percentage of these students actually enroll in four-year institutions and progress toward degree completion. Native American youth, for example, leave high school at a rate of 60 percent and junior high school at a rate of 40 percent. In 1982, only 31 percent of Native Americans enrolled in college, of which 39 percent actually received a four-year degree (Wiley, 1989). In 1988, sixty-four percent of Euro-American college students attended four-year institutions compared to 60 percent of Asian Americans, 58 percent of African-Americans and 44 percent of Latino Americans (NCES, 1990). Of the students that received high school diplomas and enrolled in four-year colleges in 1980, only 10 percent of African-Americans as compared to 21 percent of Euro-Americans had earned a college degree or more education in 1986 (American Council on Education, 1988). Similarly, of individuals between 25 and 29 years old in 1987, only 14 percent of African-Americans and 15 percent of Latinos had earned a four-year degree or more education as compared to 27 percent of Euro-Americans (NCES, 1990).

A review of the literature also reveals that the experiences of nonwhite students on predominantly Euro-American campuses differ significantly from those of their Euro-American counterparts (e.g., Allen, 1988; Harris & Nettles, 1991; Hsia, 1988; Mow & Nettles, 1990; Oliver, Rodgriguez & Mickelson, 1985; Sanders, 1987; Suzuki, 1990; Webster, 1984). African-American students, for example, have been shown to report: feelings of alienation, isolation, and social estrangement; limited dating opportunities; interpersonal dissatisfaction; experiences of harassment and racism; and restricted involvement in nonAfrican-American oriented campus activities (DeSousa & King, 1992; Loo & Rolison, 1986; Mitchell & Dell, 1992; Nottingham, Rosen, & Parks, 1992; Steward, Jackson, & Jackson, 1990). Although Euro-Americans appear to hold more favorable evaluations of Hispanic than African-American students, Hispanic students also experience oppression on predominantly Euro-American campuses (White & Sedlacek, 1987). Cultural and language barriers impede relationships with nonHispanic faculty and staff, and enrollment in English non-credit hours delay graduation and financial assistance (Florida State Commission on Hispanic Affairs, Tallahassee, 1984). Whereas Asian American students are more likely than other nonwhite groups and Euro-Americans to graduate from college and major in career areas that offer greater economic returns (Suzuki, 1990), they are also more likely to show decrements in college success as length of residency in America increases (Sue, Sue, & Wong, 1985). Likewise, the psychosocial climate on the college campus appears to be hostile to lesbian, gay and bisexual students (D'Augelli & Rose, 1990; Herek, 1989). International students also express concerns with academic demands and American norms such as competitiveness, individualism and assertiveness (Parr, Bradley & Bingi, 1992; Pruit, 1978). In addition, students with disabilities experience difficulties meeting tasks associated with the transition from high school to college (Hahn, 1985; McGuire, Hall, & Litt, 1991; Siperstein, 1988).

Results of racial-comparative studies which show academic and social adjustment differences between nonwhite and Euro-American students have been used to develop programs and services to alleviate these concerns (Levin & Levin, 1991). The numerous descriptions offered in the literature give witness to the frequency with which these interventions are implemented on college campuses. Yet, few methodologically sound investigations have been conducted to examine program effectiveness. Kulik, Kulik and Shwalb (1983) conducted a meta-analysis of 500 studies of retention programs for minorities and found that only 12 percent used somewhat adequate designs. Some of the flaws that make the results uninterpretable include: general program descriptions rather than data, failure to use appropriate comparison groups, neglect in assigning participants to groups, and variation in participants' degree of exposure to program services. The absence of process and summative evaluative data, inappropriate research design, and failure to attend to issues of internal and external validity make it difficult to determine the actual worth of these services. In addition, results of the few well-controlled evaluations that have been conducted do not unequivocally show retention services to effectively meet their objectives (Oliver, Rodgriguez, & Mickelson, 1985). Concern for the accurate identification of student difficulties and appropriate design of services have led staff and administrators to turn toward needs assessment methodologies.

HISTORY AND DEFINITIONS:
THE CONCEPT OF NEEDS ASSESSMENT

Theoretically, needs assessment represents a fundamental aspect of program planning and is conducted to generate information for program development and implementation. According to Murrell (1977), needs assessment is:

> one of many different approaches to collecting systematic information that may be conducted under the general rubric of "program evaluation" (p. 461).

Stewart (1979) offers a more detailed description by defining needs assessment as:

> . . . an activity through which one identifies community problems and resources to meet the problems, develops priorities concerning problems and services, and is part of program planning and development of new or altered services (p. 294).

Needs assessment, then, is concerned with the acquisition of objective, valid and reliable data to form questions and provide information for program development and implementation.

Although calls for assessment data are relatively recent, the development of and emphasis on needs assessment closely parallels the historical trends of program evaluation. Reliance on this process to obtain information can be attributed to several educational, social and political phenomena: (1) changes in the nature and role of the federal government, (2) social problems of different time periods, and (3) advances in social science research. Because the interrelationships among these factors are too varied and complex to describe here, only a brief discussion is offered.

Prior to World War I, evaluation efforts were primarily related to educational programs, occupational training and public health interventions. Following World War II, the role of the federal government expanded and large scale programs were implemented to meet needs related to family planning, health and rural community development. This new role of the government raised questions about the value of major expenditures and the worth of social programs, such that many large scale program evaluations were in effect near the end of the 1950's. As the federal government continued to assist with social concerns, demands for large-scale evaluative studies also increased. Economic problems and inflation of the 1970's combined with outcomes which demonstrated the ineffectiveness of programs implemented during the 1960's to contribute to skeptical views of social programs. These views, in turn, placed greater emphasis on program accountability and effectiveness.

Advances in research methods and theory also spurred the emphasis on assessment. After the war, for example, interest in the number of military personnel who were found mentally unfit for military duty led mental health officials to focus on the identification of military persons with mental illness. The large number of persons found unsuitable for duty and the use of epidemiological survey data to identify those with mental health problems set the stage for the use of survey instruments as assessment tools in general.

Statutes that were enacted for the federal Community Mental Health Centers (CMHCs) also influenced the use of needs assessments. As early as 1963, legislation required applicants to show need before receiving financial services for center requests. Public Law 89-749 in 1966, for example, required these agencies to identify and clarify needs as well as the relationship between the reported needs and specific services. Public Law 94-63 (1975) went further with the requirement that the National Institute of Mental Health (NIMH) devise accreditation standards for mental health agencies. Planning, evaluation and assessment were to serve as prerequisites to all center funding requests. The requirement that centers obtain input from service users for allocation requests contributed to community mental health centers' dependence on needs assessment data. The implications of these statutes generalized beyond mental health centers to exert effects on college counseling centers. Community mental health legislation indirectly increased counseling center staffs' interest in meeting the personal, social and academic needs of students. The civil rights requirement for institutions of higher education to educate African-American students and the federal mandate that mental health centers assess needs combined to promote a proliferation of needs assessments on predominantly Euro-American campuses during the seventies (Benedict, Apsler, & Morrison, 1977; Carney & Barak, 1976; Fullerton & Potkay, 1973; Westbrook, Miyares, & Roberts, 1978). More recently, the educational agendas of the Reagan-Bush administrations accentuated the importance of assessment as a step in the direction of greater educational accountability.

Despite the emphasis on assessment, several criticisms have been levied against the needs assessment process. Kimmel (1977), for example, reports that needs assessment is:

> a kneejerk response to perplexing problems of public policy which are poorly understood (p. 6).

In general, needs assessment has been criticized on numerous grounds: use of global and nonspecific instruments (Brown, 1981; Hanson, 1982), failure to identify implications of assessment results (Hanson, 1982), collection of data at single points in time, infrequent use of data for decision purposes (Murrell, 1977), inability of respondents to identify needs (Wilson & Yaeger, 1981), and the use of questions based on needs of program developers (Aponte, 1978; Warner, 1975). These criticisms are applicable to needs assessments conducted on college campuses and are partly attributable to the continued reliance on unidimensional and monocultural conceptualizations of the needs assessment process.

Since the 1960's advances have been made on several college campuses which have as objectives the recruitment, retention and graduation of nonwhite students. Needs assessment is one area of importance. Data from needs assessments have generally been used for decisions that enhance the probability that these educational objectives are accomplished. The climate and organizational structure of Euro-American universities, however, are incompatible with the needs of many nonwhite students and create barriers to the accurate identification of student needs for preventive efforts. Needs assessment represents an honorable attempt to provide *objective* information but the process and method cannot be isolated from the political, cultural and structural makeup of educational institutions. Marti-Costa and Serrano-Garcia (1983) suggest that this "myth of neutrality" is inappropriate because it confuses the reality of the process. They state:

> ... needs assessment is an integral part of community [university] development, the process of consciousness-raising. It implies a political commitment which undermines the traditional view of a neutral science and a firm commitment to the exploited, underprivileged, and powerless groups in society. (p. 77)

Without a commitment to educational objectives for nonwhite students, existing institutional norms and values are perpetuated in policies and programs; and mere *lip service* is given to racial and ethnic inclusiveness. The provision of programs consistent with skills and interests of university staff has been the traditional institutional response to the presence of nonwhite students. Concentration on student characteristics to the exclusion of the campus ethos has led to a focus on the role of students' internal factors within cognitive, interpersonal and behavioral realms. Consistent with this model, assessors ask, "What are the deficiencies of this student group?" and then proceed to design services consonant with a deficit perspective. That students' difficulties may arise from institutional qualities is often overlooked or treated as an afterthought.

The tendency for assessors to neglect environmental conditions and instead concentrate on student factors is reflected in the components that comprise the preponderance of university programming for nonwhite students. For instance, many program descriptions include components designed to eradicate academic deficiencies (e.g., study skills, academic advising) (Garcia & Presley, 1981) but few build in university-related services to modify institutional deficits that exacerbate or create problems for students. In a discussion concerning African-American students, Cheatham, Tomlinson & Ward (1990) summarize this matter as follows:

> Many of the failing programs have been devised and implemented without a clear demonstration of African American students' [nonwhite students'] developmental needs or of the environmental influence on personality development and psychological functioning (p. 492).

The risk that methods of data collection and applications of the results will be ineffective are maximized when student needs are reduced to a single explanation. Simplistic explanations do not capture the complexity of nonwhite students' needs on predominantly Euro-American campuses. Rather, needs are influenced by interdependent cognitive, physical, sociocultural, and psychoemotional variables that cross "general" and "specific" domains and these should be considered in any determination of needs (Harding, Baldwin & Baser, 1987). To further complicate this matter, these needs must be translated into useful programs and services. Results that arise from one-sided assessment efforts can contribute to limitations that emerge at various phases of the needs assessment process. For example, specification of assessment goals in the pre-assessment phase without consideration of previous traditions and future objectives of a particular institution can thwart tasks of the dissemination phase because conflicts of interest arise between assessors and university administrators. Moreover, assessors' failure to account for ecological factors (e.g., university mission, observable artifacts, university traditions) distorts students' problems and omits valuable information about the context from which these needs originate. Consequently, needs assessment data may have several shortcomings and perhaps present an obstacle to the adequate redress of students' needs.

Several studies show that personal characteristics and background information influence students' in-college experiences (Harris & Nettles, 1991; Nettles, 1988). Students' pre-college and in-college experiences have also been shown to affect progress and graduation. Yet, few needs assessment survey instruments are designed to request descriptive data other than basic identification information (e.g., race). Personal characteristics that can influence performance and adjustment are rarely considered. Even the survey instruments that are designed to obtain sociodemographic information assess only a select set of characteristics. Many assessors restrict personal information to those qualities that obviously pertain to the academic objectives of university environments (e.g., choice of major, grade point average, SAT scores). Simplistic instruments are less costly and time consuming than those of more depth and breadth of coverage but the use of inadequate measures promotes program development based on skewed information. Initial efforts to assess the complexity of student problems may be more cost-beneficial in the long term than measures that discount the importance of intragroup variation.

In addition, staff often neglect the relevance of intergroup variability and consolidate the responses of diverse nonwhite populations. Clearly, adjustment to unfamiliar expectations, values and behaviors are experiences that nonwhite student groups share on predominantly Euro-American campuses. Dissimilarities in campus experiences, however, evolve from social class factors, racial identity attitudes, cultural value orientations, and quality and quantity of previous experiences with Euro-American culture. For example, Sue and Zane (1985) examined the achievement and adaptation of Chinese university students and found them to receive higher grades than other student groups (including Euro-Americans). The use of global assessments obscures these types of intergroup variability and actuates service designs that may effectively meet needs of some student groups, yet offer little of advantage to others (Keller, Piotrowski & Sherry, 1982). Aggregate level data also perpetuate institutional references and responses to nonwhite students as "minorities" which show little regard for the values and worldviews of individual groups.

THE CONCEPT OF CULTURE

Whereas student background factors and personal qualities are frequently included as predictors of in-college experiences and outcomes, cultural values are virtually ignored. Because studies on the experience and progress of these students rarely include cultural variables, planners of needs assessments are also unlikely to consider the importance of cultural characteristics and treat the definitions of needs, views of assessment and procedures for data collection as *culture free.* The advancement of assessment as value-free misrepresents the assumptions and practices of university systems and indirectly makes it difficult to remedy student difficulties.

Strong (1986) proposes that

> The multicultural organization is one which is genuinely committed to diverse representation of its membership; is sensitive to maintaining an open, supportive and responsive environment; is working toward and purposefully including elements of diverse cultures in its ongoing operations; and . . . is authentic in its response to issues confronting it. (p. 7).

It follows then, that culturally-relevant needs assessments are best conducted on college campuses that adhere to similar principles.

Sensitivity to the cultural characteristics of students is extremely important in the needs assessment process. Because many assessments of needs originate in the counseling centers on university campuses, and counselors are obligated to "the enhancement of the worth, dignity, potential, and uniqueness of each individual and thus to the service of security" (American Association for Counseling and Development [AACD], 1988); it appears that needs assessors would logically integrate cultural factors in the needs assessment process. Ethical guidelines offered by national accreditation bodies appear to have had little effect on this process. As early as 1973 the American Psychological Association (APA) developed and proposed ethical guidelines for cross-cultural counseling. The basic proposal was that a lack of staff members who were *competent* to offer culturally related services would be viewed as unethical (Paradis, 1981). The absence of specific reference to racial and ethnic minorities, however, resulted in great variability in the degree to which university counseling staff in particular designed services with cultural concerns in mind (Sue, Arredondo & McDavis, 1992). More recently, guidelines have been put forth by APA's Board of Ethnic Minority Affairs (BEMA) for Providers of Psychological Services to Ethnic, Linguistic, and Culturally Diverse Populations (APA, 1991). These guidelines have opened the floodgate for more important discussions and a multitude of perspectives on culture.

Culture has traditionally been used to refer to patterns of behavior and shared ways of living for groups of individuals. Whereas some theorists emphasize customs, rituals, architecture, products, language, and observable indications of group commonalities, others focus on ethnographic factors (Bennett, 1990). Because culture is complex, several definitions based on multidimensional perspectives have been put forth (Pedersen, 1988). Yet, arguments have been made against the use of too broad a definition. To expand the meaning of culture to include all variables and all people who view themselves as oppressed dilutes the boundaries such that culture becomes synonymous with individual differences (Brislin, 1990; Lee, 1991). The more recent emphasis on the differentiation of cultural groups as a function of values or worldviews reduces this problem and includes visibly different groups *and* universal concerns.

Worldviews or value orientations are implicit frames of reference that assist in interpreting the world, mediating behavior and environmental phenomena and giving meaning to observable differences in group patterns of behavior. Kluckhohn and Strodbeck's (1961) model of cultural values or value-orientations emphasizes groups' solutions to five common problems: Human Nature, Person-Nature Relationship, Human Activity, Time, and Social Relations. These solutions can also be viewed as five questions which all groups must answer: (a) what is the character of human nature? (Good, Mixed, or Evil); (b) what is the relationship of people to nature? (Mastery, Harmony, or Subjugation); (c) what is the appropriate emphasis of time? (Future, Present, or Past); (d) what is the appropriate vein of personal expression? (Doing, Being, or Being-in-Becoming); and (e) what is the emphasis of social relations? (Individual, Lineal, or Collateral). Although common to all societies, variations in the solutions chosen to resolve these problems are assumed to reflect cultural differences. Kluckhohn (1962) describes culture as

> ... patterns, explicit and implicit, of and for behavior acquired and transmitted by symbols, constituting the distinctive achievement of human groups, including their embodiments in artifacts; the essential core of culture consists of traditional (i.e., historically derived and selected) ideas and especially their attached values; culture systems may, on the one hand, be considered as products of action, on the other as conditioning influences upon further action (p. 73).

Schein (1993) defines culture as

> the sum total of what a given group has learned as a group, ... usually embodied in a set of shared, basic underlying assumptions that are no longer conscious, but are taken for granted as the way the world is (p. 705).

According to Poortinga (1990), culture represents

> shared constraints that limit the behavior repertoire available to members of a certain sociocultural group in a way different from individuals belonging to some other group (p. 6).

Jackson and Meadows (1991) suggest that cultural worldviews consist of six basic assumptions that lead to different conceptual systems which in turn, give rise to different group behaviors, perceptions and experiences. A group's nature of reality, however, serves as the foundation for the evolution of the remaining five assumptions. The philosophical assumptions identified by Jackson and Meadows are the following:

1. Ontology (the nature of reality). What is reality? Who is right? What perspective is real? How do nonwhite students and Euro-American students and administrators see situations and events in the classroom and residence hall? For example, nonwhite students may not voluntarily speak in class because the perspective of the professor denies their history.

2. Cosmology (the order and pattern of reality). How do students, program planners and faculty view the nature of society? Is society good, bad, both, or neutral? What is the relationship between these views and academic performance or interpersonal satisfaction?

3. Epistemology (the nature of knowledge). How does one know? Where does knowledge come from? What are the channels or mechanisms through which knowledge is acquired? In some instances, references are cited by students as evidence of the validity of their comments. However, for some nonwhite students, to offer references is viewed as irresponsible because one's experience is valid in and of itself.

4. Axiology (the nature of values). What is "most important" to a student group? What is valuable? In African culture, for example, interpersonal harmony and respect are most valuable. Among Native Americans, a harmonious universe in which objects and beings have a sacred life and humans are not superior is most important (Herring, 1990).

5. Logic (the nature of reasoning). What is the appropriate way of thinking? How are inferences formed? Is reasoning a dichotomous or diunitial process? Among African-Americans, expressive and instrumental role behaviors are expected and accepted for males and females.

6. Process (methods of producing action or change). How does change occur? For example, nonwhite students may desire to withdraw from a course and consider this process complete after receiving an instructor's permission, although the Euro-American college system functions in a less interpersonal manner and relies upon technology (i.e., computer information to indicate withdrawal).

Characteristics and Culture of Students

Although the general scarcity of discussions on culture, worldviews and values addressed in the college student literature is quite obvious, a few studies have recently been conducted on college campuses. Carter (1990) found that African-American and Euro-American students hold different cultural beliefs. The cultural values for African-American students were preferences for Evil Human Nature, Past Time Preference, Subjugation to Nature, Being-in-Becoming Activity Preference, and Lineal or Authority based social relations. To be sure, some commonalities may exist among students who are of the same ethnicity or race but these characteristics are not necessarily satisfactory criteria for cultural value similarities. The sociocultural and socialization experiences of some nonwhite students may make them similar in beliefs, values and attitudes to Euro-Americans. Thus, program planners and developers must avoid the mistake of assuming that all students of a particular race or ethnic group perceive the university environment the same. Several intervening factors make blanket generalizations about race and ethnicity inappropriate. Central to this issue is the theory of acculturation which posits an avenue for understanding nonwhite students' needs on predominantly Euro-American campuses.

Some theorists define acculturation as a process of assimilation whereby nonwhite students adopt the behaviors, attitudes and mannerisms of Euro-American culture and relinquish patterns unique to their own culture (e.g., Garcia & Lega, 1979). Others view acculturation as a multi-faceted process that involves a dynamic exchange or transformation of values among or between groups with different values and cultural practices (Berry, 1980; Berry, 1983; Gordon, 1978). According to Berry (1980), the group with the greatest power, however, maintains the most control over this process and the weaker group adapts in several ways including: assimilation, integration, rejection, and deculturation. Bogardus (1950) defines acculturation as

> a process of developing one culture system out of two or more culture systems whose human representatives are in contact with each other . . . a new culture mosaic becomes accepted before its subjects are aware of its adoption (p. 203).

As a result, some nonwhite student groups experience more distress adapting to Euro-American university environments than do others. For example, Sodowsky, Ming Lai and Plake (1991) found Asians more than

Hispanics to perceive racial discrimination and to score lower on acculturation. Within the Asian group, Vietnamese members were least acculturated and Japanese the most acculturated. First-generation immigrants, political refugees and those who adhered to Eastern religions also scored lower on acculturation than later-generation immigrants, voluntary immigrants and Protestants, respectively. Students with cultural values or worldviews that differ from the mission and assumptions of the university as compared to those whose values better fit the institutional culture are especially likely to have social and academic difficulties. Sodowsky and Plake (1992) studied the acculturation of African, Asian, South American, and European international students in a midwestern university and found students of color more than Europeans to report prejudice and preference for their native culture. However, Africans perceived more prejudice than Europeans and the other student groups. Residence status, length of residence, and religion were also related to degree of student acculturation. Ironically, students who are most discrepant in values from those of the college environment are also least likely to benefit from university services when cultural value differences go unrecognized by needs assessors.

Failure to acknowledge within group differences is also obvious in other instances. Consider that "Hispanic" has been used to refer to several groups of people who differ in important ways, yet a comparison of Mexican American and Hispanic, nonMexican American college students reveals that Mexican Americans report lower socioeconomic status levels for parents and lower educational aspirations than do Hispanic, nonMexican Americans (Arbona & Novy, 1991). Arbona and Novy (1991) also report that Cubans and Hispanics from Central and South America are higher in socioeconomic status than are Mexicans or Puerto Ricans. Even students of a similar racial group respond differently to some environmental conditions. For example, African-American students report a preference for same-race counselors but rate values, age, education, and personality of counselor as more important than racial similarity (Atkinson, Furlong, & Poston, 1986).

Because cultural values may vary to the extent with which group members psychologically identify with their group, theorists have examined the role of racial identity in intragroup differences. Parham and Helms's (1981) revision and examination of Cross's (1971) Black identity model shows that the racial identity of African-American and Euro-

American students is characterized by developmental stages. For African-Americans, the developmental process involves four stages which include: Preencounter, Encounter, Immersion/Emersion, and Internalization. In the first stage, African-American students reject or deny their Blackness but idealize Euro-American culture and Whiteness. In the Encounter stage, students are interested in learning of African-American culture and have positive feelings toward their Blackness. The Immersion/Emersion stage is characterized by a rejection of Euro-American culture and increased awareness of prejudice, racism and discrimination. In the Internalization stage, students integrate Blackness into their total identity and accept self as African-American but also recognize Euro-American culture. These stages can be used to develop more suitable needs assessment instruments for African-American students. For example, encounter, immersion and internalization racial attitudes have been shown to relate positively to African-American students' participation in African-American oriented activities.

For Euro-Americans, racial identity development includes five stages: Contact, Disintegration, Reintegration, Pseudo-Independence, and Autonomy. The Contact stage is characterized by naivete of one's own race and other racial groups and interactions with African-Americans for the first time. In the Disintegration stage, Euro-American students become aware of racism and experience internal conflicts that are expressed in various ways (e.g., withdrawal, immersion into African-American culture). The Reintegration stage is basically characterized by withdrawal and denial of human similarities between racial groups. In the Pseudo-Independence stage, Euro-American students develop a cognitive understanding and factual knowledge of racial differences but continue to hold questions about racial similarities and differences. In the Autonomy stage, the cognitive understanding becomes acceptance and differences are not denied or minimized but recognized and appreciated for the diversity brought to interracial or interethnic interactions. White racial identity attitudes have also been found to predict racism for Euro-American college students (Carter, 1990) and Euro-American faculty (Pope-Davis & Ottavi, 1992). Several types of identity models have been developed. For example, the Minority Identity Development Model (MID) developed by Atkinson, Morten and Sue (1983) is based on types of oppression and includes five stages: Conformity, Dissonance, Resistance and Immersion, Introspection, Synergistic Articulation and Awareness. Meyers (1988) also describes a phase model of identity development (i.e., Optimal Theory Applied to Identity Development) based on assumptions of optimal theory which consists of seven phases: Absence of Awareness, Dissonance, Immersion, Internalization, Integration, and Transformation. Models have also been tested with ethnic/racial groups other than African-Americans (Sue, 1981; Keefe & Padilla, 1987) and nonethnic/racial groups such as feminists and gay and lesbian populations (Cass, 1979; Downing & Roush, 1985). Degree of acculturation and stage of racial identity contribute to intragroup variability but characteristics of the institutional context interact with these cultural patterns to affect students' satisfaction, adjustment and performance.

Institutional Characteristics and Culture

University characteristics have a significant impact on students' performance and personal development (Pascarella & Terenzini, 1991). Tinto (1982) proposes that students assimilate into the culture of a university via two primary mechanisms: social and academic integration. Social integration refers to interactions with others and academic integration refers to intellectual and cognitive performance. Failure to integrate at either level can lead to student difficulties and subsequent attrition. Nonwhite students are especially likely to experience integration problems on these campuses but intragroup and intergroup variance can result in different student experiences. For example, Steward, Germain and Jackson (1992) found no difference in alienation or interactional styles among successful Euro-American, Hispanic American or Asian American students, however, successful African-American students varied their interactional style as a function of the racial composition of the campus environment.

The several elements that constitute the university environment influence students' level of social and academic integration. Kuh and Whitt (1988) describe three major dimensions of college campuses that make each unique: college/university itself; subcultures within the college/university; and the external environment that surrounds the college/university campus.

College/University

Kuh (1993) proposes that three sets of properties make up the character of institutions of higher education: mission, philosophy, and culture. The *mission* describes long-range institutional objectives and represents the philosophy of education which motivates operations, customs, rules, and expectations for students, faculty and administrators. Rules and procedures related to curriculum requirements, course content, employment policies, and acceptable conduct originate from the mission and exert direct and indirect influences on nonwhite students. The overriding mission is based on institutional history and tradition and may or may not be reflected in the actual university mission statement. Yet, some institutional missions are more obvious than others. For example, Howard University located in Washington, D.C. and Lincoln Memorial University located on the borders of Kentucky, western Virginia and Tennessee were both founded to educate impoverished and oppressed groups; African-Americans and Euro-Americans of rural Appalachian regions, respectively. However, the mission of Howard University, unlike its original sister institution, Lincoln Memorial University, has expanded since its development to emphasize research and grant productivity, although service to the African-American community remains the thrust of research activities. Additionally, other American nonwhite student populations, Euro-Americans and international students are considered as part of the university's mission of diversity.

The *philosophy* of an institution is characterized by values and underlying assumptions regarding the education of students. Unconscious assumptions guide the values that dictate daily operations and practices of the institution. These values can be observed in the actual operation of the university because stated values may have little to do with what actually occurs. For example, most predominantly Euro-American institutions give mention to plans and goals of diversity, yet few act in ways to make this a reality. Why? Because educational processes and goals on many of these campuses evolve from and adhere to Eurocentric perspectives and principles.

Several researchers have studied the value system of Euro-American *culture*. According to these findings, the Euro-American value orientation emphasizes a doing form of self-expression which is noticeable in external actions (e.g., achievement). Individuals are expected to subdue natural forces and materials for purposes of the group and the future is regarded as more significant than events of the past or present (e.g., graduation, retirement). From this worldview, people are also seen as basically good and the group is viewed as less valuable than the individual (i.e., personal strivings often outweigh group objectives).

Hall (1966) refers to the values and norms of this culture as "low context" and discusses differences between this type of culture and "high context" cultures characteristic of Native Americans, African-Americans and Mexican Americans. These differences in values give rise to overt, covert and subtle differences in areas of interpersonal/social relations, time perspectives, preferred reasoning processes, forms of communication, and overall cultural tempo. Low-context cultures emphasize direct communications, rules and procedures, adherence to time and associated schedules, and analytic ways of processing information. In contrast, high context cultures express less regard for rules and standard schedules, value flexible rules and procedures, allow more time interruptions for unplanned events, respect other ways of knowing (e.g., intuition), emphasize feelings, and attend to needs that promote group harmony.

Based on suggestions of Dyer (1985) and Schien (1985), Kuh (1993) discusses five assumptions that are thought to comprise the essence of a university's character. The assumptions to be considered, as outlined by Kuh, are the following:

1. Relationship between people and nature. What is the relationship between the university and the surrounding natural context as viewed by institutional administrators and officials?

2. Nature of reality and truth. What are the norms, rules and procedures that determine what is "real," how is truth assessed (e.g., research results or personal experiences)?

3. Nature of human nature. What assumptions are made about humans as regards the university structure? How are students perceived? For example, traditionally African-American universities assume that all students can learn with support and encouragement.

4. Nature of human activity. What actions are viewed as appropriate within the college environment? For example, are students to be active or passive learners? Where do play and academic studies fit?

5. Nature of human relations. How are students, faculty, staff, and administrators to relate? Do faculty expect to be distant from students? Are students expected to compete for course grades? How much emphasis is placed on a normal distribution of grades? What is the appropriate manner of relating?

Assumptions that underlie Euro-American values also influence course offerings, student interactions, lectures, design of buildings, and dynamics of residence halls and classrooms. Conflicts that emerge from different value systems and variance within each also contribute to unsettling incidents of intolerance which challenge administrators to examine campus values from the eyes of nonwhite students.

University Subcultures

Various groups can be found within the larger structure of the university environment. These "subcultures" share norms and values that may not be similar to those of the university governance structure. Colleges within the university (e.g., Liberal Arts, Business, Education), departments within each college (e.g., Psychology, Sociology, Curriculum and Instruction, Management), sorority and fraternity groups, racial/ethnic cultural centers, counseling centers, athletic teams, and many others develop a perspective that determines what is acceptable behavior.

Student subcultures are major socialization units for college students. Nonwhite students gravitate toward each other on predominantly Euro-American campuses to seek support in an environment viewed as different and uninviting or intolerant. Group members experience the freedom to express themselves within these enclaves in culturally distinct ways that may go unsupported among nonminority students (DePalma, 1991; Nagasawa & Espinosa, 1992). Murguia, Padilla and Pavel (1991) found the restricted interactions of Hispanic and Native American students on predominantly Euro-American campuses to originate from forced segregation and personal choice as well. African-American more than Euro-American students have also been found to involve themselves in campus activities, although primarily within predominantly African-American clubs and organizations (DeSousa & King, 1992; Mitchell & Dell, 1992). Thus the social integration of nonwhite students primarily involves campus subcultures rather than the campus as a total environment.

The values of some student subcultures are more consistent with those espoused by the university administrators and faculty than are others. Research has shown, for example, that Asian American students' peer culture on Euro-American campuses consist of traditional Asian values that promote academic integration (Butterfield, 1990). These same characteristics, however, deter social integration because they are unable to provide middle-class Euro-American social skills and norms on predominantly Euro-American campuses that fail to recognize the worth of diverse cultures (Nagasawa & Espinosa, 1992). In contrast, African-American students appear to be more socially integrated than their Asian American counterparts but less well academically integrated (Nettles, 1988). For example, race has been found to contribute to grade point average on predominantly Euro-American campuses but not traditionally African-American campuses. Even when SAT scores, high school grades, study habits, socioeconomic status, and academic integration are equal, African-American students receive lower grades on predominantly Euro-American campuses. Although ethnic/racial enclaves are usually homogeneous as regards race or ethnicity, other forms of oppression may be implicated. At the same time that students belong to a social milieu based on racial similarity, they may also identify with enclaves of gay students, international students, or students with disabilities (Chan, 1989; Loiacano, 1989). This overlap among groups makes the needs assessment process even more complex.

External Community

The community that surrounds a particular university is also important to the well-being of nonwhite students. Qualities of the community including racial/ethnic composition, values and beliefs, race relations, and laws and rules exert powerful influences on the university that indirectly affect nonwhite students. Community characteristics also exert direct influences on nonwhite students' sense of belonging, social integration and overall adjustment. For example, universities are often embedded in geographical locations in which residents share similar customs, traditions and values that evolve into norms over the years. These rules and expectations determine whether and which newcomers are accepted and under what conditions.

These norms also influence the college environment in numerous ways. First, universities located in certain areas are more likely to encounter difficulties attracting nonwhite students. Second, for those who enroll in the university, many may fail to progress to graduation because of conflicts with values of the community (e.g., prejudice, racism) and the absence of nonwhite community support (e.g., place of worship). Third, any negative views held by community members toward nonwhite groups may generalize to levels within the university. Many colleges also employ residents of the surrounding community which provides a mechanism for these values to become intertwined with those of the university. Finally, public institutions primarily recruit local students and those from within the state such that diversity in perspective is minimized. Thus, universities located in pluralistic regions may be more successful in the recruitment, retention and graduation of nonwhite students because needs unmet by the university itself can be met via community affiliations.

A MODEL OF NONWHITE STUDENTS' NEEDS

Figure 1 presents a conceptual model combining factors that affect the needs of nonwhite college students. The broken oval drawn around the factors represents the influence of macrolevel events and changes across time that modify interrelationships among the factors within the overall model. Factors on the left are posited to precede those at the immediate and far right. The first two sets of factors in the model are Euro-American cultural values and cultural values of nonwhite American populations. Euro-American values include competition, achievement, individualism, materialism, meritocracy, and a future orientation. Non-white cultural values vary according to the race/ethnic identification of the student populations involved but refer to the values of African-American, Asian American, Hispanic American, and Native American students. The second set of factors, students' background characteristics and cultural values, reflect qualities that students bring to the university setting. The broken boundary around these two sets of factors represents a strong relationship between the two. Different background factors (i.e., socialization, family income, parents' educational level, type of high school attended, academic preparedness, and previous interactions with Euro-Americans) are associated with differences in students' cultural values. However, both are directly determined by the values and worldviews of nonwhite students' racial and ethnic group membership. Students' background characteristics and values also influence the campus and the surrounding community environment, albeit to a lesser extent than the environmental influences exerted on nonwhite students as indicated with the broken arrow. The campus environment is also closely related to the surrounding community and both are directly influenced by Euro-American cultural values of mainstream America as indicated with the solid line. Finally, cultural values of nonwhite groups have a minor effect on the predominantly Euro-American college climate. Theoretically, student needs are the products that derive from the dynamics involved in the numerous reciprocal transactions among social, institutional, and student factors. As the spirit of the times (i.e., *zeitgeist*) changes, so too do

Figure 1
Model of Factors Influencing Nonwhite Students' Needs

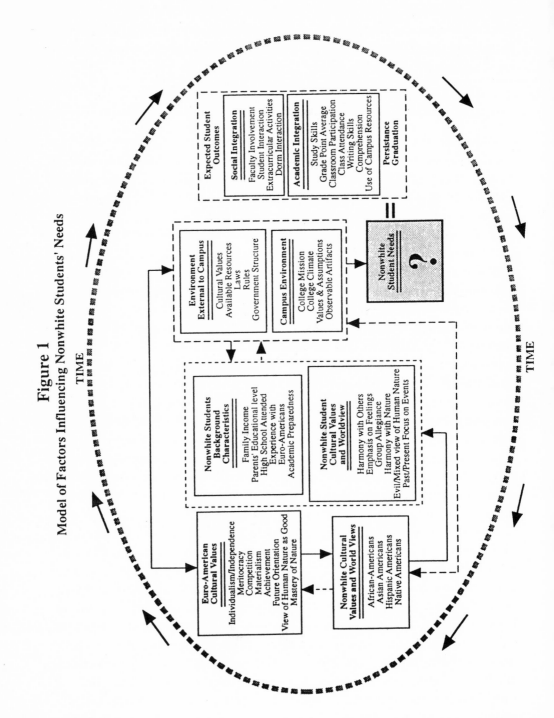

the mechanisms through which these factors influence students and their needs. Unmet needs can thwart social and academic integration which, in turn, prevent outcomes of persistence and graduation.

INTEGRATING CULTURE INTO NEEDS ASSESSMENTS FOR STUDENTS

Based on the previous discussion and model of nonwhite students' needs, general guidelines are offered to university staff and administrators to assist with the integration of cultural variables into the needs assessment process. Because needs are perceived through filters that are culturally mediated and individuals of different cultural backgrounds identify needs that are consistent with their values, it is recommended that assessors conceptualize the needs assessment process, methods and techniques from a culture-specific framework. This approach assumes that needs assessment information is more useful when the perspective of nonwhite students' culture and that of their university are considered. Such a process involves an examination of nonwhite students' behaviors, cognitions and feelings as if the assessor is an outsider looking in. This type of assessment plan encourages the examination of major aspects of students' culture with attention to each group's way of handling academic and social interactions. Based on the primary values identified during this phase, needs are targeted for further understanding. A question that guides this approach asks, "Are there other programs and services that might be more beneficial for this specific student group given their cultural frame of reference?" Culture-specific needs assessment can minimize cultural distortions and account for the numerous factors that make needs assessment a complex process.

Previous assessments have relied on racial-comparative results that yield deficit based data because of comparisons against Euro-American standards of performance and adjustment. A more useful approach assumes that nonwhite student groups possess certain culturally based skills that can be used to assist with needs identification. This way of handling needs is important because the term is vague and open to culturally encapsulated interpretations. The numerous definitions of need also complicate existing biases (e.g., see Bloom, 1976; Stewart, 1979). Different types of needs may emerge when students' perceptions of their unit's functioning are assessed. The goal is to understand the group, especially as regards their problem solving strategies and the influences of any intragroup variables. Related to this objective is the need to examine the university and external community. The task at all three levels is the identification of salient values and assumptions that hinder or enhance the social and academic integration of nonwhite students.

A cultural approach to needs assessment raises several issues. University officials, faculty or staff usually pursue needs assessment data because of experiences or perceptions that a particular student group has problems or concerns. What may be considered as problematic by university observers, however, may not be considered a problem from the perspective of the targeted student group. Likewise, variance in values among certain racial/ethnic groups can affect needs. Stage of racial identity and degree of acculturation into the Euro-American value structure can lead to varied perspectives of a particular concern. For example, a freshman student who is African-American and attended a predominantly African-American high school and who has attitudes characteristic of the encounter stage of racial identity might describe concerns quite differently than a student of the same racial background and academic status who has preencounter racial attitudes and attended a predominantly Euro-American high school.

In addition, students may have difficulties of which observers are unaware. Research also suggests that these subjective methods of establishing needs may be unreliable when the opinions and feelings solicited are not those of the target population that would receive the services. For example, Henggeler, Sallis and Cooper (1980) compared ratings of mental health professionals and students on the seriousness of mental health concerns among students and their families and found disagreement in ratings of the two groups. The professionals were more likely than the students to see needs that approximated existing campus services. Program rationales based on staff's perceptions can especially be inappropriate and ineffective when the worldviews and values from which they originate differ from those of the targeted groups.

A culture-specific approach to needs assessment assumes that students are best at identifying their needs. The generation of items for instruments by assessors may be unnecessary because the methods will evolve from the assumptive framework of the students. Pen-and-paper data collection procedures that require students to respond without interactions with others may be culturally undesirable for some students. With Asian American or African-American students, it may be more appropriate and beneficial to orient toward an interpersonal/social approach rather than the use of standardized instruments. For other student groups, or subgroups of these populations, instrument assessment may be consistent with their values and assumptions. Some points should be kept in mind when survey instruments are used regardless of worldviews and values. This topic is thoroughly covered in Chapter Three and only a few relevant issues are discussed here. First, students should be included in the construction of measures before their development. The inclusion of these group(s) enhances the likelihood that their values, worldviews and assumptions are represented in the item pool and sentence structure of statements. Assessors should also recruit members of the actual groups of interest in order to obtain input into the actual administration of measures when surveys are used. Second, many measures developed for needs assessment purposes are not designed to elicit cultural information about students. These instruments focus on needs but set arbitrary limits on what students may report. Students cannot respond to needs that are not represented. The needs assessment instruments should also reflect the various levels from which needs can evolve (e.g., family concerns, interpersonal relations).

Related to this step in the assessment process is the selection of an assessor who has some fundamental understanding of the different cultures that comprise the student population. This individual should have personal awareness of racial and ethnic biases that could potentially stagnate the flow of information among the students. A positive view of differences in styles of communication, preferences for word choice and language and degree of emotional expressiveness or inexpressiveness is also important for this role. Although an assessor does not have to be of the same racial or ethnic background as the student group, this person should also have a wealth of culturally based information and the ability to feel comfortable with views that might significantly differ from his/her own. Skills that allow the assessor to understand and to be understood are also needed. The ability to engage in active listening, empathic relating, behavioral modeling, and related interpersonal communication skills assist with the acquisition of information. In instances that student groups prefer to use their primary language (e.g., Spanish), the presence of an interpreter who is a member of the student groups' culture would provide a more welcoming forum. Finally, the assessor should be thoroughly knowledgeable of the operations, practices, traditions, values, and rules of the academic institution. To more objectively assess needs, the assessor should ideally be external to the institution but have access to the mission statement and associated institutional policies and practices. In conjunction with the written documentation, nonwhite staff, faculty and administrators might also offer a perspective on these issues. In practice, however, the acquisition of this data can be difficult because many university employees may be reluctant to speak authentically about university values. On the other hand, the role of the assessor as an objective agent may increase their feelings of security, and thus engender more cooperation. Attention should be given to the interdependence of students and the campus ethos. It is essential that the assessor listen to students' and university representatives' views of the conditions under which nonwhite students and institutional qualities interact in relation to academic and social objectives of the university (e.g., grade point average, timely progress, friendship formation) in order to understand this bidirectional relationship. The overt expressions of each assumption within the university culture should be examined. Congruence of espoused and articulated objectives which stem from these assumptions should also be determined. Whether a program or service exacerbates or alleviates nonwhite students' needs may relate to transactions between these underlying assumptions and values of the students. Careful attention should be given to students' values as related to needs associated with different sectors of the institution. Student-faculty, student-administrator/staff and student-student dimensions are important in this regard. Assumptions of students and those of residents within the macrosystem surrounding the institution must be included to understand the interrelationships that influence needs. The location of the university and students' relationships with nonwhite and Euro-American community members and organizations should offer insight into other university dynamics.

CONCLUSION AND SUMMARY

Several benefits are associated with conducting needs assessments from a cultural perspective. First, the inclusion of culture encourages program planners and developers to integrate characteristics of the college climate, students, and program staff as relevant dimensions in the analysis of need. Observable and unobservable student variables can also be allowed under the rubric of needs for students who do not appear to be culturally different from the Euro-American norm (e.g., Appalachian students) but who, in fact do differ. A broad conceptualization of the needs assessment process raises the conscious awareness of administrators such that a greater willingness to understand the impact of institutional culture is promoted. A more dynamic picture of students' needs representative of the natural ebb and flow of development can also be considered from this perspective. The rationale for a cultural-specific perspective in needs assessment methods and processes is to increase the effectiveness of services for students who are dissimilar in culture from the pervasive Puritan ethic (Takaki, 1979). The incorporation of students' level of cultural identification and worldviews at each stage of the needs assessment process can lead to a more precise identification of factors that influence students' experiences and perceptions of the college environment. Because students' needs arise from contextual and personal factors, an understanding of needs must involve an assessment of the transactions that occur at the institutional, community and student levels. Thus, interrelationships among students' cultural values, ideologies, norms and philosophies of educational institutions deserve acknowledgement at each stage of the assessment process. Yet, it is important to recognize that student needs, institutional variables and the needs assessment process are influenced by the climate of society.

REFERENCES

Allen, W. (1988). The education of Black students on White college campuses: What quality the experience? In M. T. Nettles (Ed.), *Toward Black undergraduate student equality in American higher education.* (pp. 57–85). Westport, CT: Greenwood Press.

American Association for Counseling and Development. (1988). *Ethical standards.* Alexandria, VA: Author.

American Council on Education. (1988). *Minorities in higher education* (Fourth annual status report). Washington, DC: Author.

American Psychological Association. (1991). *Guidelines for providers of psychological services to ethnic, linguistic, and culturally diverse populations.* Washington, D.C.: Office of Ethnic Minority Affairs.

Andersen, P. (1991). 7.3 million Asian and Pacific Islanders in the U.S. *Asian Week, 12,* 1–17.

Aponte, J.F. (1978). A need in search of a theory and an approach. *Journal of Community, 6,* 42–44.

Arbona, C., & Novy, D.M. (1991). Hispanic college students: Are there within-group differences? *Journal of College Student Development, 32,* 335–341.

Atkinson, D.R., Furlong, M.J., & Poston, W.C. (1986). Afro-American preferences for counselor characteristics. *Journal of Counseling Psychology, 33,* 326–330.

Atkinson, D.R., Morten, G., & Sue, D.W. (1983). *Counseling American minorities: A cross-cultural perspective.* (3rd ed.). Dubuque, IA: William C. Brown.

Benedict, A.R., Apsler, R., & Morrison, S. (1977). Student views of their counseling needs and counseling services. *Journal of College Student Personnel, 18,* 110–114.

Bennett, C. (1990). *Comprehensive multicultural education.* Boston: Allyn & Bacon.

Berry, J.H.W. (1980). Acculturation as varieties of adaptation. In A.M. Padilla (Ed.), *Acculturation: Theory, models and some new findings* (pp. 9–25). Boulder, CO: Westview Press.

Berry, J.H.W. (1983). Acculturation: A comprehensive analysis of alternative forms. In R.J. Samuda & S.L. Woods (Eds.), *Perspective in immigrant and minority education* (pp. 65–78). Lanham, MD: University Press.

Bloom, B.L. (1976). The use of social indicators in the estimation of health needs. In R.A. Bell, M. Sundel, J.F. Aponte, and S.A. Murrell, (Eds.), *Need assessment in health and human services: Proceedings of the Louisville conference.* Louisville, KY.

Bogardus, E.S. (1950). Intercultural education and acculturation. *Sociology and Social Research, 34,* 203–208.

Brislin, R.W. (1990). *Applied cross-cultural psychology.* Newbury Park, CA: Sage.

Brown, R.D. (1981). The student development educator role. In U. Delworth et al. (Eds.), *Student services: A handbook for the profession* (pp. 191–208). San Francisco: Jossey-Bass.

Butterfield, F. (1990, January 21). Why they excel. *The Parade,* pp. 4–6.

Carney, C.G., & Barak, A. (1976). A survey of student needs and student services. *Journal of College Student Personnel, 17,* 280–284.

Carter, R.T. (1990). The relationship between racism and racial identity among White Americans: An exploratory investigation. *Journal of Counseling and Development, 69,* 46–50.

Cass, V.C. (1979). Homosexual identity formation: A theoretical model. *Journal of Homosexuality, 4,* 219–235.

Chan, C.S. (1989). Issues of identity development among Asian-American lesbians and gay men. *Journal of Counseling & Development, 68,* 161–20.

Cheatham, H.E., Tomlinson, S.M., & Ward, T.J. (1990). The African self-consciousness construct and African American students. *Journal of College Student Development, 31,* 492–499.

Cross, W.E. (1971). The Negro-to-Black conversion experience. *Black World, 7,* 13–27.

D'Augelli, A.R., & Rose, M.L. (1990). Homophobia in a university community: Attitudes and experiences of heterosexual freshmen. *Journal of College Student Development, 31,* 484–491.

DePalma, A. (1991, May 18). Separate ethnic worlds grow on campus. *The New York Times,* pp. 1,7.

DeSousa, D.J., & King, P.M. (1992). Are white students really more involved in collegiate experiences than black students? *Journal of College Student Development, 33,* 363–369.

Downing, N.E., & Roush, K.L. (1985). From passive acceptance to active commitment:

A model of feminist identity development of women. *The Counseling Psychologist, 13,* 59–72.

Dyer, W.G., Jr. (1985). The cycle of cultural evolution in organizations. In Kilmann, R., Saxton, M., Serpa, R., & Associates (Eds.), *Gaining control of the corporate culture* (pp. 200–229). San Francisco, CA: Jossey-Bass.

Florida State Commission on Hispanic Affairs: Eighth Annual Report (1984). *The Hispanic student in Florida's university system.*

Fullerton, J.S., & Potkay, C.R. (1973). Student perceptions of pressures, helps and psychological services. *Journal of College Student Personnel, 14,* 355–361.

Garcia, M., & Lega, L.I. (1979). Development of a Cuban ethnic identity questionnaire. *Hispanic Journal of Behavioral Sciences, 1,* 247–261.

Garcia, S.A., & Presley, K. (1981). An assessment and evaluation program for Black university students in academic jeopardy: A descriptive analysis. *Journal of Community Psychology, 9,* 67–77.

Gordon, M.M. (1978). *Human nature, class, and ethnicity.* New York: Oxford University Press.

Hahn, H. (1985). Changing perception of disability and the future of rehabilitation. In L.G. Perlman & G.F. Austin (Eds.), *Social influences in rehabilitation planning: Blueprint for the 21st century* (pp. 53–64). A report of the Ninth Mary E. Switzer Memorial Seminar. Alexandria, VA: National Rehabilitation Association.

Hall, E.T. (1966). *The hidden dimension.* New York: Doubleday.

Hanson, G.R. (1982). *New directions for student services: Measuring student development.* San Francisco: Jossey-Bass.

Harding, K., Baldwin, S., & Baser, C. (1987). Towards multi-level needs assessment. *Behavioural Psychotherapy, 15,* 134–143.

Harris, S.M., & Nettles, M.T. (1991). Racial differences in student experiences and attitudes. In J.C. Dalton (Ed.), *Racism on campus: Confronting racial bias through peer interventions.* New Directions for Student Services, no. 56 (pp. 25–38). San Francisco: Jossey-Bass.

Henggeler, S.W., Sallis, J.F., & Cooper, P.F. (1980). Comparison of university mental health needs priorities identified by professionals and students. *Journal of Counseling Psychology, 27,* 217–219.

Herek, G.M. (1989). Hate crimes against lesbian and gay men: Issues for research and social policy. *American Psychologist, 4,* 948–955.

Herring, R.D. (1990). Understanding Native American values: Process and content concerns for counselors. *Counseling and Values, 34,* 134–137.

Hsia, J. (1988). *Asian Americans in Higher Education and at Work.* Hillsdale, NJ: Lawrence Erlbaum Associates.

Jackson, A.P., & Meadows, F.B., Jr. (1991). Getting to the bottom to understand the top. *Journal of Counseling & Development, 70,* 72–76.

Keefe, S.F., & Padilla, A.M. (1987). *Chicano ethnicity.* Albuquerque: University of New Mexico Press.

Keller, J., Piotrowsky, C., & Sherry, D. (1982). Perceptions of the college environment and campus life: The Black experience. *Journal of Non-White Concerns in Personnel and Guidance, 10,* 126–132.

Kimmel, W.A. (1977). *Needs assessment: A critical perspective.* Office of Program Systems, OPS for Planning and Evaluation, Department of Health, Education and Welfare, Washington, D.C.

Kluckhohn, C. (1962). The concept of culture. In R. Kluckhohn (Ed.), *Culture and behavior* (pp. 19–73). New York: Free Press.

Kluckhohn, F.R., & Strodtbeck, F.L. (1961). *Variations in value orientations.* Evanston, IL: Row Paterson.

Kuh, G.D. (1993). Appraising the character of a college. *Journal of Counseling & Development, 71,* 661–668.

Kuh, G.L., & Whitt, E.J. (1988). *The invisible tapestry: Culture in American colleges and universities.* Washington, D.C.: ASHE–ERIC Higher Education Report Series #1.

Kulik, C.C., Kulik, J.A., & Shwalb, B.J. (1983). College programs for high risk and disadvantaged students: A meta-analysis of findings. *Review of Educational Research, 53,* 397–414.

Lee, C.C. (1991). Promise and pitfalls of multicultural counseling. In C.C. Lee & B.L. Richardson (Eds.), *Multicultural issues in counseling: New approaches to diversity* (pp. 1–13). Alexandria, VA: American Association for Counseling and Development.

Levine, A. & Associates (1989). *Shaping higher educations' future: Demographic realities and opportunities, 1990-2000.* San Francisco: Jossey-Bass.

Levin, M.E., & Levin, J.R. (1991). A critical examination of academic retention programs for at-risk minority college students. *Journal of College Student Development, 32,* 323–334.

Loiacano, D.K. (1989). Gay identity issues among Black Americans: Racism, homophobia, and the need for validation. *Journal of Counseling & Development, 68,* 21–25.

Loo, C., & Rolison, G. (1986). Alienation of ethnic minority students at a predominantly white university. *Journal of Higher Education, 57,* 59–77.

Magner, D.K. (1989). Blacks and Whites on the campuses: Behind ugly racist incidents, student isolation, and insensitivity. *The Chronicle of Higher Education, 35,* 28–33.

Marable, M. (1988). Race and the demise of liberalism: The 1988 presidential campaign reconsidered. *Black Issues in Higher Education, 5,* 76.

Marti-Costa, S., & Serrano-Garcia, I. (1983). Needs assessment and community development: An ideological perspective. *Prevention in Human Services, 2,* 9–33.

McGuire, J.M., Hall, D., & Litt, A.V. (1991). A field-based study of the direct service needs of college students with learning disabilities. *Journal of College Student Development, 32,* 101–108.

Meyers, L.J. (1988). *Understanding an Afrocentric world view: Introduction to an optimal psychology.* Dubuque, IA: Kendall/Hunt.

Mitchell, S.L., & Dell, D.M. (1992). The relationship between black students' racial identity attitude and participation in campus organizations. *Journal of College Student Development, 33,* 39–43.

Mow, S.L., & Nettles, M.T. (1990). Minority student access to, and persistence and performance in, college: A review of the trends and research literature. In J. Smart (Ed.), *The Handbook of Higher Education* (pp. 35–105). New York: Agathon Press.

Murguia, E., Padilla, R.V., & Pavel, M. (1991). Ethnicity and the concept of social integration in Tinto's model of institutional departure. *Journal of College Student Development, 32,* 433–439.

Murrell, S.A. (1977). Utilization of needs assessment for community decision-making. *American Journal of Community Psychology, 5,* 461–468.

Nagasawa, R., & Espinosa, D.J. (1992). Educational achievement and the adaptive strategy of Asian American college students: Facts, theory and hypotheses. *Journal of College Student Development, 33,* 137–142.

National Center for Education Statistics. (1990). *Trends in racial/ethnic enrollment in higher education: Fall 1978 through Fall 1988.* Washington, DC: U.S. Government Printing Office.

National Institute Against Prejudice and Violence. (1987). *Ethnoviolence on campus: The UMBC study* (Institute Report No. 2). Baltimore, MD: Authors.

Nettles, M.T. (1988). Black and White students' performance and experiences at various types of universities. In M.T. Nettles (Ed.), *Toward Black undergraduate student equality in American higher education* (pp. 35–56). Westport, CT: Greenwood Press.

Nottingham, C.R., Rosen, D.H., & Parks, C. (1992). Psychological well-being among African American university students. *Journal of College Student Development, 33,* 356–362.

Oliver, M.L., Rodgrieguez, C.J., & Mickelson, R.A. (1985). Brown and Black in White: The social adjustment and academic performance of Chicano and Black students in a predominantly White university. *Urban Review, 17,* 3–23.

Paradis, F.E. (1981). Themes in the training of culturally effective psychotherapists. *Counselor Education and Supervision, 21,* 136–151.

Parham, T.A., & Helms, J.E. (1981). The influence of Black students' racial preferences for counselor's race. *Journal of Counseling Psychology, 28,* 250–257.

Parr, G., Bradley, L., & Bingi, R. (1992). Concerns and feelings of international students. *Journal of College Student Development, 33,* 20–25.

Pascarella, E.T., & Terenzini, P.T. (1991). *How college affects students.* San Francisco, CA: Jossey-Bass.

Pedersen, P. (1988). The triad model of multicultural training. *A handbook for developing multicultural awareness.* Alexandria, VA: American Association for Counseling and Development.

Poortinga, Y.H. (1990). Towards a conceptualization of culture for psychology. *Cross-cultural Psychology Bulletin, 24*(3), 2–10.

Pope-Davis, D.B., & Ottavi, T.M. (1992). The influence of White racial identity attitudes on racism among faculty members: A preliminary examination. *Journal of College Student Development, 33,* 389–394.

Pruitt, F. (1978). The adaptation of foreign students on American campuses. *Journal of NAWDAC, 41,* 144–147.

Sanders, D. (1987). Cultural conflicts: An important factor in the academic failures of American Indian students. *Journal of Multicultural Counseling and Development, 15,* 81–90.

Schien, E.H. (1993). Legitimating clinical research in the study of organizational culture. *Journal of Counseling and Development, 71,* 703–708.

Siperstein, G.N. (1988). Students with learning disabilities in college: The need for a programmatic approach to critical transitions. *Journal of Learning Disabilities, 21,* 431–436.

Sodowsky, G.R., Ming Lai, E.W., & Plake, B.S. (1991). Moderating effects of sociocultural variables on acculturation attitudes of Hispanics and Asian Americans. *Journal of Counseling & Development, 70,* 194–204.

Sodowsky, G.R., & Plake, B.S. (1992). A study of acculturation differences among international people and suggestions for sensitivity to within group differences. *Journal of Counseling & Development, 71,* 53–59.

Steward, R.J., Germain, S., & Jackson, J.D. (1992). Alienation and interactional style: A study of successful Anglo, Asian, and Hispanic University students. *Journal of College Student Development, 33,* 149–156.

Steward, R.J., Jackson, M.R., & Jackson, J.K. (1990). Alienation and interactional style in a predominantly white environment: A study of successful Black students. *Journal of College Student Development, 31,* 509–515.

Stewart, R. (1979). The nature of needs assessment in community mental health. *Community Mental Health Journal, 15*(4), 287–295.

Strong, L.J. (1986). *Race relations for personal and organizational effectiveness.* Unpublished manuscript.

Sue, D.W. (1981). *Counseling the culturally different: Theory and practice.* New York: Wiley.

Sue, D.W. (1991). A conceptual model for cultural diversity training. *Journal of Counseling & Development, 70,* 99–105.

Sue, D.W., Arredondo, P., & McDavis, R.J. (1992). Multicultural counseling competencies and standards: A call to the profession. *Journal of Counseling & Development, 70,* 477–486.

Sue, S., Sue, D., & Wong, H. (1985). Where are the Asian American leaders and top executives? *Pacific/Asian American Mental Health Research Center Research Review, 4,* 13–15.

Sue, S., & Zane, N.W.S. (1985). Academic achievement and socioemotional adjustment among Chinese university students. *Journal of Counseling Psychology, 32,* 570–579.

Suzuki, B. (1990). Education and the socialization of Asian Americans: A revisionist analysis of the "model minority" theses. In R. Endo, S. Sue, & N. Wagner (Eds.), *Asian-Americans: Social and psychological perspectives* (pp. 155–178). Palo Alto, CA: Science and Behavioral Books.

Takaki, R. (1979). *Iron cages.* New York: Oxford University Press.

Tinto, V. (1982). Limits of theory and practice in student attrition. *Journal of Higher Education, 53,* 687–699.

U.S. Department of Commerce, Bureau of the Census, Current Population (April, 1988). *School enrollment-social and economic characteristics of students: October 1975 and 1984.* (Series p-20, No. 426).

U.S. Department of Commerce, Bureau of the Census. (1991). *Statistical Abstracts of the United States.* Washington, DC: Author.

Warner, R.W., Jr. (1975). Planning for research and evaluation: Necessary conditions. *Personnel and Guidance Journal, 54,* 10–11.

Webster, D.S. (1984). Chicano students in American higher education. *Integrated Education, 22,* 42–51.

Westbrook, F.D., Miyares, J., & Roberts, J.H. (1978). Perceived problems areas by black and white students and hints about comparative counseling needs. *Journal of Counseling Psychology, 25,* 119–123.

White, T.J., & Sedlacek, W.E. (1987). White student attitudes toward Blacks and Hispanics: Programming implications. *Journal of Multicultural Counseling and Development, 15,* 171–183.

Wiley, E., III. (1989). Native American educational plight described as national disgrace. *Black Issues in Higher Education,* 6(3), 8–9.

Wilson, F.R., & Yaeger, G.G. (1981). A process model for prevention program research. *Personnel and Guidance Journal, 59,* 590–595.

Chapter 3

NEEDS ASSESSMENT METHODOLOGIES

SALLY D. STABB

This chapter is intended to give the reader an overview of needs assessments methodologies—traditional/quantitative, qualitative, and mixed model approaches. A careful reading of the chapter should give student service professionals enough information to design a needs assessment project by adapting the guidelines herein and modifying the examples given to suit their unique institutional context. There is a particular emphasis on the political nature of needs assessment—how to make it work in a system with diverse, and sometimes conflicting, constituencies. Additionally, the interaction between methodology and majority/minority issues is discussed at some length.

Of course, there are also sections specific to basics such as instrumentation, data collection, and analysis from a variety of perspectives. However, the chapter is not meant to be either a mini-statistics text or an in-depth review of all possible research designs. The chapter concludes with a recommendations section, in which particularly salient points from the body of the work are highlighted.

TRADITIONAL METHODS

Traditional needs assessment from a quantitative paradigm is likely the most familiar to student service professionals. Some notable leaders in the area have been well published and often cited—George Kuh (1982) and Oscar T. Lenning (1980a, 1980b). These foundational works will form the basis for the initial discussion of classic needs assessment methodologies in this chapter. The incorporation of other researchers will extend and refine their needs assessment work.

Definitions

Most discussions of traditional needs assessment methodologies start with definitions and ask the question "What are needs?" Lenning (1980a) defines two types of needs. Met needs are necessary or desirable conditions that already exist in actuality. Unmet needs arise when there is a discrepancy between desirable conditions and current actuality. These needs would be judged by multiple, objective criteria that have been agreed upon by the relevant parties involved.

These definitions highlight two important points: that needs can be met or unmet, and that they are determined in part by consensus and in part by objective measures. Lenning also distinguishes between needs and wants or demands. He sees wants and demands as the vocal expression of unmet needs: "Wants are most often than not indications that a real need is present . . . especially if those wants become expressed in terms of strong and critical demands or expressions of anguish and of grave concern" (p. 265). However, he also cautions against equating a vocal outcry for something students want with a legitimate need: "There have been occasions when some students demanded something merely because other students had it . . . primarily to attract attention . . . or to keep other students from having it" (p. 266). Lenning essentially sees needs as related to issues that have "primary or critical statuses, conditions, and situations, not with superficial or trivial matters" (p. 265)—those judged to be necessities rather than luxuries. In a general sense, he notes that students have educational needs as well as needs placed on them through eventual employers, industries, communities, and family, friends and peers.

Lenning (1980a, 1980b) also reviews the concept of need as seen through the eyes of various psychological theorists, such as Murray's classification of needs, Maslow's hierarchy of needs, and needs suggested by developmental theorists. Any of these theories may serve as a conceptual basis for a needs assessment, although a detailed discussion of each is beyond the scope of this chapter (the reader is advised to consult primary sources for such elaboration). Lenning also notes that needs can be conceptualized in terms of student problems, which might be evaluated using a problem checklist. Lenning and others (Humm-Delgado & Delgado, 1986) review the schemes for categorizing types of needs. These types include (1) normative needs, based on an absolute standard of adequacy, such as professional standards for adequate housing, (2) felt need, such as a wanted or desired service, (3) expressed need, which reflects an active demand such as a waiting list for an agency's services, (4) comparative needs, which are determined by comparisons of analogous groups, in which one group is typically underserved in relation to the other, and (5) future needs—those which are anticipated or projected.

Kuh (1982) also reviews definitions of needs. In addition to those discussed, he notes democratic needs—a change desired by the majority of some reference group, and discrepancy needs—the difference between a present state of functioning and an ideal or acceptable level of functioning. Many of the needs in Lenning's (1980a) discussion also fall into this latter category. Kuh additionally reviews the terminology of maintenance needs and incremental needs. Maintenance needs are similar to met needs—the need exists, but without apparent gap or shortfall, such as students needing to have study time, and having adequate time. Incremental needs exist when a gap exists—the student needs study time, but not enough is available. Kuh also recognizes that needs can be short-term or long-term, generic or specific. Other definitions reviewed include the idea that needs are an interaction of level of necessity and discrepancy of some dimension(s).

While the multitude of definitions and typologies of need may seem overwhelming, in practice, needs assessments most often converge on some type of unmet need/discrepancy need evaluation. Although the other types of needs should be assessed, practical reality often dictates that some types of needs, such as met needs or future needs, will not receive attention. Student service professionals will often ignore long-term needs in favor of short-term needs in an attempt to meet immediate, high profile demands on campus. However, there is nothing wrong with meeting short-term needs, and there is near universal recognition of needs assessment as an ongoing, dynamic process that responds to shifts in the local context. For example, Mayes and McConatha's (1982) survey of student needs compared 1980 data to that researchers gathered using the same instrument four and eleven years earlier. Clear shifts in students' priorities were observed on a number of items.

Purposes

Needs assessments can serve a variety of purposes and determining that purpose is the next conceptual step in the planning process. Kuh (1982) identifies five possible purposes for needs assessment. The first is to monitor stakeholder perceptions. The purpose here is to generate ideas and document perceptions about various issues. Perception monitoring tends to be exploratory in nature and relatively non-threatening, although it may fail to differentiate wants and needs or be directly linked to action. The second purpose is program or policy justification. The purpose here is to determine whether presently available services, options, etc. are acceptable or to gather support for possible alternatives. This is more likely to involve people in decision making, but still may not differentiate wants and needs. The third purpose for needs assessment is to develop a satisfaction index. The purpose here is to estimate the relative acceptability of various potential alternatives/solutions. This can clarify potentially controversial issues, especially if a variety of subgroups are assessed, but tends to highlight wants over needs. The fourth purpose is to actually select the most acceptable policy or program from among alternatives. This allows stakeholders to influence institutional response to needs. (Depending on your perspective, this level of influence may be viewed as highly desirable or as threatening). The fifth purpose of a needs assessment is to determine if needs have been met. The focus is on evaluating programs or services that are already in place and documenting their effectiveness—or lack thereof. This type of needs assessment focuses on previously identified concerns (e.g., How are we doing?) rather than needs that arise. Kuh clearly recognizes that these purposes can overlap. In fact, a number of these purposes are often met simultaneously in the course of a single needs assessment.

Planning

This stage involves developing resources and support for the needs assessment, planning and outlining the process, coordinating personnel/ participant involvement, and selecting a specific methodology and/or assessment instrument(s). Lenning (1980a) notes that as formal planning proceeds, informal networks should be kept active. "The needs assessors . . . should attempt to, in various ways, keep the communication channels open to all areas and levels of the campus community and remain alert for impromptu evidence that needs of a particular group or in a particular area are changing and need in-depth assessment" (p. 275). Decisions also should be made about who will actually conduct the assessment, and whether coordination will occur through a central office on campus, such as an institutional research office, or through the staffs of specific departments and/or programs. Lenning gives an excellent overview of these processes:

> In the first case, economies of scale can occur and institutionwide coverage of programs is assured. Although a central office, usually institutional research or academic planning, is coordinating and carrying out most of the needs assessment activities, program planners and administrators will be using the information for planning and operational decision making, respectively. This means they should be intimately involved in needs assessment planning, deciding what information should be collected and how it should be analyzed and reported. In the second case, activities will be taking place largely within the department or program; but the institutional research office should be proactive in providing technical consultation as needed about useful measures, data collection methodology, analysis, and application to program planning and decision making. Furthermore, all programs will need common data (broken down by program) about students, the external environment (including campus data), the total institutional situation, and so forth that is already being collected or gathered from other collection sources by the institutional research office or would best be collected or gathered by it (p. 276).

The specific choices made will reflect the goals, organizational structure, patterns of staff expertise, and politics of the particular institution/ departments wishing to carry out the needs assessment. Lenning implies that typically one individual will be a project coordinator, who after laying some initial groundwork, would then construct a planning committee, composed of representatives of all relevant and interested constituencies. He stresses the political nature of the process at this point, noting that personalities, expertise, motivation, and commitment should be taken into account. Typical lines of authority in the system should not be ignored. The committee should not get too large, or it will become ineffective. Lenning notes that students should have some representation on the planning committee:

> Full student involvement (by perhaps a couple of students) in the planning committee deliberations is essential for the success of an effort that is attempting to collect and use information about student program needs ... student members ... if they are chosen carefully, may be able to provide valuable input, effectively communicate the importance of the study to their fellow students, and elicit student support for and cooperation in the data collection from students (p. 277).

It will be the mission of the planning committee to agree on specific purposes, goals, and objectives of the needs assessment. The planning committee should come to some consensus about what types of needs are of concern and for whom, what data is to be collected and why, and how the data will relate to programs and be used. Lenning recommends developing a list of factors that will facilitate the needs assessment process and those that will hinder it.

The planning committee will also determine what specific assessments are to be used and how data will be collected. This is essentially the "research design and instrumentation" part of the process. In selecting instruments, reliability and validity are primary criteria. Lenning (1980a) recommends the use of multiple measures due to the strengths and weaknesses of specific individual assessment tools. Reliability and validity can vary across different groups of students and instruments may or may not have appropriate norms for subgroups of students; thus, an appropriate review of a potential instrument's psychometric properties is essential. Lenning states:

> The use of quick and inexpensive data collection methods, such as student self-report (which much research has found to be generally reliable and valid) and data collected for other purposes (secondary data), may provide a valuable supplement to data provided by more expensive and sophisticated data collected with tests and psychometric inventories (p. 279).

The most typical types of assessment instruments chosen are paper-and-pencil measures. Because group data is usually used, reliability coefficients of these instruments need not be tremendously high (e.g., down to .6 is considered acceptable). However, the measures should be carefully examined to see if the items specifically target the types of needs the committee has agreed to assess. Often, you will choose to develop your own instrument. Rather than starting from scratch, many needs assessment researchers chose to modify instruments already developed at other institutions. Access to these assessment tools usually may be obtained through collegial networking or through literature reviews of already published needs assessments, which often list the entire contents of the surveys in the articles. Of course, appropriate permissions should be obtained. Committee members or consultants with expertise in test development and measurement should be intimately involved with the creation of the new instrument, and can give assistance with issues such as norm-referencing or criteria referencing, reliability, and pilot testing of face/content validity.

If you are developing your own instrument, one of the fundamental questions you will need to address is "What exactly do we ask and how?"

Some, such as Evans (1985), recommend using a specific theory base (such as her use of Chickering's developmental vectors) to guide choices for specific item selection and content. As mentioned earlier, reviewing pertinent literature and examining others' needs assessment instruments can also give leads. Another extremely important point regarding item selection/wording comes from Friedlander (1978), who notes that needs assessors are likely to get very different responses depending on whether students are asked to rate the importance of needs or to rate their actual intent to use services targeting these needs. Vastly different information—and consequently, program decisions—might be made. Many students will rank items such as "need to develop good study skills" very high on importance, but when asked if they will commit to attend a workshop on the topic, or if they can envision using academic services over the next year for assistance, indicate that they do not plan to participate. Clearly, it is a massive waste of resources for student service professionals to design and implement programs which students do not plan to use, even though they rate the needs as important. Social psychologists have reliably documented this fundamentally low relationship between attitudes and behavior for years, and efforts should be made to use this information in constructing your needs assessment instrument. The personal experiences of the editors of this book also strongly support this recommendation. In our needs assessment work in counseling centers, we asked students to rate both importance of and intent to use services, as well as their preferred format (individual counseling, group counseling, or presentations in dorms). These three types of information gave a more comprehensive, realistic, and practical assessment than if we had asked only for importance ratings.

In addition to standardized paper and pencil inventories and locally developed questionnaires, standardized interviews may be conducted. These interviews typically follow a highly prescribed and agreed-upon format. Interviewers are typically trained to administer the interview in a standardized format, including how questions are asked, how much and what type(s) of prompts are given, and how interviewee questions are to be handled. Traditionally, questions are structured so that clear and quantifiable responses can be generated.

Although Lenning (1986a) clearly advocates traditional methods and expresses concern about classic issues such as reliability and validity, he also acknowledges that non-traditional forms of assessment, such as the effective use of archival data, may yield valuable supplemental information.

However, a detailed discussion of these methods will be presented in the next section on qualitative methodology.

It should be noted at this point that the planning committee is also responsible for determining a method of data collection. Needs assessments are not the kind of research in which experimental and control groups are involved, and that would be in fact, an inappropriate conceptualization. They are not experimental designs at all. No interventions are introduced or compared; no one group of students serves as a control group against which other students are judged (particularly such as judging minority students needs against those of majority students). Needs assessments can perhaps best be described as correlational designs. The real choices at this stage involve selecting and gaining access to appropriate samples.

Data Collection

The next major step in needs assessment is data collection. As an overview, Lenning (1980b) notes:

> The proper measures and data collection methods are of no avail if one does not plan well and use care in the actual data collection. For example, a poorly worded cover letter sent out with a questionnaire can easily cut the response rate in half or more; so can sending the questionnaire shortly before midterm exams. Much time, money, and frustration can be saved if one takes pains to have well-designed interview forms, written instructions for test administrators, careful selection of samples, questionnaire items free of bias, well designed pilot tests to try out procedures for maximizing response rate (such as showing the need for such data and promising—and giving—respondents feedback about the results), sensible coding and data formatting rules, careful editing procedures, and so forth (p. 241).

Some of these issues have been considered already. Let us turn our attention to selection of samples and strategies for actual data collection.

Often, a traditional needs assessment will attempt a random selection of all university students or a random selection within a certain group, such as freshmen. This is typically determined by such methods as computer-generated lists or taking every 10th name in the student directory, etc. The benefits of random selection are well documented, and if such a sample can be obtained, will theoretically result in a sample that is representative of the population. Often, however, samples of convenience are used instead, such as all freshmen at a particular orientation meeting, students in large introductory courses easily accessible to the assessors, students who attend regular meetings of a certain student organization, or students who agree to take a survey in the student union during lunch hours over a two-week period. This is particularly true if personal administration of surveys (i.e., handing them out) is used as a distribution method. Occasionally, a needs assessor may attempt to survey an entire population, such as all handicapped or international students on campus. Thus, needs assessors should carefully note the composition and demographics of their samples, particularly non-random and/or small samples, since interpretations of data from such samples is likely to be skewed or to have limited generalizability.

As far as specific data collection techniques are concerned, the major, traditional strategies include mailing questionnaires, using telephone surveys, handing out questionnaires, and conducting standardized interviews. Each of these techniques has its pros and cons.

Mailing surveys is relatively quick and efficient, although production and postal costs (including return postage) are high when large samples are involved. Mailing also is conducive to random selection strategies, at least in terms of initial distribution. Perhaps the most serious drawback to using mail surveys is the typically low rate of return. Many researchers report return rates in the 25–35% range. With such low response rates, one must question whether the initial random selection of participants makes any difference. Furthermore, it is often difficult to determine what distinguishes those who respond from those who do not. Even if demographic data are available, the psychosocial or environmental factors that mitigate a participant's choice whether or not to respond may remain unknown. Return rates for mail surveys can be enhanced by inclusion of a convincing cover letter, providing clear instructions, developing a questionnaire of moderate length, and by sending least one, and often two, reminder/follow-up postcards. Some method of coding surveys is needed, both to keep track of data flow and to ensure the confidentiality and/or anonymity of participants. If true and complete anonymity is desired, however, selective follow-ups of those who failed to respond may not be possible. Yet, the anonymous nature of mail questionnaires permits assessment of sensitive information which a participant might be reluctant to disclose face to face.

Telephone surveys have the advantage of greater return rates than mail surveys. In their comparison of the two strategies, Talley, Barrow, Fulkerson, and Moore (1983) obtained a 34.5% return rate on mail-out questionnaires in contrast to a 79.2% response with telephone surveys. Phone surveys also allow participants to ask questions, to get clarification, and perhaps to feel more involved than those receiving mail surveys. The disadvantages lie in the time and training involved; interviewers must learn the assessment protocol, schedule time to make calls, conduct the telephone interview, and keep track of who didn't respond or who need to be called back—each a potentially lengthy process. An additional issue that may arise in phone interviews is social desirability bias, in which respondents may feel uncomfortable talking about negative, critical, or highly personal matters.

Direct handing out of questionnaires has the benefit of assuring large numbers of respondents in short periods of time, particularly if a captive audience is allowed to complete the instrument immediately. Alternately, respondents may be asked to return the survey the next class period or to bring it to a specific location, although this procedure usually produces a considerable reduction in response rates. Like phone interviews, this method potentially allows a certain amount of interaction between assessor and participant. Social desirability pressures are also less likely than in phone surveys, although more likely than with mailing. In addition, scheduling can be an issue with this method, and permission should be obtained from faculty or other agency staff to contact "their" students. As noted earlier, this technique rarely captures a random sample of students.

Finally, structured interviews may be used to collect needs assessment data. Social desirability factors are likely to be at a high point, and the ability of interviewers to develop trust and rapport will be a crucial skill. However, response rates are often high and comprehensive data may be collected. In addition, structured interviews often elicit useful information which is not part of the protocol. This method also demands that interviewers are trained in the standard administration and coding of responses. It is a time-consuming, but often profitable and gratifying procedure which lies closest to the non-traditional methods discussed later in this chapter.

Interpretation, Analysis and Distribution of Data

Obviously, the type of interpretation and analysis of data depends a great deal on the type of data you collect and on the goals of the needs assessment planning committee. In the most typical case scenario, a series of needs are rated as to their importance, usually on Likert type scales. For example, services are rated on the likelihood of being used, etc. Demographics such as age, sex, ethnicity, and class are also typically available. Commonly, this type of data is analyzed with descriptive statistics, including means, ranges, frequencies, percentages and rank orderings. A variety of breakdowns are also possible, such as reporting needs of males and females, freshmen and seniors, female freshmen and male freshman, etc. With regard to averages, "those items having an average score above a certain threshold level (that is logically or definitionally determined) can be considered to indicate needs" (Lenning, 1980a, p. 282). For example, depending on the resources and climate of your institution and the orientation of its needs assessment committee, if one's rating scale for each item is as follows: 1 = not a need at all, 2 = once in awhile is a need, 3 = sometimes a need, 4 = often a need, and 5 = always a need, then a criteria of a mean of 3.5 or 4.0 or 4.5 might be selected.

If different constituencies have responded to the needs assessment, the items ranked at high levels can be viewed as strong and converging evidence that the need is real and intense. Patterns of conflicting needs can also be identified by examining the results from differing subgroups.

In terms of more complex analyses, Lenning (1980a) states:

> . . . statistical tests separately on each scale, and across scales that are equivalent in nature, can be helpful in assessing amplitudes, amplitude discrepancies, and amplitude similarities. The use of profile and graphical analyses can highlight such patterns and make them more understandable. Intercorrelations where there is continuous data or discrete data with a number of points on the scale, and correlations with other student or program factors, can suggest possible reasons for needs. So can multivariate analyses, such as analysis of variance, analysis of covariance, and discriminant analysis (p. 283).

Lenning discusses a number of other more esoteric data analysis procedures; the reader is referred to his work, to basic statistics texts, or to your local statistician for consultation in these matters, as a detailed elaboration of statistical techniques is not the focus here.

Appropriate interpretation and use of secondary data, such as institutional records, in combination with specific needs assessment data can also be effective. For example, in a study by the first author and a colleague (Stabb & Cogdal, 1992), archival data from counseling center records on presenting problems of African-American men in personal counseling were compared with needs assessment data that had been recently obtained. Interesting discrepancies were found between what

African-American males said they needed in counseling on the needs assessment and what concerns they actually talked about once there. Likewise, information gathered during the needs assessment that is not necessarily quantifiable should be evaluated, such as responses to open-ended questions, comments written by students, or remarks noted by researchers in data collection.

There is always a certain amount of subjective analysis that occurs and the interpretation or meaning attached to results is clearly a judgement call. There is likely to be disagreement about what the numbers really mean, and different groups may idiosyncratically interpret the results. If the needs assessment planning team has agreed upon the objective criteria in advance, some of this potential conflict may be avoided. Still, one should expect a good deal of discussion about priorities, especially if funding to implement programs is tight.

Regardless of the specific decisions made, the results of the needs assessment study should be made readily available to all those who have an interest and those who participated. This includes the students themselves as well as administrators, staff and faculty who may have been involved in the process. The report may be presented somewhat differently depending on the specific audience, but basic information should be available to all.

Program Implementation and Evaluation

While perhaps not actually a phase of needs assessment itself, program implementation is the logical and intended outcome of such an endeavor. In fact, if program implementation is not feasible for financial, political, or other reasons, the needs assessment should probably not be undertaken as it will result only in frustration, both for those who have wasted their time doing the assessment and for those who had hoped for change as a result of it. Once programs are in place, they will have to be evaluated in an ongoing way—a process that is a very close cousin to needs assessment (as a quick check back at the "purposes" section will verify). These interrelated processes form part of the continuous cycle of feedback and modification that will always be a part of student services if we are to meet the shifting needs and context of our academic communities.

QUALITATIVE METHODS

Qualitative methodologies and the philosophy that underlies them may be less familiar to many readers than more traditional formats such as those described in the previous section. Therefore, a somewhat more lengthy discussion of these techniques is in order. While some of the content that follows is general, in the sense that the foundations of qualitative inquiry will be outlined, the application of these concepts to needs assessment per se will be made in appropriate sections. Some concluding remarks about the applicability of these methods to assessing the needs of diverse groups of students in particular will close the qualitative methods component of this chapter.

It is difficult to summarize the variety of possible qualitative approaches available, but some attempt will be made to do so, along with the identification of common themes that run through all these methods. For the reader who is interested in pursuing these topics at greater depth, a number of excellent books are now available on qualitative inquiry. In particular, I would recommend Patton's (1990) *Qualitative Evaluation and Research Methods,* Lincoln and Guba's (1985) *Naturalistic Inquiry,* and Marshall and Rossman's (1989) *Designing Qualitative Research.* Complete citations for these references are available at the end of this chapter.

What is Qualitative Inquiry?

For those who have no familiarity with qualitative inquiry, the best place to start is in answering the question "What is it?" Qualitative inquiry, in general, is research that minimizes how much the investigator manipulates and controls the environment and its subjects, and places none or few prior constraints on what the outcomes of the process will be. In traditional designs, the researcher tries to "control for" external influences and to measure narrow, specific, quantifiable outcomes. In many ways, qualitative inquiry is in sharp contrast to the traditional "scientific method" into which most of us were indoctrinated. There are many varieties of qualitative research, and the terminology can be confusing. The broadest terms seem to be "qualitative," "new paradigm research," "post-positivist" or "naturalistic," although the later is sometimes used to refer to more specific methods. However, they all share notable differences with traditional research designs and assumptions.

These contrasts are summarized below in Table I, taken from the work of Lincoln and Guba (1985):

Table I: Contrasting Positivist and Naturalist Axioms

Axioms About	Positivist Paradigm	Naturalist Paradigm
The nature of reality	Reality is single, tangible and fragmentable	Realities are multiple, constructed, and holistic
The relationship of knower to the known	Knower and known are independent; a dualism	Knower and known are interactive, inseparable
The possibility of generalization	Time- and context-free generalizations (nomothetic statements) are possible	Only time- and context-bound working hypotheses (idiographic statements) are possible
The possibility of causal linkages	There are real causes, temporarily precedent to or simultaneous with their effects	All entities are in a state of mutual simoultaneous shaping, so that it is impossible to distinguish causes from effects
The role of values	Inquiry is value-free	Inquiry is value laden

From Lincoln, Y. S. and Guba, E. G. (1985). *Naturalistic Inquiry.* (p. 37). Reprinted by permission of Sage Publications, Inc.

A thoughtful examination of this brief table highlights how the fundamental assumptions of the two paradigms differ. Based on these underlying tenets, Lincoln and Guba elaborate on the general ways in which actual research operations would be conducted. These include use of naturalistic settings, the researcher as the primary tool for data-gathering, the legitimate use of tacit/intuitive knowledge, preference for qualitative over quantitative data/methods, purposive rather that random sampling, preference for inductive vs. deductive analysis, the development of theory as it emerges from the data itself—usually termed "grounded theory," emergent design—rather than predetermined research design, negotiated outcomes, case study reporting modes, idiographic interpretation, tentative application, focus determined boundaries, and special criteria for trustworthiness.

A similar, related group of themes of qualitative inquiry have been developed by Patton (1990). His ten themes are reproduced in Table II. There is general agreement on these themes, with the possible exception of number 9, as quite a few qualitative researchers actively support the use of research for advocacy and political change (e.g., Cook & Fonow, 1990; Reinharz, 1992).

Table II: Themes of Qualitative Inquiry

1. Naturalistic inquiry	Studying real-world situations as they unfold naturally; non-manipulative, unobtrusive, and non-controlling; openness to whatever emerges — lack of predetermined constraints on outcomes
2. Inductive analysis	Immersion in the details and specifics of the data to discover important categories, dimensions, and interrelationships; begin by exploring genuinely open questions rather than testing theoretically derived (deductive) hypotheses
3. Holistic perspective	The whole phenomenon under study is understood as a complex system that is more than the sum of its parts; focus on complex interdependencies not meaningfully reduced to a few discrete variables and linear, cause-effect relationships.
4. Qualitative data	Detailed, thick description; inquiry in depth; direct quotations capturing people's personal perspectives and experiences
5. Personal contact and insight	The researcher has direct contact with and gets close to the people, situation, and phenomenon under study; researcher's personal experiences and insights are an important part of the inquiry and critical to understanding the phenomenon
6. Dynamic systems	Attention to processes; assumes change is constant and ongoing whether the focus is on an individual or an entire culture
7. Unique case orientation	Assumes each case is special and unique: the first level of inquiry is being true to, respecting, and capturing the details of individual cases being studied; cross-case analysis follows from and depends on the quality of individual case studies
8. Context sensitivity	Places findings in a social, historical, and temporal context; dubious of the possibility of meaningfulness of generalizations across time and space

Table II: (Continued)

9. Empathic neutrality	Complete objectivity is impossible; pure subjectivity undermines credibility; the researcher's passion is understanding the world in all its complexity—not proving something, not advocating, not advancing personal agendas, but understanding; the researcher includes personal experience and empathic insight as a part of the relevant data, while taking a neutral, non-judgemental stance toward whatever content may emerge
10. Design flexibility	Open to adapting inquiry as understanding deepens and/or situations change; avoids getting locked into rigid designs that eliminate responsiveness; pursues new paths of discovery as they emerge

From Patton, M. Q. (c 1990). *Qualitative Evaluation and Research Methods.* (pp. 40–41). Reprinted with permission of Sage Publications, Inc.

The reader should now have a flavor for what qualitative inquiry is all about. However, there is often skepticism about these methods, which seem so different from what most of us are used to. Thus, a brief discussion of the rationales for qualitative inquiry are presented next. It is also worth mentioning that these reasons may come in handy if and when you decide to do a qualitative needs assessment—chances are, you too will have to justify these methods to various colleagues, administrators, or funding agencies (Marshall & Rossman, 1989).

Rationales for Qualitative Inquiry

Why use qualitative methods at all? Primarily, because human problems and human nature have a hard time fitting into the traditional scientific method. We don't stand still to be counted, we change, we do alot inside our heads that no-one sees. There is a clear belief in the new paradigm that research methods need to match the nature of the beings participating in that research.

Hoshmand (1989) and Polkinghorne (1991) discuss a number of specific rationales. Among these, there is a recognition that human observation is rooted in context, presumptions, worldview, and language. Qualitative design can use this contextuality, rather than view it as a threat to validity. In a related vein, the traditional idea that the observer and the observed are unaffected by each other seems unrealistic. Human beings are not anywhere near as predictable as the laws derived from the scientific methods would deem desirable; the standard methods of reductionism and constancy in measurement are not possible with covert human processes such as perception, inference and intention. Yet processes such as intentionality and the construction of meaning are qualities that are fundamentally human and important. These authors argue that due to our self-constructing nature and ability to create change, human nature is basically not amenable to study using traditional methods.

Idealogically, there is also a sense that traditional methods reflect a world view that is too deterministic; that fails to acknowledge the human ability for self-determination (Hoshmand, 1989). Also, many assert that research in the conventional sense often exploits people (Cook & Fonow, 1990; Lincoln & Guba, 1985). (This has historically been particularly true in the case of majority researchers studying minority groups, and will be discussed in more depth at the end of this chapter). Reason (1988) states that traditional research methods alienate research participants from both the actual work of the research and its eventual product. In doing so, it has the potential to alienate research participants from others and themselves. He talks about doing research "*with* and *for* people, rather than *on* people" (p. 1, emphasis in original). It is easy to envision this negative process in needs assessment research; with little or no input regarding what is to be asked or to whom, students are surveyed with a questionnaire developed and distributed by people they may never meet or interact with, and consequent decisions about programs are made with out further input from them. An example of how to use qualitative methods to remediate these potential difficulties will be presented shortly.

When to Use Qualitative Inquiry

While proponents of new paradigm research are clearly enthusiastic, most agree that there are certain types of situations and research questions that are more amenable to qualitative inquiry than others. The work of Patton (1990), Williams (1986a), and Peshkin (1993) will be integrated to help answer the question "When should I use a qualitative design?"

Qualitative designs are good to use when your goal is to describe a system, group of people, individuals, etc. in their natural state. Complex processes and interpersonal relationships are difficult to capture with traditional methods, but may come alive through thick, detailed description. These methods are also good to use when exploration and discovery are goals, when little is known about a topic, system, subculture and so forth, or when breaking established organizational/program routines to gain new insights. A determination must be made if the situation will permit intensive inquiry.

Qualitative designs are also excellent strategies for a variety of program evaluations at a variety of stages. These may include implementation evaluation, formative evaluation, process evaluation, quality assurance, program quality or quality of life, prevention evaluations, policy evaluation, and practice evaluations.

Qualitative designs are recommended when there is a need for unobtrusive measures or reducing the potential reactivity of participants. In a related vein, these methods are also recommended when there is an emphasis on facilitating collaboration, participation, personalization, and/or empowerment as a part of the research process and its eventual products. They are good for documenting diversity, reporting on multiple perspectives, and when the use of individual case information is desirable to learn about special interests or knowledges.

Finally, qualitative inquiry is useful in the development of or verification of assumptions and theories. It may complement traditional designs by adding depth, detail, and meaning to statistical data. Similarly, when there is no proven quantitative instrumentation available to do the job, qualitative methods may be useful. Mixed qualitative/quantitative models will be discussed further on in this chapter.

Thus, both the research question asked and the context in which it is to be answered will determine your choice of methodology. Of course, practical concerns, such as the funding for an in-depth study or the availability of properly trained/knowledgable personnel could be issues. It should be noted at this point that needs assessment research fits in quite well with a number of the criteria listed above. For example, it is closely related to program evaluation, requires the input of multiple constituencies, there is a desire to know about student needs in their natural environment, to attend to student diversity, and often to empower students. Williams (1986b), reached a similar conclusion after a highly detailed analysis of the "intersection" of 30 program evaluation criteria and 17 aspects of naturalistic inquiry; only 3% of intersections proved an incompatibility of the two.

Types of Qualitative Inquiry

This section will give an overview of the types of qualitative inquiry available, but due to space limitations and the focus of this book, cannot give an in-depth description of all that is available. Those types of inquiry that seem most suitable to needs assessment will be given more detailed attention. Borrowing again from Patton's (1990) excellent resource, Table III is offered as a summary of the major varieties of qualitative inquiry.

Additionally, Jacob (1987) describes the disciplines of cognitive anthropology (also called ethnoscience and new ethnography) and ethnography of communication (also called microethnography or constitutive ethnography). Cognitive anthropology studies culture in purely mentalistic terms, by studying culturally defined categories, semantic systems, and the relationships within and between them. The field of ethnography of communication focuses on the patterns of social interaction among members of a cultural group, and are interested in specifying how processes of face-to-face interaction are related to larger issues of culture and social organization. There are variations in terminology, such as the use of "holistic ethnography" for "ethnography" as Patton (1990) describes it, or limiting the term "hermenuetics" specifically to the study of texts or transcriptions (Hoshmand, 1989).

Amidst all the overlapping terminology and occasional disciplinary turf wars (or in spite of it), there are clearly some of these varieties of qualitative inquiry that would be more appropriate for a needs assessment than others. These include ethnography, phenomenology, ecological psychology, and systems theory. Each of these will be discussed in more detail below.

In the ethnographic paradigm—or what Hoshmand (1989) calls the naturalistic-ethnographic paradigm, "Primary importance is granted to the worldview and constructs of the persons under study, as expressed through the interaction between researcher and informant. Intersubjectively shared experiences and the personal meanings and perceptions of actors and participants constitute the data of interest" (p. 16). Inquiry is always carried out in its natural setting, and attempts are made to give a holistic description of the phenomenon of interest in its context. The quality of the data obtained is often crucially linked to the relationships developed between the investigator—who is an outsider, and the participants—who are insiders. Rapport and trust will be vital, as will be an

Table III: Variety in Qualitative Inquiry: Theoretical Traditions

Perspective	Disciplinary Roots	Central Questions
1. Ethnography	Anthropology	What is the culture of this group of people?
2. Phenomenology	Philosophy	What is the structure and essence of experience of this phenomenon for these people?
3. Heuristics	Humanistic Psychology	What is my experience of this phenomenon and the essential experience of others who also experience this phenomenon intensely?
4. Ethnomethodology	Sociology	How do people make sense of their everyday activities so as to behave in socially acceptable ways?
5. Symbolic Interactionism	Social Psychology	What common set of symbols and understandings have emerged to give meaning to people's interactions?
6. Ecological Psychology	Ecology, psychology	How do individuals attempt to accomplish their goals through specific behaviors in specific environments?
7. Systems theory	Interdisciplinary	How and why does this system function as a whole?
8. Chaos theory: Nonlinear dynamics	Theoretical physics, natural sciences	What is the underlying order, if any, of disorderly phenomenon?
9. Hermeneutics	Theology, philosophy, literary criticism	What are the conditions under which a human act took place or a product was produced that makes it possible to interpret its meanings?
10. Orientational, Qualitative	Ideologies, political economy	How is x ideological perspective manifest in this phenomenon?

From Patton, M. Q. (c 1990). *Qualitative Evaluation and Research Methods.* (p. 88). Reprinted with permission of Sage Publications, Inc.

open, non-judgemental attitude. In terms of a needs assessment, this would mean investigating student needs in the natural environment of the campus-at-large (not just in a classroom, or in your office), and to completely and thoroughly record students' own experiences, opinions, perceptions, and meanings of their various needs, how they meet those needs, etc. This would be accomplished by developing genuine relationships with students, with prolonged contact and immersion in their world. Specific methods related to this paradigm will be covered in the next section.

The second likely paradigm for needs assessment is phenomenology. In many ways, it is similar to ethnography, except the focus is narrower. Whereas almost any kind of data—behavioral, verbal, non-verbal, interactional—that is observed by the researcher or reported by the participant is included in the broad scope of ethnography, the phenomenological paradigm concentrates specifically on issues of meaning and uses almost exclusively verbal data (although written text or transcriptions might also be included, such as a student's journal). The focus is on the comprehension of the meaning of another person's experience (Hoshmand, 1989). The major specific method involved is the qualitative interview, which will be detailed in the section on specific qualitative methods.

The third model that seems to hold particular promise for needs assessment work is ecological psychology. The description of this model will be taken primarily from Jacob (1987). The focus in this model is on naturally occurring human behavior and the relationships between human behavior and its environment. It recognizes both the objective environment and persons' subjective, emotional reactions to their environments, and that these components interact with each other. Behavior is viewed as being primarily motivated by a person's perceptions, but also molded by the environment. The environment can include the actual physical properties of settings (location, amount and arrangement of space, furniture, temperature, etc.), human aspects of the environment, such as the variety of roles or density, and specific programs that are in place (e.g., a lesson plan or agenda). Ecological psychologists are interested in describing people's behaviors and the emotional qualities attached to their behaviors. They are likewise interested in how environments differ in their standing patterns of behavior, how environments select and shape individuals in them, and the properties of environments to which people must adapt. It would seem that this type of qualitative research strategy would lend itself well to determining what behaviors students actually engage in to meet their needs on campus, and how they feel about those behaviors. Additionally, this perspective would be excellent for systematically helping to determine what concrete aspects of the campus environment either contribute to or hinder the meeting of students' needs. For example, it is quite conceivable that services offered in a building that is remote, physically unpleasant, or with limited hours might affect student use of services, even if needed, or that programs/personnel already in place contribute to a negative environment in some way. As with the other models, specific techniques associated with the ecological psychology paradigm will be noted shortly.

The last qualitative strategies to be considered in depth are those based on systems theory. In general, systems theory involves the idea that wholes are in some sense greater than the sum of their parts; systems function to maintain their own equilibrium or homeostasis through an ongoing process of error-activated feedback and change (Hoshmand, 1989). The parts of the whole system are all interdependent, and cannot be understood independent of their systemic context. A change in any one aspect of the system will affect all other components of that system. Systems theories also recognize that many systems may be imbedded in each other. Thus, a student's internal self-system is embedded in a family system and a peer system; the peer system may be embedded at least partially in the dorm system, the dorm system is situated in the campus system, etc. Hoshmand explicitly relates these ideas to what has been termed "action research", stating "Action research as a model of inquiry has a pragmatic focus on needs assessment, problem diagnosis, planned interventions, and evalution of changes . . . Because action plans are modified in the context in which they are tested, a cyclical feedback process is entailed" (p. 33). Thus, needs assessment from a systems point of view would attempt to describe both the parts and the whole of the student/student services system, their interrelationships, what constitutes disruptions in the equilibrium of this system, and how the system "rebounds" from these disruptions to maintain itself. Therefore, there would also be a focus on what effects modifying the system would have in each of its components and as a whole, and how the system can be changed in a way that does not disrupt its fundamental stability (or the changes will not be accepted).

We turn now to a discussion of specific techniques associated with each of these four paradigms. In many ways, they constitute a good review of qualitative methods in general, as most of the major techniques are involved.

Specific Methods of Qualitative Inquiry

In this section, the specific methodologies associated with the ethnographic, phenomenological, ecological psychology and systems paradigms will be covered. Additionally, issues of sampling, qualitative interviewing and "fieldwork" techniques will be presented in some depth. Data analysis will also be covered.

As in more traditional models, a planful approach is necessary. Before a specific method is chosen, the usual steps of determining what your research questions are, developing a rationale for the project, and choosing a workable overall design must be carried out (Marshall & Rossman, 1989). Following this general planning, specific methodological issues can be addressed.

Sampling

One of the primary issues to be considered is sampling. Sampling methods in qualitative inquiry are quite different from the traditional random selection of the scientific method. Typically, these alternate sampling techniques have a rational or theoretical basis, rather than a statistical or random basis. A clear summary of these sampling methods has been presented by Patton (1990) and is reproduced in Table IV. Traditional methods are under heading "A"; qualitative methods, which Patton terms "purposeful sampling" are under heading "B."

Many general qualitative data collection techniques use combinations of these sampling strategies, such as the "key informant" approach, which can combine critical case sampling, typical case sampling, and chain sampling, or the "field survey" approach, which may use random, purposeful sampling, maximum variation sampling, and typical case sampling (Humm-Delgado & Delgado, 1986).

Data Collection

When the sampling question "From whom shall we collect data?" is answered, the next step is the method question: "How do we collect data?". The specific methods associated with the four models of qualitative inquiry best suited to needs assessment will be detailed below.

The ethnographic-naturalistic paradigm requires prolonged contact

Table IV: Sampling Strategies

Type	Purpose
A. Random probability sampling	Representativeness: Sample size a function of population size and desired confidence level
1. Simple random sample	Permits generalization from sample to the population it represents
2. Stratified random and cluster samples	Increases confidence in making generalizations to particular subgroups or areas
B. Purposeful sampling	Selects information-rich cases for in-depth study. Size and specific cases depend on study purpose
1. Extreme or deviant case sampling	Learning from highly unusual manifestations of the phenomenon of interest, such as outstanding successes/notable failures, top of the class/dropouts, exotic events, crises
2. Intensity sampling	Information-rich cases that manifest the phenomenon intensely, but not extremely, such as good students/poor students, above average/below average
3. Maximum variation sampling—purposefully picking a wide range of variation on dimensions of variation on dimensions of interest	Documents unique or diverse variations that have emerged in adapting to different conditions. Identifies important common patterns that cut across variations
4. Homogenous sampling	Focuses, reduces variation, simplifies analysis, facilitates group interviewing
5. Typical case sampling	Illustrates or highlights what is typical, normal, average.
6. Stratified purposeful sampling	Illustrates characteristics of particular subgroups of interest; facilitates comparisons
7. Critical case sampling	Permits *logical* generalization and maximum application of information to other cases because if it's true of this one case it's likely to be true of all other cases
8. Snowball or chain sampling	Identifies cases of interest from people who know people who know people who know what cases are information-rich, that is, good examples for study, good interview subjects
9. Criterion sampling	Picking all cases that meet some criterion, such as all children abused in a treatment facility. Quality assurance.

Table IV: (Continued)

Type	Purpose
10. Theory-based or operational construct sampling	Finding manifestations of a theoretical construct of interest so as to elaborate and examine the construct
11. Confirming and disconfirming cases	Elaborating and deepening initial analysis, seeking exceptions, testing variation
12. Opportunistic sampling	Following new leads during fieldwork, taking advantage of the unexpected, flexibility
13. Random purposeful sampling (still small sample size)	Adds credibility to sample when potential purposeful sample is larger than one can handle. Reduces judgement within a purposeful category (Not for generalizations or representativeness)
14. Sampling politically important cases	Attracts attention to the study (or avoids attracting undesired attention by purposefully eliminating from the sample politically sensitive cases)
15. Convenience sampling	Saves time, money and effort. Poorest rationale; lowest credibility. Yields information-poor cases
16. Combination or mixed purposeful sampling	Triangulation, flexibility, meets multiple interests and needs

From Patton, M. Q. (c 1990). *Qualitative evaluation and research methods.* (pp. 182–183). Reprinted with permission of Sage Publications, Inc.

in the natural setting or community of interest. Immersion is necessary to describe and analyse observed patterns, and first-hand data collection by the researcher is the norm. This also allows for ongoing clarification and elaboration of new questions or incomplete information. Typically, copious field notes must be taken, and verbatim statements of participants are highly desirable (taken either by hand or audio/video recorded). A concerted effort is made to present situations as seen from the native's point of view. Participant observation, interviewing, oral histories, and descriptions of critical incidents are all common (Hoshmand, 1989; Jacob, 1987). This may be supplemented with archival data, such as institutional records for demographics or evaluations, program descriptions, organizational minutes, etc. — anything that would help to give a reliable, up-to-date, valid, and representative indicator of the students themselves or help to document their need (Humm-Delgado & Delgado, 1986; Midkiff & Burke, 1987). Multiple methods are recommended in this approach.

In conducting a naturalistic-ethnographic study, overall guidelines for fieldwork include the following (Patton, 1990, p. 273–274):

(1) Be descriptive in taking field notes.

(2) Gather a variety of information from different perspectives.

(3) Cross-validate and triangulate by gathering different kinds of data—observations, interviews, program documentation, recordings, and photographs—use multiple methods.

(4) Use quotations; represent program participants in their own terms.

(5) Select key informants wisely and use them carefully. Draw on the wisdom of their informed perspectives, but keep in mind that their perspectives are limited.

(6) Be aware of and sensitive to the different stages of fieldwork.

    (a) Build trust and rapport at the entry stage. Remember that the evaluator-observer is also being observed and evaluated.

    (b) Stay alert and disciplined during the more routine, middle phase of fieldwork.

    (c) Focus on pulling together a useful synthesis as fieldwork draws to a close.

    (d) Be disciplined and conscientious in taking field notes at all stages of fieldwork.

(7) Be as involved as possible in experiencing the program as fully as possible while maintaining an analytical perspective grounded in the purpose of the fieldwork.

(8) Clearly separate description from interpretation and judgment.

(9) Provide formative feedback as a part of the verification process of fieldwork. Time that feedback carefully. Observe its impact.

(10) Include in your field notes and evaluation report your own experiences, thoughts, and feelings. These are also field data.

Furthermore, as Jacob (1987) reminds us, being a participant observer usually means becoming personally involved with the day-to-day activities of the community under study. This helps reduce reactivity, makes the researcher's presence less obtrusive, and helps him/her to understand participants' views of their own worlds. Following these recommendations will help assure that solid data emerge from the naturalistic-ethnographic model.

In the phenomenological paradigm, the qualitative interview is the primary vehicle for data collection. This technique is described in some detail here, as it is commonly used in most qualitative designs. The qualitative interview has a theme (such as student needs), but is neither standardized nor non-directive. Although no pre-set number, wording, category, or hierarchy of questions is used, neither is the interview completely "free form" since the theme serves as a focus. The goal of the interview is to articulate the essential meanings of students' experience, by having them "think aloud" and clarify ambiguities as they arise. The interviewer must approach the interview with an open attitude, which is enhanced by a process of self-reflection in order to identify his or her own biases and preconceptions. An attempt is made to suspend one's own preconceptions during the interview, a process qualitative interviewers call "bracketing" (Hoshmand, 1989).

This type of interview is similar to Patton's (1990) description of the "informal conversational interview" where "Questions emerge from the immediate context and are asked in the natural course of things; there is no predetermination of question topics or wording" (p. 288). He also notes that somewhat more structured variations of these procedures are available, such as the "interview guide approach," which uses a rough outline of topics or issues to be covered in advance, but no set order of presentation. Another more structured variation is the "standardized, open-ended interview," in which the exact wording and sequence of questions are predetermined, but the questions are in an open format that allows for elaboration without "leading" the interview. Finally, there are "closed, fixed-response" interviews, in which response categories as well as questions are predetermined, and the interviewee chooses from among fixed responses. The more highly structured formats are less common in qualitative designs.

Using a slightly different framework, Patton (1990) notes that questions can be asked over a variety of domains. He suggests behavior/ experience questions, opinion/value questions, feeling questions, knowledge questions, sensory questions, and demographic/background questions. These may be explored in a past, present, or future time frame.

All sources agree that good interviewing skills are essential. These skills include the ability to establish trust and rapport, to encourage and prompt, to ask open-ended questions (which usually begin with "How?" or "What?" rather than "Do, don't" or "Is, isn't", for example), to express single ideas clearly, and to accurately follow content and process. Interviewing is both a skill and an art; selection/training of interviewers can make or break an attempt at phenomenological inquiry.

The third model to be discussed is ecological psychology. This model uses two principal approaches to data collection, the specimen record and the behavior setting survey (Jacob, 1987). Specimen records are narrative descriptions of the actual behavior of an individual, as well as observers' inferences about the meaning of the behavior to the individuals. For example, a researcher might observe students in a career library, noting not only what aspects of the library are being used, but also the types of reactions an individual has to different kinds of materials, such as smiles or looks of disgust.

The behavior setting survey focuses on a particular, delimited, environmental setting which naturally occurs in the environment, such as a student lounge, a financial aid office or a classroom. To be designated as a behavior setting, the environment in question must involve " . . . a bounded pattern of behavior that occurs independently of the particular persons involved and anchored to a particular milieu at a particular time and place. Moveover, the behavior must be similar in structure to the milieu, and the milieu must surround or enclose the behavior" (Jacob, 1987, p. 8). Descriptions of the behavior setting are then made according to such factors as occurrence and duration of behaviors, sex, ethnicity, or social class of participants. Specimen records and behavior setting surveys are then typed and coded into logical units for analysis.

The last methods to be covered are those tied to the systems theory paradigm. This is possibly the area in which methods are least well developed; although there seems to be a consensus that evaluation criteria and targets should reflect a systems view, specificity is difficult. An attempt is made to " . . . provide detailed documentation of the contributions and coinfluence of all participants in a given case . . . " (Hoshmand, 1989, p. 32). A variety of techniques might conceivably be used, if tailored to assess all components of the system, as well as the system itself, including its embeddedness in larger systems. Systemic interviewing techniques have been developed by some family therapists, and may be modified to needs assessment purposes. Systemic interviews involve asking the same question to each member of the system who is present, and then following up with questions about how each member views each other member's response. In this manner, multiple perspectives are given on a topic, and the subjective perceptions of each member are placed in the context of others' reactions and elaborations. In a similar vein, Hoshmand suggests the use of audio or video tape-assisted recall to facilitate such processes. In spite of the methodological ambiguities, the systems perspective has a great deal to offer.

The techniques of data collection listed here are by no means exhaustive. Many others have been developed, such as the use of nominal groups (Skibbe, 1986), text analysis, and autobiographies (Hoshmand, 1989).

Data Analysis

It is helpful to have an overall strategy for data analysis, typically based on the purpose of the study and a consideration of how it might be most helpful to present results. For example, observational data could be analyzed by chronology, key events, settings, people, processes, or issues (Patton, 1990). Interviews may be analyzed case by case, or compared with each other through cross-case analysis or both (Husband & Foster, 1987). Often, entire records (such as interview transcripts) are made available, although this level of detail may not be needed by all constituencies. More commonly, data are categorized and coded, sorted, recategorized and recoded, and resorted in a process of refining meanings and determining themes and patterns from data. This is not a simple process. It requires conscientious effort and a considerable amount of time. The coding and categorization of data should be cross-checked by independent raters as well as with actual participants to ensure minimal bias and maximum truth-to-the-community under study (Hoshmand, 1989).

It is often helpful to ask yourself and others, "What could be taken out of this 'picture,' or changed in it, and still have an accurate view of the topic or situation?" Another effective technique is to search for negative cases. That is, while coding and developing thematic categories, and generating theory or relationships between variables as you sift through the data, you should constantly be on the alert for disconfirming data or for cases that most strongly test the limits of your emerging theories. If your data collection and sampling have been thorough, no negative cases will be found. This type of process may demand an ongoing exchange between data collection and data analysis—not necessarily a sequential process. Both may occur simultaneously, especially in the middle and later stages of an investigation.

Qualitative data analysis may lead to some quantitative results. Certainly, frequencies of occurrences of categories are easily reported, for example. Some strategies, such as the methods of ecological psychology, lend themselves more readily than do others to this type of analysis. In ethnographic strategies, verbatim representations of participants' points of view are more important. The recommendation for the use of multiple methods holds for both data collection and data analysis.

Presentation of Data

A great deal of effort will be expended in synthesizing the results of a qualitative inquiry into presentable form for various audiences. Much of what occurs here is similar to what happens in traditional models; the reader is referred to that section and to the section on "Politics: Who is the Client?" for a detailed discussion of these follow-up issues. However, there are aspects of presentation that are unique to qualitative design, particularly because of their non-traditional nature. Often, the issue of justifying qualitative conclusions is paramount.

Standards of Proof

One of the ongoing issues for those involved in qualitative inquiry is justifying their methods and conclusions in a paradigm that differs fundamentally from the traditional scientific method. The long touted standards of rigor—internal validity, external validity, reliability, and objectivity—simply cannot be transferred to a paradigm based on radically different assumptions. Still, standards of proof are necessary. As Smith (1987) notes, people are prone to equate the relativistic nature of qualitative inquiry with an "anything goes subjectivism," and he argues that the type of relativism in naturalistic evaluations " . . . still holds that reason and rationality are crucial." He concludes, "This definition of relativism does not release us from the obligation to make the best case possible for our knowledge claims and evaluative conclusions" (p. 354).

The most thorough work on standards of proof in qualitative inquiry has been done by Lincoln and Guba (1986). These researchers define two major standards—trustworthiness and authenticity. The trustworthiness criteria were designed to parallel the traditional standards of internal and external validity, reliability, and objectivity. Their four parallel constructs are termed credibility, transferability, dependability, and confirmability. Credibility can be established by prolonged engagement and persistant observation of the phenomena/respondents in the field; by cross-checking data with different sources, methods, times, and investigators; through peer debriefing—processing information and biases with others; by negative case analysis—the active search for disconfirming evidence; and by member checks—soliciting the reactions of participants to get feedback on the researcher's reconstruction of data. Transferability typically is established through dense descriptive data, which have sufficient detail, depth, and clarity that it could be applied elsewhere, in whole or part. Dependability and confirmability are established by the creation of an audit trail carried out by a competent external and disinterested auditor. Audits of process result in dependability judgements; audits of products (data and reconstructions) result in confirmability judgments.

Lincoln and Guba's (1986) second major standard for qualitative inquiry is authenticity. This standard is unique to new paradigm research and has no parallel in the traditional scientific method. It has five components: fairness, ontological authenticity, educative authenticity, catalytic authenticity, and tactical authenticity. Fairness refers to the equal representation of multiple perspectives, the inclusion of all stakeholders in the process of making recommendations and subsequent action, the open and complete disclosure of data to all, and the use of informed consent and member checks. Ontological authenticity is a criterion that the research should improve the group's or individual's experiencing of the world, and reflects an opportunity for growth and development as a result of interaction with others. Educative authenticity refers to a goal of understanding others, appreciating the constructions made by diverse others and how they are rooted in value systems. This appeciation, however, should not be equated with agreement. Catalytic authenticity is the part of the standard that says qualitative research should facilitate and stimulate action. Tactical authenticity asks the question, "Did action result in a desired change?" Several authors have clearly supported these authenticity standards for qualitative research, especially with regard to open disclosure and action/change (Cook & Fonow, 1990; Reinharz, 1992; Williams, 1986a).

Additionally, Pearsol (1987) emphasizes the unique role of the primary researcher or evaluator in justifying conclusions in qualitative inquiry. In many ways, this person serves as interpreter and negotiator, with a great deal of responsibility for the reconstruction of the data gathered. He states, "From an interpretive perspective, bias exists and claims for evaluation conclusions rest on an evaluator's efforts to mediate among biased perspectives and to present a persuasive analysis of selected evidence and claims" (p. 335–336). The personal accountability of the researcher is on the line, and her/his persuasive and analytic abilities are key.

Hopefully, this brief overview of the standards of proof for qualitative methods will help to ease researchers' concerns about implementing new paradigm investigations. As Reason (1988) concludes, "In human inquiry it is better to be approximately right than precisely wrong. It is also better to initiate and conduct inquiry into important questions of human conduct with a degree of acknowledged bias and imprecision, than to bog the whole thing down in attempts to be prematurely correct or accurate" (p. 229).

Mixed Models

There is a great deal of support for the idea of combining qualitative and quantitative methods. While purists in each camp view the models as fundamentally incompatible, particularly on philosophical/theoretical grounds, there are strong arguments for the combined use of the methods of each paradigm. As Polkinghorne (1991) states:

> Both systems used by the human sciences are empirical, their conclusions based on and informed by data. The criteria for accepting knowledge claims is not adherence to a particular method but evidence that the knowledge-generating process (a) coheres to the particular logic used in drawing together its conclusion, (b) passes the muster of public scrutiny, and (c) provides a particular partial display of the phenomenon under study that is useful to the field. Quantitative and qualitative methods are not oppositional; they are merely different (p. 112).

Some aspects of human experience and action are best tapped by quantitative methods, others by qualitative ones.

The most common way in which this combination is discussed is via "triangulation"—the use of multiple methods and specific assessments that offset each other's strengths and weaknesses. Smith (1986) notes that the use of multiple methods is most fruitful when good description is needed, particularly to bring comprehension and meaning to the context in which quantitative data have been collected. Qualitative data extend quantitative data, and can illustrate important points with case material. Mixed methods are particularly valuable when a variety of perspectives are called for and when increases in validity, the capacity for mutually informative reporting, and the needs of differing audiences are at stake. Jick (1983) elaborates on the concept of triangulation:

> . . . the most popular use of triangulation . . . is largely a vehicle for cross validation when two or more distinct methods are found to be congruent and

to yield comparable data. For organizational researchers, this would involve the use of multiple methods to examine the same dimension of a research problem.... It can also capture a more complete, holistic and contextual portrayal of the unit(s) under study. That is, beyond the analysis of overlapping variance, the use of multiple measures may also uncover some unique variance which otherwise may have been neglected by single methods. It is here that qualitative methods, in particular, can play an especially prominent role by eliciting data and suggesting conclusions to which other methods would be blind. Elements of context are illuminated. In this sense, triangulation may be used not only to examine the same phenomenon from multiple perspectives but also to enrich our understanding by allowing for a new or deeper dimensions to emerge. In all the various triangulation designs, one basic assumption is buried. The effectiveness of triangulation rests on the premise that the weaknesses in each single method will be compensated by the counterbalancing strengths of another (pp. 136–138).

The author is in agreement with these researchers that mixed models are workable, and in many cases better, than the use of a single methodology. The use of a carefully considered mixed model in planning a student needs assessment is recommended.

Concluding Remarks on the Application of Qualitative Inquiry to the Needs Assessment of Diverse Student Groups

There are a number of reasons why qualitative methods are an excellent fit for a needs assessment of diverse student groups. In terms of themes of qualitative inquiry, the holistic, naturalistic, contextual and personal aspects of these methods are likely to reflect a sensitivity to diversity not common in traditional methods which separate researcher and subject and reinforce power and status differences. Unique meanings and perspectives are not made to "fit" pre-existing categories based on majority culture, but can be taken verbatim from participants. The principles of design flexibility and empathic neutrality help to keep researchers responsive to the participants involved. The self-reflection recommended by paradigms such as the phenomenological model ensures that researchers have examined their own biases and attitudes before engaging in contact with participants. Data analysis techniques which demand cross-checking and validation by members of the group under study enhance the credibility of results. Sampling methods that are specifically designed to assess diversity—such as maximum variation sampling—are clearly compatible.

In addition to this, the authenticity criteria (Lincoln & Guba, 1986) which conceptualize action and desired change as integral parts of qualitative methodology are clearly in line with calls from feminist and multicultural researchers to "give something back" to the communities studied (Cook & Fonow, 1990; Mio & Iwamasa, 1993; Ponterotto, 1988; Reinharz, 1992). Many ethnic and cultural minority student groups have needs and perceptions that are seldom fully appreciated by majority researchers or student service professionals. McCarl-Nielsen (1990) describes this in terms of "standpoint epistemology," which

> ... begins with the idea that less powerful members of society have the potential for a more complete view of social reality than others, precisely because of their disadvantaged position. That is, in order to survive (socially and sometimes even physically), subordinate persons are attuned to or attentive to the perspective of the dominant class (for example, white, male, wealthy) as well as their own. This awareness gives them the potential for ... double consciousness —a knowledge, awareness of, and sensitivity to both the dominant world view of the society and their own minority (p. 10).

These unique perceptions seem far more amenable to qualitative interviews or ethnographic methods than paper and pencil surveys, no matter how well constructed. Given even this brief analysis of the fit between qualitative inquiry and the nature of diversity on campus, it seems clear that compatibility exists. The author highly recommends the use of these methods when conducting a needs assessment of diverse student groups. The methods can be incorporated into mixed models combining qualitative and quantitative methods to produce a thorough and respectful assessment which allows multiple voices both to speak and to be heard.

SOME EXAMPLES

In the following section, examples of needs assessments and evaluations using the various methods previously discussed are presented. Samples of research using traditional methods are illustrated first, followed by qualitative and mixed models. Diversity in the settings, populations, and methods are reviewed, especially in the qualitative and mixed models. By examining these different strategies, a wide range of techniques and applications is made available to persons wishing to conduct their own needs assessments. The studies reviewed are not exhaustive, but rather, selections are chosen to illustrate particular methods, strengths and weaknesses, or to show the wide range of possible applications.

Traditional Methods

As noted earlier, the most common form of needs assessment has undoubtedly been a written survey, administered either directly or mailed to the populations of interest. Items are traditionally developed through literature reviews and/or by "experts" (usually the researcher), rather than through contact with the group itself. Data are collected and analyzed, and recommendations are made from the quantitative analysis of responses. Follow-up in terms of action and program or policy change may or may not be pursued.

Occasionally, the group of interest will be consulted in item development or to help assess the face validity of the instruments developed. Some open-ended questions may be included on questionnaires so that participants may comment on their needs in an unstructured way. To the extent that these procedures are incorporated, they would represent a mixed model. Often, however, even this minimal amount of involvement or free response is neglected. This was especially true in earlier needs assessment work. By way of illustrating some traditional needs assessments, the following examples are offered.

Harris and Anttonen's (1986) study of male and female college freshman presents a prototypical traditional needs assessment. The senior author developed a 70-item instrument "tailored to fit the clientele of a medium-sized, state-owned, 4-year institution of higher learning" (p. 277). Items were rated on 5-point Likert scales by a sample of 356 incoming freshmen during summer orientation, and responses were analyzed using Chi-square statistics. Implications were discussed, though in general terms. No follow-up was reported.

In a similar vein, Helwig and Vidales (1988) used traditional methods to study differences in the needs of minority and white counselors. Again, items were developed by the researchers after a review of the literature. No pilot study or face validity checks were made. The survey was then mailed to 1,946 counselors in various settings, with one follow-up postcard sent to those who failed to respond within three weeks. Of these, 1,121 counselors (59%) returned the survey; 76.1% of the respondents were white and the remaining 23.9% were minority counselors. Chi-square analyses were used to determine differences on items between minority and white counselors' needs, and implications were noted. No follow-up was reported.

A somewhat more substantive study is presented by Minatoya and

King (1984), who assessed the needs of minority undergraduates by developing a 68-item questionnaire developed from a literature review on the counseling needs of ethnic-minority students. The content validity of the instrument was checked using a sample of 38 minority students, and the instrument was then administered to a random sample of 100 minority undergraduates. Nearly equal numbers of males and females were obtained, and proportions of Asian American, African-American, Hispanic American, and Native American students were representative of their distribution on campus. Data were analyzed using descriptive statistics and Chi-squares. Responses to open-ended questions about suggestions for design and delivery of services were categorized by themes and recorded using percentages. Data were then reported in a minority student newsletter, to residence life, to academic affairs, and to counseling center staff, interns, and practicum students. Services to ethnic minority students were expanded to include a series of articles in the minority student newsletter, additional outreach programs, and the development of a mentoring program.

More recently, a basically traditional approach was used by Stabb and Cogdal (1990) in assessing the needs of African-American and international students at a mid-sized state university in the South. The researchers used an instrument previously developed and tested through literature review and used validity checks with both student groups at a second university. The researchers then took the instrument to both African-American and international student organizations on their own campus to further test its validity in the new setting. Some modifications were made in items to reflect the unique culture of the particular campus and community. The instrument was then administered directly to as many students as possible by handing the survey to students during organizational or social meetings, through residence hall assistants, and by distributing them at the student union building. Traditional statistical analyses were used to handle the data and specific recommendations were given to counseling center personnel and other student affairs professionals. This approach represents a more proactive method of encouraging use of services. Presentations of the results of the study were also offered to African-American and international student groups.

As summarized in the section on traditional needs assessment methods, many of the strengths and weaknesses of these traditional designs can be noted in the studies presented. Strengths include ease/speed of development, administration, and analysis, as well as random sampling or large samples (in some cases). Empirically-based data are used to offer specific recommendations or to implement change.

On the other hand, these studies also highlight the relative lack of involvement of the groups they are intended to serve during the processes of item development and administration, the interpretation of results and the process of program recommendations and change. Little attention typically has been paid to the differences within the groups studied, and upon careful examination, some have fallen prey to the "different is deficit" thinking discussed earlier (e.g., Ponterotto, 1988; Zuckerman, 1990).

Qualitative Methods

Because qualitative methods are less familiar to many readers, examples of these studies will be covered in more detail. It should be kept in mind that qualitative studies, by nature, tend to be highly tailored to the populations and settings in which they occur. Techniques may share a common philosophy and emphasis on participant-researcher interaction, but vary considerably from study to study. Also, few actual examples of "pure" qualitative methods used in needs assessment or program evaluation have been published (or perhaps even attempted). This is perhaps due to conservative editorial policies of professional journals, as well as to the nature of qualitative inquiry itself, which tends to be time-consuming and highly detailed/lengthy in reporting, as noted in earlier sections of this chapter.

Lorion, Hightower, Work, and Shockly (1987) describe an action research approach to the design and evaluation of an academic skills enhancement program for at-risk elementary school students. The study begins with a detailed description of the community, the school population, and the key teachers and administrators, as well as with the researchers. This depth of description is common in qualitative research and provides a vivid, comprehensive understanding of the setting.

The evolution of the Basic Academic Skills Enhancement (BASE) program is then described. Teachers, administrators, parents, and researchers met extensively to discuss the needs of each constituency and of the children involved. For example, kindergarten teachers expressed dissatisfaction with the current system, which allowed for long delays between referral, testing, and identification of remedial interventions. The solution generated in this collaboration was to design a comprehensive screening program for all children entering kindergarten. This procedural change had the additional benefits of decreasing stigma and potential self-fulfilling prophesies for those children who otherwise would have been singled out for special testing.

The development of the comprehensive screening itself also involved a variety of "players." Teachers needed understandable and instructionally relevant information. There were "turf wars" to be negotiated between the researchers and school special education personnel regarding who would interpret and disseminate screening data. Lorion et al. (1987) detail the decision-making process surrounding this issue. It was finally decided that the researchers would provide summary data to the school psychologist and the educational diagnostic team, who would then make recommendations to teachers. A thorough screening procedure was developed to include information from parents, teachers and children.

The screenings are designed to take place during the first week of school and to provide rapid and integrative feedback on strengths and weaknesses of all incoming kindergartners to the teachers. This early assessment gives an opportunity for early instructional planning to meet specific needs of individual children. Teachers also use this information in early teacher-parent planning conferences. Lorion et al. (1987) also report "ripple effects" from the program, such as increases in teachers' collaboration, increased consultative involvement of the diagnostic teams, earlier identification and remediation of learning difficulties, and increased parental involvement. They note that while "for the applied researcher, such unplanned and uncontrolled variables represent methodological 'noise' that must be explained in attempts to delineate the effects of program procedures . . . for the community practitioner, such . . . effects are highly desirable for both political and programmatic reasons" (p. 71).

These action researchers document how the BASE program is evaluated over time to account for and describe both planned and unplanned effects. For example, the psychometric properties of all new assessment measures used by teachers and parents are continually monitored and revised. Analyses of actual processes, such as teacher-child interactions or child-child interactions, via behavioral observation are being developed, as are content analyses for teacher-team meetings. Traditional measures such as numbers of children certified for special educational services, along with data about their disorders are also tracked, and comparisons are made between schools with and without the BASE program. In keeping with a qualitative paradigm, the researchers conclude that

"... interventions must focus their impacts on evolving developmental processes rather than on the end-state conditions that they are designed to avoid" (p. 74) and that "enhancing a community's competence, empowering its members, and leaving it with the responsibility and credit for resolving its own problems" (p. 75) are unique contributions of action research in a community psychology framework.

A study of community health needs and programming by Aubel, Alzouma, Djabel, Ibrahim & Coulibaly (1991) offers another clear example of qualitative research. They note that:

> Programs that have demonstrated the best results are those which built their strategies on a systematic knowledge of the local belief systems, social organization, and existant health strategies. There is an increasing awareness, as well, that the assessment of community health problems by health professionals who have a narrow clinical perspective is insufficient as a basis for program planning. It has been suggested that the scope of preliminary data collection should include information of social, cultural, and economic factors related to the health problem or situation of concern. There is a growing consensus that ... quantitative survey data are insufficient and that in-depth qualitative data are necessary (p. 346).

Based on a model implemented to study health needs in a Nigerian community, these researchers also provide practitioners with details on the importance of making research results understandable and usable. Data collection teams and planning teams involve service providers working in the target community (as opposed to the exclusive use of outside "experts"), making "a conscious effort to step outside their own professional culture" (p. 349) in order to see the issues through the community's point of view.

Data collection involved the use of semi-structured interviews. Teams were prepared for data collection by intensive study of the available data on the community, as well as though interviewing techniques/communication skills, and small group exercises to help team members assess and confront their attitudes towards the group with whom they would interact. This approach involved far more preparation than is typical in quantitative designs, and yet it took only three days. Teams then spent three days in each of the villages surveyed. Initial contacts were made with village leaders, followed by interviews conducted individually or in small groups. Analysis of the data was performed within 24 hours of collection, allowing immediate identification of areas requiring follow-up for clarification or elaboration.

The teams then prepared summaries of their findings for presentation to regional planners, and continued to be involved in the design of interventions to address the villagers' health needs. The qualitative interviews identified several crucial processes that would not have been discovered had traditional survey methods been used. For example, it became clear that management of health concerns was primarily determined by family and close friends, while traditional healers were consulted next, and health social workers had least influence on villagers' points of view. The structure of the male and female communication networks in the community also became apparent. Such information was later used in designing and implementing health interventions, for example, by primarily targeting mothers and fathers of young children, and older women (especially grandmothers), over other village members. Teams also made recommendations for better interpersonal communication skills to be taught to health workers.

In the final phase of the project, researchers implemented their recommendations and received feedback from the communities about the programs developed. After formal meetings with village leaders, informal sessions were held in which family members observed and discussed role plays and stories related to their health needs and interventions. Many of the modifications suggested by the families later were incorporated into the recommended health strategies. Aubel et al. (1991) report that these non-directive, participative health education techniques and the genuine, respectful involvement of the villagers in all phases of the project resulted in high levels of cooperation, encouragement, and action in fulfilling the health needs of these Nigerian communities. The entire program was grounded in qualitative philosophy and methodology; virtually no traditional methods were used.

While kindergarten childrens' academic planning needs and the health needs of Nigerian villagers may seem remote from college student services work, many of the issues and methods described in these two studies are readily transferable to the university campus arena. These include the awareness and appropriate use of the socio-political and cultural context in which needs are assessed, interview/discussion techniques in data collection, participation of the group under study in identifying their needs, involvement of the group in planning intervention strategies, and returning for feedback in order to make modifications on the implementation. The rich level of description afforded by qualitative methods also tends to uncover processes, rather than exclusively content, which can be crucial in the effective response to a group's needs.

For an example of qualitative needs assessment on the college campus, Skibbe's (1986) use of nominal groups presents a different, but relatively simple and workable design. Nominal groups are small, relatively homogenous discussion groups, typically consisting of five to nine members. For example, a nominal group might consist of a group of freshmen, or a group of a particular racial/ethnic background, or perhaps a group having a particular problem in common. Members may or may not have contact with each other outside of the needs assessment group. One person is chosen as leader and one as a recorder for each group. Leaders and recorders participate in short training sessions on managing and facilitating group interactions, and are given an overview of the nominal group technique. Overall, the method is similar to that of "brainstorming" groups developed originally in the 1950's.

Once back in their groups, leaders give a brief introduction to the topic and structure of the sessions, which typically run 45–90 minutes (Skibbe used the 50-minute undergraduate class period standard). Next, the leader initiates a writing phase, in which each group member generates as many responses as possible to open-ended questions. Skibbe used, "What are the mental health and personal development needs or problems of students [at this university]?" (p. 532). Questions during this phase are met with noncommittal responses by the leader, in order not to limit responses in any way. In the third phase, the recorder notes all ideas, which are publically listed (e.g., on a blackboard or on large sheets of paper) and each idea is briefly described; new ideas may be added at this time, but none are explicitly evaluated. In the evaluation phase, the group generates pros and cons for each of the ideas listed. The recorder documents these as well. The evaluation phase tends to be the least structured aspect of the group process, and will demand the most skill from leaders in managing group conflict, keeping on track, ensuring all members are heard, etc. Last, the leader asks the group to rank the five most important needs, although all will be eventually presented to those conducting the needs assessment.

In discussing the assets of the nominal group method, Skibbe notes that arranging groups on a college campus is relatively simple, and that

If five pairs of leaders are used, a class of 50 can be broken down into five nominal groups that can perform their task within the 50 minute class time limit. Because the process is quite structured, both graduate and undergraduate students can be taught to conduct the groups with about five hours of classroom training. Despite the process structure, the output is totally up to individual group members. Needs that are totally unanticipated by the counseling center staff members occasionally emerge, particularly needs that apply to only a select group on campus. Finally, in most cases group members seem to enjoy the process . . . If the counseling center or any other helping organization on campus desires detailed input from any portion of the community, the process can be geared up, implemented, and completed within a month (p. 533).

Skibbe describes the successful use of this process over a two year period at his university:

On the liabilities side, there is the recognition that nominal group process data is not easily quantified or statistically analyzed, and may not come from a representative sample of students. However, Skibbe comments that "this can be viewed as an asset . . . because campus subgroups' needs can easily be buried in statistical averages" (p. 533). Other difficulties may arise from leaders who are not well skilled in negotiating group dynamics, and end up with little input or excessive conflict.

Mixed Models

Most of the qualitative research published in the needs assessment area actually would be better described as mixed model work. Most of the studies reviewed in this section have a strong qualitative bent, but use some combination of quantitative and qualitative techniques. Until pure qualitative models gain more acceptance, and because they aren't appropriate in all situations, mixed models are likely to remain popular. They often combine the qualitative aspects of participant involvement, giving back to the community, and socio-cultural/political awareness with more traditional methods of data collection and analysis. A variety of examples are presented below.

Schuh and Veltman (1991) describe the application of an ecosystem model to meeting the needs of handicapped students on campus. The ecosystem model involves not only having group members identify needs, but then having them make recommendations about interventions. This is clearly in line with qualitative philosophy. The authors developed a survey in coordination with the Office of Handicapped Services, and chose to include as possible needs all of the types of services the office had previously made available (a total of 30 services and activities). The survey was then mailed to potential participants. Students were asked to rate each item quantitatively, then to go back through the survey and to discuss in an open-ended format any items about which they felt particularly strongly, and to make recommendations for changes. The empirical data were analyzed with descriptive statistics and the comments by content analysis. The data and recommendations were taken back to the Office of Handicapped Services, where "workable solutions suggested by the disabled clients" (p. 238) were implemented around a variety of specific needs.

A good example of mixed model action research is described by Sloboda (1990), in his work with test anxiety in British university students. Under the British system, undergraduate students are given a set of comprehensive examinations at the end of three years of study, and these "finals" tend to be highly anxiety-provoking. Sloboda describes his study as " . . . a piece of action research within a specific institutional context . . . " and that "although it had academic aims, its principal motivation was political" (p. 125). The goals of the research were as follows:

(1) To raise the awareness of students and staff about the existence and effects of finals examination anxiety.
(2) To elicit, from the students themselves, their perceptions of the sources of distress, their coping strategies, their use of formal helping agencies, and their suggestions for alleviating the problems.
(3) To initiate an institution-wide debate on the issues raised.
(4) To promote policy decisions concerning (a) the nature and extent of support offered by the institution to students facing examination anxiety, and (b) the possible introduction of inherently less stressful assessment arrangements (pp. 125–126).

Goal (2) of this action research plan is essentially a needs assessment component, although the other goals reflect common aspects of qualitative methods, which include a recognition of socio-political context and a need to use the results of research to implement positive change for the parties involved. Sloboda describes in detail the process used for obtaining institutional support to conduct the study, which was based on an appeal to the university's dedication to good academic performance (and consequent reputation and funding), to cost effectiveness, and to humanitarian ideals. The needs assessment component was relatively traditional: a paper-and-pencil survey was given to all students taking finals in the year of the study. The survey contained both open-ended and fixed-format questions on demographics, use of medical and counseling services, physical/emotional stress symptoms during finals year, factors contributing to stress, strategies for coping, and what recommendations the students would make to deal with their needs in relation to the anxiety of final exams. Data were analyzed using descriptive statistics for quantitative items and content/theme analysis for open-ended questions. While the return rate was not as high as might be desirable (26.8%), the author identified some strong trends in the data, such as students' need for earlier and more formative evaluation and a complete lack of support for the system as it stood. Sloboda distributed his report to all levels of the university. He notes "some departments used the survey to instigate internal discussion between staff and students...others claimed they were already practising the major recommendations of the survey" (pp. 126–127). He concludes that his action research made a "small but significant impact on the institution" (p. 127).

A third example comes from Masi and Goff's (1987) description of the evaluation of employee assistance programs (EAPs). These researchers used a combination of quantitative and qualitative techniques to evaluate the effectiveness and appropriateness of the EAPs in 15 governmental agencies under the U. S. Department of Health and Human Services (USDHHS). Here, needs have been identified and a system is in place to meet those needs, but evaluation of the program must be implemented. This is one of the last, but crucial, steps in a thorough needs assessment. The evaluation phase is always necessary to determine if interventions are working (and if so, for whom, at what level), and what modifications in the system might need to be made. Quantitative data collected included demographic information on clients using the EAPs, empirical supervisory ratings (taken at EAP intake, three months after intake, and nine months after intake), and number of days of sick leave and other absences from employment. These data were compared to similar information from an aggregate personnel profile of employees who had not participated in EAPs.

Qualitative data collected were derived from a peer review process. Psychiatrists, social workers, and psychologists participated with equal input by reviewing actual case files. Data were recorded in tables, narratives, and in descriptions of strengths and weaknesses; recommendations were then made. It should be kept in mind that the evaluation is thus done with the USDHHS as the "client," rather than the persons who participate in the EAPs. The issue of multiple constituencies is often noted in qualitative research, and is discussed in greater detail in other sections of this chapter.

ADDITIONAL CONSIDERATIONS

Politics: Who is the Client?

Whether your needs assessment is a traditional, qualitative, or mixed model, the fact that it will be conducted in a social, political, and cultural context demands attention if you are to construct meaningful and successful programs. While your goal as a student service professional may be to meet the needs of Hispanic American students or student athletes or underachievers, etc., a great number of others have interests and needs that can "make or break" your program if ignored. To some, you will be directly accountable; to others, indirectly so. These constituencies may include other agency personnel, clerical/support staff, administrators at various levels in your college or at the state level, faculty, parents, community members and organizations, and other student groups, to name a few. Many researchers and needs assessment theorists, particularly those who work from qualitative bases, have discussed these issues in detail. The various illustrations that follow may serve as potential frameworks for dealing with these political issues. The terms "constituencies," "stakeholders," and "audiences" refer to these interrelated yet diverse groups who share a claim in the needs assessment endeavor.

Humm-Delgado and Delgado (1986), in discussing gaining access to Hispanic communities to assess their service needs, indicate four areas of consideration: interagency collaboration, contact with natural support systems, community member involvement, and use of local Hispanic media and institutions. Besides enlisting the cooperation of these sources in needs assessment, the authors stress that "people who participate in needs assessments do so most readily when they see the outcome of the process—the product, such as a new program, employment opportunity, skill—is likely to benefit them" (p. 88). They further caution that meeting the researchers' or academic institutions' needs for scholarly productivity cannot take precedence over the needs of the assessed community, and that an agency should only do a needs assessment if it has the resources to actually follow through and develop services that the needs assessment identifies. Needs assessment findings should be distributed throughout the community, in Spanish as well as in English.

Elias (1991), in his analysis of action research in middle schools, notes that researchers, parents, teachers, principals, school boards, and children are all accountable to each other in complex ways. Furthermore, these constituencies speak different languages, so to say, and respond to information in different formats:

> The university and certain basic-research oriented funding sources evaluate the success of the action research efforts in terms of products commensurate with the experimental paradigm. Community mental health centers and state- and county-level sources are more attuned to data within the pragmatic paradigm. Colleagues, staff, and especially students make many of their evaluative judgments on the basis of less formal and less quantitative information, focusing on vivid, dramatic, clinical, and anecdotal examples of the program's functioning (p. 399).

Attention to each group, with communication in the mode its members best understand, is thus implied. This sentiment is echoed by Smith (1986), who comments that some audiences are likely to find qualitative results more persuasive, while others will respond best to quantitative presentations. However, she makes the point that "there is currently no adequate means of classifying audiences according to which form of report they believe or whose recommendation they accept" (p. 43). Smith also reviews literature indicating that tacit or working knowledge is more readily affected by stories and anecdotes than by statistical results. Psychologists studying social cognition have recognized this bias for quite some time. Smith recognizes that despite this bias, formal authorities in institutions "may feel obliged to base final decisions on the results of a rigorous experiment or survey" (p. 43). In the end, Smith recommends using both tacit and propositional—qualitative and quantitative—data in presenting results to all stakeholders.

Brown and Barr (1990), in reviewing the student affairs field in general and its relationship to developmental theory, shed additional light on the issue of bringing research results to varied student service professionals. They argue that part of the difficulty is that this audience often lacks a shared understanding of underlying developmental theory, as well as coming from diverse academic backgrounds. Their argument serves as a reminder that we can't really even generalize about audiences like "administrators" or "counseling center staff" or "faculty"; there is often great variation within these groups as well as within the student groups they seek to serve.

Bridges, Elliott, and Klass (1986), reporting on the use of naturalistic inquiry for pupil performance appraisal in elementary and secondary school settings, note that "multiple perspectives might have a proper and useful place in pupil assessment" and that "the generation and availability of several diverse, even conflicting evaluations of an object of inquiry, far from constituting a methodological problem, is precisely what is expected, sought, and valued" (p. 225). However, while this approach is methodologically sound, it is politically difficult. The authors note that dialogue is necessary to gain "a clearer perception of the . . . assessment of pupils and a richer view of the valuation or interpretation which might be set on this evidence" (p. 226). They caution that this exchange may not, and need not, end in consensus or compromise, but little is offered in the way of concrete ways to resolve these political differences.

Additionally, Bridges et al. raise a number of other essentially political questions. The implementors of any ethically sound needs assessment will have to grapple with these issues and address them in its design and methods. The questions include:

—How can . . . assessment serve the purpose of human development as against that of social selection and control?
—Should . . . assessment be private or public?
—Who owns assessment data: the assessors or the assessed?
—To what extent should the assessed have a say in the outcome of the assessment?
—How can . . . assessment systems prevent unfair comparisons of individuals being drawn from assessment data?
—How can . . . assessments . . . portray individuals holistically?
(p. 230).

Some of their solutions involve refraining from overgeneralization and from taking data out of the context in which it was assessed, and from using predetermined categories to structure judgments. Instead, they recommend collecting a wide range or variety of data, making the reasons for assessment explicit and tied to appropriately justified goals, expressing assessment data in a positive framework, and allowing themes to emerge contextually—which ensures that participants' own understanding of self is incorporated into the assessment.

Feminist researchers (Cook & Fonow, 1990; Reinharz, 1992) explicitly acknowledge the political nature of assessment, and actively support the

use of research for socio-political change. While feminist researchers
may use a number of traditional, qualitative, and mixed methodologies,
there is a distinct tendency to favor the assumptions, if not the methods,
of qualitative assessment. For example, involvement of the researcher as
a person in close interaction and relationship with those assessed is
highlighted, as opposed to more traditional/male models in which there
is a strict split between "subject" and "object." Special efforts are made to
involve participants in the determination of their own needs. Additionally, information is made available to all constituencies throughout
the duration of the research—planning, collection, interpretation, and
recommendations/action. Often, changes will be made as shifts in the
context arise. Attention to multiple perspectives and diversity is also
explicit. In fact, Reinharz states that an attitude has developed among
many (typically white) feminist researchers that

> producing research that is inadequately diversified with regard to race, age,
> ethnicity, and sexual preference has become a sign of methodological weak-
> ness and moral failure, and impermissible reflection of a lack of effort and
> unwitting prejudice (p. 255).

More on the issue of majority researchers and minority participants is
found in the next section of this chapter.

Feminist researchers are well aware that their agendas, the agendas of
those whose needs are assessed, and the agendas of those in positions of
power may differ. They acknowledge that being political involves risks.
Thus, on the whole, the feminist perspective tends to handle political
issues by confronting them directly, with the hope that the act of
doing/participating in research itself will raise the consciousness of
those involved. Often, forging direct links with individual policy makers,
the media, and other policy-relevant organizations is beneficial. Again,
these political links are probably most effective if integrated at all stages
of a needs assessment project.

Pearsol (1987) brings yet another perspective to the issue of data
interpretation with varying constituencies. He argues that the personal
effectiveness of the evaluator is crucial, especially in justifying results of
naturalistic assessments to those who may be less familiar with or receptive to these strategies. He states that

> ...reconstruction, rather than direct representation, is what an evaluator
> does...he or she is always operating from a position of reconstructing context,
> issues, and perspectives [and thus] it is diligent negotiation that shapes the
> nature and scope of naturalistic evaluation conclusions...By defining the

evaluator as interpreter, one recognizes that assuming the mantle of naturalistic evaluator carries profound responsibilities... Of course, credibility is an issue, but from an interpretive perspective, credibility is defined in terms of the evaluator, not the methodological technique... The bottom line in naturalistic evaluation becomes the persuasiveness of the evaluator in reconstructing a telling tale (pp. 336–338).

Very similar conclusions are reached by Smith (1987), who states "all one can do, and this is all that should be expected, is to make the best case possible for one's conclusions" (p. 356). This appears to be a politically astute observation, regardless of the methodology used. Needs assessment researchers must carefully choose who is to represent them and their findings. The person(s) selected must not only be able to speak the language of particular stakeholders, but do so in a convincing manner.

While the preceding discussion has predominantly centered on qualitative researchers' viewpoints on the politics and management of the "Who is the client?" questions, more traditional needs assessment researchers have not neglected this area. In fact, two of the most well known and often cited traditional needs assessment experts have commented on this dilemma. Kuh (1982) captures the issues succinctly:

> To be politically and logically defensible, needs assessment must be a public and conscious effort to understand the requirements and perspectives of all students and groups associated with the problem. This approach requires collaboration: .... a common problem-solving effort. Voting to determine needs is not usually defensible because it is not public. A more justifiable strategy uses collaborative decision making and prioritizing through an apportioning process to achieve a reasoned consensus about how to proceed... Problem focused needs assessment requires expertise, public involvement, and recognition of the pluralistic value orientations of various stakeholders.... An effective needs assessment process requires the participation of a variety of persons with vested, and perhaps, competing interests (pp. 207–208).

Kuh recommends that needs assessments thus be closely tied to unique local conditions, context, and institution in order to maximize the benefits to all constituencies. He also recognizes that needs assessment is a value-laden process, even in the context of more traditional data collection techniques or designs.

Lenning (1980a), after detailing a variety of traditional methodologies for assessing student program needs, concludes:

> Once the results, interpretations, and judgments coming from the needs assessment are developed and refined, they need to be fed effectively into the program planning process... Their format and content should be tailored for

the decision makers at whom the report is aimed. In many cases, it will be preferable to send different reports to different people. They must be read and be fully meaningful to each person if the needs assessment is to have significant impact on program planning (p. 284).

Thus, regardless of the methodological orientation of the researchers, all seem to acknowledge some aspect of the political nature of needs assessment work. Student services professionals who are planning their own needs assessments clearly should take heed of the consensus of opinion on this issue. While the majority of researchers cited focus on the use of needs assessment data once it is gathered, it also seems wise to consider these political issues at all levels of needs assessment. Input in the planning stages, design, and actual data collection procedures could— and perhaps should—involve multiple constituencies. This would serve to ground support for the needs assessment project in a variety of campus "communities" and increase investment by involving them in actual collection, interpretation, and use of the information obtained.

Majority Professionals Working with Minority Students

A large proportion of professionals who read this book will be majority culture student service personnel. Many will not be members of any of the groups that are covered. The general ramifications of this fact have been discussed in Chapter 2. However, specific implications for methodology will be covered here. The generic stages of needs assessment design and implementation will serve as a framework for discussing the majority/minority issue, and each will be addressed in turn. These broad phases include 1) development of a conceptual base for the needs assessment and the consequent choice of a research strategy, 2) developing support and resources to carry out the assessment, 3) actual data collection, 4) interpretation of results, 5) presentation of results to various constituencies, 6) action: implementation of programs, and 7) ongoing feedback and evaluation. In reviewing the literature for this section, it is apparent that more has been suggested in reference to some items than to others. For example, steps 6 and 7 are less explicitly addressed than others, while step 1 has generated a great deal of commentary.

Some suggestions cross all stages of needs assessment. The predominant recommendations here are for majority researchers to work with minority members at all phases. Teams should be constructed which directly and seriously involve minority student service professionals and/or faculty, administrators, students, and/or community members (Mio & Iwamasa, 1993; Rave, 1990; Sue, 1993; Wright, 1987). In addition, training current personnel in multicultural issues is imperative (Casas, 1985; Casas & San Miguel, 1993; Shang & Moore, 1990; Stone & Archer, 1990). The professional ethical codes of most mental health professions virtually require attention to such issues (e.g. American Psychological Association, 1991). Many of the majority/minority conceptualization issues discussed next also have relevance for other stages in the needs assessment process. Therefore, it is the most detailed, and perhaps most important, section included here.

As just noted, the conceptual basis for needs assessment research and the choice of a research strategy which would flow from that base are prime areas for majority/minority issues consideration. One's conceptual base is the stone thrown in the water of the campus environment: all else ripples out from its center. For this reason, it is absolutely essential that one's conceptual base be solid when as a majority researcher, one ventures into the realm of assessing the needs of various minority student groups. The variety of knowledge bases that are considered desirable are broad indeed.

First of all, there should be an awareness of the social, historical, and economic context in which various minorities live every day. There are sources of stress that minority students face simply because of their minority status, including stigma, value conflicts with majority culture, and in-group and out-group acceptance/rejection issues. These affect all aspects of life—family, workplace, and school (Carter, 1991; Payton, 1985; Smith, 1985; Wright, 1987).

Student service professionals should also have a basic knowledge of various minority groups, especially those groups who have large representation on their particular campuses and in their communities (Jones, 1990; Smith, 1985; Smith, 1991). However, it must be stressed that a good proportion of the available literature grossly overgeneralizes about groups of minority students. This failure to identify the differences within groups has been a major criticism of multicultural research. Additionally, there has been a neglect of potentially confounding variables, such as socio-economic status, in much of this research. Every precaution should be taken not to repeat these errors in either conceptualization or design (Boyd, 1990; Parham, 1993; Ponterotto, 1988; Zuckerman, 1990).

Another issue which demands attention at the conceptualization phase is the lack of a sound theoretical base to guide minority research. While advocates of theory-based research are many, the use of untested theories that have been derived almost exclusively from majority culture—as almost all are—is clearly inappropriate. Many of our developmental and psychological theories remain untested with minority members even today. Many of these theoretical models not only failed to incorporate minority persons in the research samples, but either implicitly or explicitly set majority culture as the norm against which minority members by definition fall short. Differences then end up being seen as deficits. Even in work which has incorporated minority samples, these samples tend to be small and skewed (Boyd, 1990; Casas, 1985; Jones, 1990; Katz, 1985; Parham, 1993; Ponterotto, 1988; Shang & Moore, 1990; Wright, 1987; Zuckerman, 1990). Thus, great caution should be exercised in the choice of a theory base for a needs assessment, and a careful review of the theory/theories chosen for minority application is in order. A number of models of minority identity development and acculturation have been established (e.g., Helms, 1990; Sue & Sue, 1990), and may serve as better jumping-off points for assessing the needs of minority students than other, more traditional student development theories.

It is also incumbent upon the majority student service professional to choose assessment instruments which have appropriate minority norms or are culturally specific. Many traditional assessment tools are as biased as the theories discussed above. While a detailed discussion of minority testing issues is beyond the scope of this chapter, if a researcher chooses an instrument for needs assessment that has been previously established, s/he should examine it carefully for its norms and conceptual biases. Minority researchers have noted a general over-reliance on paper and pencil measures, and further observe that traditional test-taking procedures may not be culturally compatible for some students. There may be variations due to levels of acculturation, language, etc. Additionally, when choosing or developing a needs assessment instrument, a researcher should consider that needs can be conceptualized on a variety of levels, from the universal needs that all humans share, to culturally/ethnically based issues, to those that are unique to an individual—or unique to the interaction of a particular environment with these levels (Casas, 1985; Lonner, 1985; Ponterotto, 1988; Silva, 1983).

Another factor that may be helpful in the conceptualization stage for the majority researcher is a knowledge of current utilization patterns and help-seeking preferences of minority students. It is well established that minority students tend to underuse student services of various kinds.

Explanations for underuse include unavailability of culturally similar or sensitive personnel, value conflicts, mismatched expectations, varying levels of acculturation/identity development, and the use of alternative sources of help (Atkinson & Gim, 1989; Atkinson, Jennings, & Liongson, 1990; Atkinson, Poston, Furlong, & Mercado, 1989; Atkinson, Whitely, & Gim, 1990; Austin, Carter, & Vaux, 1990; Carter, 1991; Gim, Atkinson, & Kim, 1991; Gim, Atkinson, & Whitely, 1990; Helms & Carter, 1991; Hess & Street, 1991; June, Curry, & Gear, 1990; Kunkel, 1990; Minatoya & King, 1984; Pomales & Williams, 1989; Ponce & Atkinson, 1989; Priest, 1991; Watkins, Terrell, Miller, & Terrell, 1989; Webster & Fretz, 1978; Westbrook, Miyares, & Roberts, 1978; Wilson & Stith, 1991). This list may highlight a variety of minority student needs that could be incorporated into a needs assessment.

It is also recommended that at the very outset, the majority researcher develop a true awareness of his or her own majority identity. As Helms (1993) succinctly states:

> ... White people are the born benefactors and beneficiaries of racism, although they may not consciously be aware of their bequest. Nevertheless, because racism causes White people to deny, distort, and repress realities of race relations in their environments, it has negative impacts on White people as well as having benefits. Therefore, for Whites to develop a healthy White racial identity in a racist society, I argue that Whites must become consciously aware of the ways in which racism works to their advantage and make a deliberate effort to abandon it in favor of positive nonracist definitions of Whiteness ... To the extent that the researcher is unable to recognize and value alternative race-related cultural perspectives, then he or she is likely to contribute to research that has little meaning for any of the racial groups. Moreover, if the researcher is unable to examine the effects of her or his own racial development on her or his research activities, then the researcher risks contributing to the existing body of racially oppressive literature rather than offering illuminating scholarship (pp. 241–242).

In a related vein, Katz (1985) presents an excellent summary of majority culture values over a broad range of domains (See Table V).

Such reviews can provide an excellent starting point for a personal examination of one's majority culture. Additionally, theories, assessment devices or surveys, or needs assessment goals could be compared against a list such as Katz' as one part of determining their appropriateness.

A few other points should be noted in relation to the issue of developing awareness of one's majority cultural identity. One such point is the importance of keeping in mind that majority culture may also entail

Table V: The Components of White Culture: Values and Beliefs

Rugged Individualism:
  Individual is primary unit
  Individual has primary
    responsibility
  Independence and autonomy highly
    valued and rewarded
  Individual can control environment

Competition:
  Winning is everything
  Win/lose dichotomy

Action Orientation:
  Must master and control nature
  Must always do something about a
    situation

Decision Making:
  Majority rule when Whites have power
  Hierarchical
  Pyramid structure

Communication:
  Standard English
  Written tradition
  Direct eye contact
  Limited physical contact
  Control emotions

Time:
  Adherence to rigid time schedules
  Time is viewed as a commodity

Holidays:
  Based on Christian religion
  Based on White history and male
    leaders

History:
  Based on European immigrants'
    experience in the United States
  Romanticize war

Protestant Work Ethic:
  Working hard brings success

Progress and Future Orientation:
  Plan for future
  Delay gratification
  Value continual improvement and
    progress

Emphasis on Scientific Method:
  Objective, rational, linear thinking
  Cause and effect relationships
  Quantitative emphasis
  Dualistic thinking

Status and Power:
  Measured by economic possessions
  Credentials, titles, and positions
  Believe "own" system
  Believe better than other systems
  Owning goods, property, space

Family Structure:
  Nuclear family is ideal social unit
  Male is breadwinner and the head of
    the household
  Female is homemaker and
    subordinate to the husband
  Patriarchal structure

Aesthetics:
  Music and art based on European
    cultures
  Women's beauty based on blond, blue-
    eyed, thin, young.
  Men's attractiveness based on athletic
    ability, power, economic status

Religion:
  Belief in Christianity
  No tolerance for deviation from a
    single god concept

From Katz (c 1985). The Sociopolitical Nature of Counseling. *The Counseling Psychologist, 13,* 618. Reprinted with permission of Sage Publications, Inc.

aspects not detailed above, such as heterosexism (Fassinger, 1991). A second important point is that even those with a strong commitment to equality, such as many feminist researchers, are not immune to racism. A number of authors have commented on White feminists' incorrect assumptions that a common feminist bond between minority and majority women somehow negates racial or ethnic distinctions (Boyd, 1990; Rave, 1990). In summary, some real effort should be devoted to majority awareness at least concurrently with, and even perhaps before, the conceptualization phase of needs assessment research.

The other specific methodological recommendation involving the conceptualization phase is to consider both traditional quantitative and newer qualitative designs (Parham, 1993). Because a large portion of this chapter has already been devoted to a detailed examination of the rationales for both methods, suffice it to say that a number of feminist and minority researchers see the philosophical and methodological bases of qualitative inquiry as a better "fit" to minority needs than traditional designs.

Step 2 in the generic needs assessment model is to develop institutional support and resources for conducting your research. Here, continued networking with minority administrators, student affairs peers, faculty, residence assistants and other students will be crucial. Minority funding sources should be explored, and peer research review boards on campus should include minority members (Casas, 1985). If your campus peer review committee has no minority members, you should seek additional feedback from minority representatives. It should be kept in mind that many minority groups may resent being used as research participants since historically, many majority researchers have made their careers on such research without giving back anything to the groups studied, or promising returns that never materialize (Mio & Iwamasa, 1993; Sue, 1993). Thus, in developing support for your project, while it is important to be optimistic about changing or increasing services to minority students, promises should not be made unless they can be kept. Humm-Delgado and Delgado (1986) give some specific recommendations that may be helpful for the majority researcher in developing support and resources. While their work is particularly targeted to the Hispanic community, a number of points are well worth considering in the university context and with other minority student groups. Their first recommendation is for interagency collaboration. Organizations that are specific to minority student groups can help take the lead in gaining appropriate access to members, particularly if the agency or persons conducting the needs assessment are unknown in the particular minority student community. Contact with minority students' natural support systems may also be helpful. If students are known, for example, to seek out particular advisors, faculty, or peer leaders, these persons could be involved as well. As mentioned earlier, and reiterated by Humm-Delgado and Delgado, community member involvement is also crucial. Thus, minority students, in particular, should be involved in this step of the needs assessment (as well as all others). Lastly, these authors recommend using local media and institutions to develop support and access. If minority student organizations have newsletters, for example, a story about the upcoming needs assessment might be useful, particularly if written by the student(s).

Most of the recommendations above would also apply to the actual data collection stage. There would be some variations, depending on the methodologies used. If face-to-face interviewing or nominal groups are used, perhaps teams of one minority/majority interviewer could be used. At least some minority participation in actual data collection is desirable if a team approach is deemed too time or cost inefficient. Additionally, majority interviewers should be specifically trained for appropriate interaction with various minority student groups, including knowledge base and actual communication skills. If survey methods are used, cover letters that indicate minority student organizational support or the endorsement of recognized/respected minority community leaders can also be helpful in ensuring better return rates.

Once data are collected, the third step in needs assessment begins—data analysis and interpretation. Cautions are in order for both processes. Probably the most often noted criticism that applies is that between-group comparisons should not be done against majority groups, with a consequent interpretation that the minority group, if found significantly different, is therefore deficient (Ponterotto, 1988). It also seems important to recognize that if minority members' scores on some instrument or item fall well above or below a mean, this does not de facto indicate "pathology." This is particularly true if the mean being referred to is derived from a predominantly majority sample or a majority norm. Basics should be kept in mind, such as the fact that correlations do not imply causality and that statistical significance may have little or no practical/clinical relevance. Broad generalizations should not be made from small or unrepresentative samples, a condition that often occurs in minority student research (Parham, 1993; Zuckerman, 1990). Ponterotto also cautions that interpretations should not overculturalize or underculturalize.

The findings from cognitive-social psychology also bring a number of important considerations to data interpretation. Many of these findings will be particularly applicable to more qualitative data analysis, where a certain amount of subjective judgment is necessary. However, one should not view quantitative data interpretation as immune from these effects. There are a number of biases in how all humans seem to process information. Both majority and minority researchers are thus vulnerable; for the purposes of this discussion, however, one should use the scenario of a majority researcher processing information about minority students. The first bias is the availability heuristic (Kahneman & Taversky, 1973). It involves basing judgments on information that is most readily accessible in memory, and failing to search for data that is less salient or inconsistent with the most easily remembered information. Secondly, there is the representativeness heuristic, which involves making judgments about information—or people—based on how well they fit a standard, typical example of the category involved. Racial and ethnic stereotypes are common bases for our "standards of a category." Both of these tendencies may lead to biased interpretations of data. Interview material, not recorded verbatim, is likely to fall prey to these heuristics. Interviewers may select certain types of information, or later remember or interpret information, based on these processes (which rarely occur on a conscious level). Additionally, people fall prey to biases based on their prior knowledge and labels attached to certain groups. Preconceptions tend not to be revised in the light of new, contradictory information; the new information is often discounted if it doesn't fit pre-existing cognitive schemas. Information obtained early on tends to carry significant weight, and may bias the interpretation of later data. This means that when researchers set out with certain hypotheses, they will tend to interpret data in order to confirm those hypotheses. Also, when details cannot be remembered, we often reconstruct them in our memory—we literally "fill in" what we think was probably missing. Obviously, this can be a highly biased process, yet it is a common one. A review of these processes is provided by Morrow and Deidan (1992), with vignettes that depict their application to the counseling process. Most basic introductory social psychology texts provide elaboration on these constructs. The major point to be made here is that data interpretation is far from the objective, straightforward process that many assume it to be. Majority researchers should familiarize themselves with these biases in social cognition, as an awareness of the effects of these biases often proves preventative.

In step 5 of the needs assessment process, interpreted data is presented to all interested parties. To a large extent, comments relevant to this section have been covered in the section on "Politics: Who is the Client?" The reader is referred to that portion of the chapter for a thorough discussion of disseminating results to various constituencies. The only addition to that information is to stress that majority researchers should highlight the strengths of minority students (Boyd, 1990; Ponterotto, 1988; Wright, 1987) and should always make results available to the students themselves who took part in the needs assessment. This later point may require more action than expected. For example, in earlier work, the first author of this chapter and a colleague (Stabb & Cogdal, 1990) offered to present the results of a needs assessment of African-American and international students to their respective student organizations. Results were also described in organizational newsletters. When there was no response to the presentation offer, we dropped the issue. No other mechanisms were in place for getting results out to other participants (not organization members) who might have been curious about the study in which they participated. In retrospect, perhaps an article in the campus newspaper, or copies of results made available in dormitories, would have been valuable additions. In terms of making results known to a wider professional audience, many minority researchers and their concerned majority colleagues note that until there are more minority editors, editorial review members, and other "gatekeepers" within our professional ranks, the dissemination of research involving minorities may continue to be hampered (Atkinson, 1993; Casas & San Miguel, 1993; Casas, 1985). Zuckerman (1990) notes that we also need to be extra critical of publishing research that supports unfounded racial theory or racist practice.

Steps 6 and 7 in the needs assessment process are, respectively, implementation of programs and services to meet identified student needs, and the monitoring and feedback/evaluation of those programs once in place. These two steps may arguably go beyond the assessment itself; we are now in the realm of program planning and evaluation. Thus, comments will be brief. There appears to be scant information available about the majority/minority issue in this regard, in contrast to program development and management in general, which have a voluminous literature associated with them. Perhaps the main point is to keep minority students and colleagues intimately involved in the design of interventions and their subsequent evaluations. It must be determined if the programs actually meet the identified needs in ways which are satisfying to their consumers. Periodic evaluation and modification are recommended. The information that is known on minority patterns of service utilization (see references in the section on conceptualization and knowledge bases) may also be of particular use in this stage. There have also been recommendations that programs be implemented early on in minority students' college careers (Payton, 1985).

Last but not least, no matter what stage of needs assessment is involved, an active, conscious anti-racist (sexist, classist, etc.) process on the part of the majority researcher working with minority students is needed (Casas & San Miguel, 1993; Parham, 1993; Rave, 1990; Sue, 1993). Individually and politically, this struggle must go on.

SUMMARY AND RECOMMENDATIONS

This chapter has covered a wide variety of methods for needs assessment with diverse student groups, methods both from a more traditional, quantitative perspective and those from qualitative paradigms. Hopefully, enough detail has been presented that the student service professional wishing to embark on a needs assessment venture can begin to do so with the resources herein. In conclusion, three major recommendations are made.

The first recommendation is to be planful—more planful than you think you have to be. Regardless of the strategies you eventually employ, planning will be crucial. This is particularly true regarding the amount of networking that will be needed and the development of relationships to gain access to diverse student groups. The generic stages of needs assessment can serve as a guide to the areas that will need attention. While described earlier, they are highlighted here due to their importance:

(1) Development of a conceptual base and rationale for the needs assessment and the consequent choice of a research strategy/ strategies (includes samples, instrumentation, and specific methods).
(2) Developing support and resources to carry out the assessment.
(3) Actual data collection.
(4) Interpretation of results.

(5) Presentation of results to various constituencies.

(6) Action: implementation of programs.

(7) Ongoing feedback and evaluation.

This deceptively simple list, if "fleshed out" in all its implications and nuances, can provide a good checklist for needs assessment planning.

The second recommendation is to use a mixed model for your choice of research strategies. As discussed in the qualitative methods section, there are strong arguments for the goodness of fit between qualitative strategies and diverse populations. While these techniques do require time and expertise, they contribute rich information on processes and perceptions that are rarely tapped by traditional methods. On the other hand, most of those on whom you will depend for financial and institutional support are likely to respond more enthusiastically to what they perceive as "hard data." Thus, the inclusion of more traditional survey or structured interview results that are easily quantifiable is also desirable. Careful consideration should be given to the selection of specific methodologies that will be combined; the strengths and weaknesses of each should be determined and used in ways that complement each other while allowing for a minimum of redundancy.

The third recommendation is to be political. This is meant in the broadest sense of the word. In this context, it means to be attuned to the multiple constituencies that your needs assessment will involve; speak to them in ways they relate to best and if you can't, find someone who can. It means going through the process of needs assessment with attention to feedback from these varied voices and the openness to consider modifications, if needed. It means an awareness of how biases in human cognition in general and in your own cultural identity in particular may skew your interpretations. It means recognizing that needs assessment is not a value-free endeavor. If assessing diverse student needs is conducted without a goal of improvement or positive change, and *if that change is not validated as positive for those whom it was designed to serve,* it is at best a wasteful exercise, and at its worst, a vehicle for maintaining an oppressive and unresponsive status quo.

REFERENCES

American Psychological Association. (1991). Guidelines for providers of psychological services to ethnic, linguistic, and culturally diverse populations. *American Psychological Association:* Washington, D.C.

Atkinson, D. R. (1993). Who speaks for cross-cultural counseling research? *The Counseling Psychologist, 21,* 218–224.

Atkinson, D. R. (1989). Asian-American cultural identity and attitudes towards mental health services. *Journal of Counseling Psychology, 36,* 209–212.

Atkinson, D. R., Jennings, G. R., & Liongson, L. (1990). Minority students' reasons for not seeking counseling and suggestions for improving services. *Journal of College Student Development, 31,* 342–350.

Atkinson, D. R., Poston, W. C., Furlong, M. J., & Mercado, P. (1989). Ethnic group preferences for counselor characteristics. *Journal of Counseling Psychology, 36,* 68–72.

Atkinson, D. R., Whitely, S., & Gim, R. H. (1990). Asian-American acculturation and preferences for help providers. *Journal of College Student Development, 31,* 155–161.

Aubel, J., Alzouma, E. H. M., Djabel, I., Ibrahim, S. & Coulibaly, B. (1991). From qualitative community data collection to program design: Health education planning in Niger. *International Quarterly of Community Health Organization, 11,* 345–369.

Austin, N. L., Carter, R. T., & Vaux, A. (1990). The role of racial identity in Black students' attitudes towards counseling and counseling centers. *Journal of College Student Development, 31,* 237–244.

Boyd, J. A. (1990). Ethnic and cultural diversity: Keys to power. *Diversity and Complexity in Feminist Therapy,* 151–167.

Bridges, D., Elliott, J. & Klass, C. (1986). Performance appraisal as naturalistic inquiry: A report of the fourth Cambridge conference on educational evaluation. *Cambridge Journal of Education, 16,* 221–233.

Brown, R. D. & Barr, M. J. (1990). Student development: Yesterday, today, and tomorrow. *New Directions for Student Services, 51,* 83–92.

Carter, R. T. (1991). Cultural values: A review of empirical research and implications for counseling. *Journal of Counseling and Development, 70,* 164–173.

Casas, J. M. (1985). A reflection on the status of racial/ethnic minority research. *The Counseling Psychologist, 13,* 581–598.

Casas, J. M. & San Miguel, S. (1993). Beyond questions and discussions, there is a need for action: A response to Mio and Iwamasa. *The Counseling Psychologist, 21,* 233–239.

Cook, J. A. & Fonow, M. M. (1990). Knowledge and women's interests: Issues of epistemology and methodology in feminist social research. In J. McCarl-Nielsen (Ed.). *Feminist Research Methods: Exemplary Readings in the Social Sciences.* (pp. 69–93). Westview Press: Boulder, CO.

Elias, M. J. (1991). An action research approach to evaluating the impact of a social decision making and problem-solving curriculum for preventing behavior and academic dysfunction in children. *Evaluation and Program Planning, 14,* 397–401.

Evans, N. J. (1985). Needs assessment methodology: A comparison of results. *Journal of College Student Personnel, 26,* 107–114.

Fassinger, R. E. (1991). The hidden minority: Issues and challenges in working with lesbian women and gay men. *The Counseling Psychologist, 19,* 157–176.

Friedlander, J. (1978). Student ratings of co-curricular services and their intent to use them. *Journal of College Student Personnel, 19,* 195–201.

Gim, R. H., Atkinson, D. R., & Kim, S. J. (1991). Asian-American acculturation, counselor ethnicity and cultural sensitivity, and ratings of counselors. *Journal of Counseling Psychology, 38,* 57–62.

Gim, R. H., Atkinson, D. R., & Whitely, S. (1990). Asian-American acculturation, severity of concerns, and willingness to see a counselor. *Journal of Counseling Psychology, 37,* 281–285.

Harris, H. J. & Anttonen, R. G. (1986). Assessing needs of male and female college freshmen. *Journal of College Student Personnel, 27,* 277.

Helms, J. E. (1990). *Black and white racial identity: Theory, research, and practice.* Greenwood: Westport, CT.

Helms, J. E. (1993). I also said, "White racial identity influences white researchers". *The Counseling Psychologist, 21,* 240–243.

Helms, J. E. & Carter, R. T. (1991). Relationships of White and Black racial identity attitudes and demographic similarity to counselor preferences. *Journal of Counseling Psychology, 38,* 446–457.

Helwig, A. A. & Vidales, J. L. (1988). Minority and white counselor differences on a needs assessment related to career development. *TACD Journal, 16,* 51–57.

Hess, R. S. & Street, E. M. (1991). Effects of acculturation and counselor ethnicity on client ratings. *Journal of Counseling Psychology, 38,* 71–75.

Hoshmand, L. S. T. (1989). Alternate research paradigms: A review and teaching proposal. *The Counseling Psychologist, 17,* 3–101.

Humm-Delgado, D. & Delgado, M. (1986). Gaining community entree to assess service needs of Hispanics. *Social Casework: The Journal of Contemporary Social Work, 67,* 80–89.

Husband, R. & Foster, W. (1987). Understanding qualitative research: A strategic approach to qualitative methodology. *Journal of Humanistic Education and Development, 26,* 50–63.

Jacob, E. (1987). Qualitative research traditions: A review. *Review of Educational Research, 57,* 1–50.

Jick, T. D. (1983). Mixing qualitative and quantitative methods: Triangulation in action. In J. Van Maanen (Ed.). *Qualitative Methodology.* (pp. 135–148). Sage Publications: Beverly Hills, CA.

Jones, W. T. (1990). Perspectives on ethnicity. *New Directions for Student Services, 51,* 59–71.

June, L. N., Curry, B. P., & Gear, C. L. (1990). An 11-year analysis of Black use of services. *Journal of Counseling Psychology, 37,* 178–184.

Kahneman, D. & Taversky, A. (1973). On the psychology of prediction. *Psychological Review, 80,* 237–251.

Katz, J. H. (1985). The sociopolitical nature of counseling. *The Counseling Psychologist, 13,* 615–624.

Kuh, G. D. (1982). Purposes and principles for needs assessment in student affairs. *Journal of College Student Personnel, 23,* 202–209.

Kunkel, M. A. (1990). Expectations about counseling in relation to acculturation in

Mexican-American and Anglo-American student samples. *Journal of Counseling Psychology, 37,* 286–292.

Lenning, O. T. (1980a). Assessing student program needs. In P. Jedamus and M. W. Peterson (Eds.). *Improving Academic Management.* (pp. 263–288). Jossey-Bass: San Francisco.

Lenning, O. T. (1980b). Assessment and evaluation. In U. Delworth & G. R. Hanson (Eds.). *Student Services: A Handbook for the Profession.* (pp. 232–266). Jossey-Bass: San Francisco.

Lincoln, Y. S. & Guba, E. G. (1985). *Naturalistic Inquiry.* Sage Publications: Beverly Hills, CA.

Lincoln, Y. S. & Guba, E. G. (1986). But is it rigorous? Trustworthiness and authenticity in naturalistic evaluation. In D. D. Williams (Ed.). *Naturalistic Evaluation: New Directions for Program Evaluation, No. 30.* (pp. 73–84). Jossey-Bass: San Francisco.

Lonner, W. J. (1985). Issues in testing and assessment in cross-cultural counseling. *The Counseling Psychologist, 13,* 599–614.

Lorion, R. P., Hightower, A. D., Work, W. C. & Shockley, P. (1987). The basic academic skills enhancement program: Translating prevention theory into action research. *Journal of Community Psychology, 15,* 63–77.

Marshall, C. & Rossman, G. B. (1989). *Designing Qualitative Research.* Sage Publications: Newbury Park, CA.

Masi, D. A. and Goff, M. E. (1987). The evaluation of employee assistance programs. *Public Personnel Management, 16,* 323–327.

Mayes, A. N. & McConatha, J. (1982). Surveying student needs: A means of evaluating student services. *Journal of College Student Personnel, 23,* 473–476.

McCarl-Nielsen, J. (Ed.). (1990). *Feminist Research Methods: Exemplary Readings in the Social Sciences.* Westview Press: Boulder, CO.

Midkiff, R. & Burke, J. P. (1987). An action research strategy for selecting and conducting program evaluations. *Psychology in the Schools, 24,* 135–144.

Minatoya, L. Y. & King, B. (1984). A systematic approach to assessment and intervention for minority undergraduates. *Journal of College Student Personnel, 25,* 272–274.

Mio, J. S. & Iwamasa, G. (1993). To do, or not to do: That is the question for white cross-cultural researchers. *The Counseling Psychologist, 21,* 197–212.

Morrow, K. A. & Deidan, C. T. (1992). Bias in the counseling process: How to recognize and avoid it. *Journal of Counseling and Development, 70,* 571–577.

Parham, T. A. (1993). White researchers conducting multicultural counseling research: Can their efforts be "Mo Betta"? *The Counseling Psychologist, 21,* 250–256.

Patton, M. Q. (1990). *Qualitative Evaluation and Research Methods.* Sage Publications: Newbury Park, CA.

Payton, C. R. (1985). Addressing the special needs of minority women. *New Directions for Student Services, 29,* 75–90.

Pearsol, J. A. (1987). Justifying conclusions in naturalistic evaluations: An interpretive perspective. *Evaluation and Program Planning, 10,* 335–341.

Peshkin, A. (1993). The goodness of qualitative research. *Educational Researcher, 22,* 23–29.

Polkinghorne, D. E. (1991). Two conflicting calls for methodological reform. *The Counseling Psychologist, 19,* 103–114.

Pomales, J. & Williams, V. (1989). Effects of level of acculturation and counseling style on Hispanic perceptions of counseling. *Journal of Counseling Psychology, 36,* 79–83.

Ponce, F. Q. & Atkinson, D. G. (1989). Mexican-American acculturation, counselor ethnicity, counseling style, and perceived counselor credibility. *Journal of Counseling Psychology, 36,* 203–208.

Ponterotto, J. G. (1988). Racial/ethnic minority research in the Journal of Counseling Psychology: A content analysis and methodological critique. *Journal of Counseling Psychology, 35,* 410–418.

Ponterotto, J. G. (1993). White racial identity and the counseling profession. *The Counseling Psychologist, 21,* 213–217.

Priest, R. (1991). Racism and prejudice as negative impacts on African-American clients in therapy. *Journal of Counseling and Development, 70,* 213–215.

Rave, E. J. (1990). White feminist therapists and anti-racism. *Diversity and Complexity in Feminist Therapy,* 313–326.

Reason, P. (1988). *Human Inquiry in Action: Developments in New Paradigm Research.* Sage Publications: Newbury Park, CA.

Reinharz, S. (1992). *Feminist Methods in Social Research.* Oxford University Press: NY.

Schuh, J. H. & Veltman, G. C. (1991). Application of an ecosystem model to an office of handicapped services. *Journal of College Student Development, 32,* 236–240.

Silva, J. S. (1983). Cross-cultural ethnic assessment. In G. Gibson, (Ed.) *Our Kingdom Stands on Brittle Glass.* (pp. 59–66). Silver Springs, Maryland: National Association of Social Workers.

Shang, P. & Moore, L. V. (1990). Applying cultural theory: The environmental variable. *New Directions for Student Services, 51,* 73–82.

Skibbe, A. (1986). Assessing campus needs with nominal groups. *Journal of Counseling and Development, 64,* 532–33.

Sloboda, J. A. (1990). Combating examination stress among university students: Action research in an institutional context. *British Journal of Guidance and Counseling, 18,* 124–136.

Smith, E. M. J. (1985). Ethnic minorities: Life stress, social support, and mental health issues. *The Counseling Psychologist, 13,* 537–80.

Smith, E. J. (1991). Ethnic identity development: Toward the development of a theory within the context of majority/minority status. *Journal of Counseling and Development, 70,* 181–188.

Smith, J. K. (1987). Commentary: Relativism and justifying conclusions in naturalistic evaluations. *Evaluation and Program Planning, 10,* 351–358.

Smith, M. L. (1986). The whole is greater: Combining qualitative and quantitative approaches in evaluation studies. In D. D. Williams (Ed.). *Naturalistic Evaluation: New Directions for Program Evaluation, No. 30.* (pp. 37–54). Jossey-Bass: San Francisco.

Stabb, S. D. & Cogdal, P. A. (1990, April). *Needs assessment and perceptions of help in a multicultural student population.* Paper presented at the meeting of the American College Personnel Association, St. Louis, MO.

Stabb, S. D. & Cogdal, P. A. (1992). Black college men in personal counseling: A 5-year archival investigation. *Journal of College Student Psychotherapy, 7,* 73–86.

Stone, G. L. & Archer, J. R. (1990). Counseling centers in the 1990's. *The Counseling Psychologist, 18,* 539–607.

Sue, D. W. (1993). Confronting ourselves: The white and racial/ethnic-minority researcher. *The Counseling Psychologist, 21,* 244–249.

Sue, D. W. & Sue, D. (1990). *Counseling the culturally different: Theory and practice.* New York: Wiley.

Talley, J. E. & Barrow, J. C., Fulkerson, K. F. & Moore, C. A. (1983). Conducting a needs assessment of university psychological services: A campaign of telephone and mail strategies. *Journal of American College Health, 32,* 101–103.

Watkins, C. E., Terrell, F., Miller, F. S., & Terrell, S. L. (1989). Cultural mistrust and expectations in Black client, White therapist relationships. *Journal of Counseling Psychology, 36,* 447–450.

Webster, D. W. & Fretz, B. R. (1978). Asian-American, Black, and White college students' preferences for help-giving sources. *Journal of Counseling Psychology, 25,* 124–130.

Westbrook, F. D., Miyares, J., & Roberts, J. H. (1978). Perceived problem areas by Black and White students and hints about comparative counseling needs. *Journal of Counseling Psychology, 25,* 119–123.

Williams, D. D. (1986a). Naturalistic evaluation. In M. W. Lipsey, (Ed.) *New Directions for Program Evaluation.* Jossey-Bass: San Francisco.

Williams, D. D. (1986b). Naturalistic evaluation: Potential conflicts between evaluation standards and criteria for conducting naturalistic inquiry. *Educational Evaluation and Policy Analysis, 8,* 87–99.

Wilson, L. L. & Stith, S. M. (1991). Culturally sensitive therapy with Black clients. *Journal of Multicultural Counseling and Development, 19,* 32–43.

Wright, D. J. (1987). Minority students: Developmental beginnings. In D. J. Wright, (Ed.) *Responding to the Needs of Today's Minority Students. New Directions for Student Services, 38,* 5–21.

Zuckerman, M. (1990). Dubious research/theory on racial differences. *American Psychologist, 45,* 1297–1303.

Chapter 4

CONCURRENT TECHNIQUES AND AFRICAN-AMERICAN STUDENTS' RESPONSES TO A PSYCHOLOGICAL NEEDS ASSESSMENT SURVEY

SHANETTE M. HARRIS AND JOSEPH E. TALLEY

The participation and performance of African-American students in academic and social domains on predominantly Euro-American university campuses has engendered heated discussions among government officials and university policy makers since increased enrollments during the sixties. Because of the complexity and controversial nature of problems that evolved from this merger, many solutions offered to address these concerns have been contaminated with emotionality and opinion. Needs assessment in higher education represents an important effort to reduce opinion and bias in the identification of problems, clarification of concerns and development of interventions that can be used to enhance desired outcomes for students and institutions.

Traditionally, needs assessors have focused on measuring African-American students' perceptions and use of university services. The preponderance of the research generated was performed during the seventies and eighties and primarily consists of one-shot evaluations. Systematic investigations of African-American students' needs are absent from the assessment literature and few longitudinal studies on a particular college campus or between colleges exist. Published accounts of these assessments are subsumed under minority student retention, needs assessment, mental health, and counseling bodies of literature. Various student groups (e.g., gifted and talented, recipients of program services, and high school students) and non-student populations (e.g., college counselors, elderly, practicing high school counselors, and trained peer counselors) have served as participants (Akah, 1990; Carey, Reinat, & Fontes, 1990; Carrington & Sedlacek, 1977; Chau, 1992; Ford-Harris, Schuerger, & Harris III, 1991; Helwig & Vidales, 1988; Miller, Springer, Milford, &

Williams, 1986; Ragan & Higgins, 1985; Ralston, 1983; Richmond, Johnson, Downs, & Ellinghaus, 1983; Shifman, Scott, Fawcett, & Orr, 1986; Westbrook & Smith, 1976). These assessments consist of students enrolled at the high school, junior college, four-year college, and graduate levels of education. Although a few published assessments include students enrolled at traditionally African-American institutions (e.g., Ragan & Higgins, 1985; Westbrook, Miyares, & Roberts, 1978), the majority have been conducted on predominantly Euro-American college campuses.

The bulk of the assessments conducted on these campuses emphasize racial differences in the use of counseling and the perceived effectiveness of services received. Numerous hypotheses could be formulated about the reasons assessors elect to largely investigate needs in relation to counseling services but three issues seem particularly relevant: early counseling programs were instituted on Euro-American campuses to enhance the greatest intellectual potential of students (Farnsworth & Oliver, 1959), tutorial and support services were traditionally sponsored by counseling centers, and results of early research showed African-Americans more than Euro-Americans to hold unfavorable attitudes toward counseling services (Brown, Frey, & Crapo, 1972; Burrell & Rayder, 1971).

The acceptance and enrollment of African-American students on predominantly Euro-American campuses introduced many concerns related to existing admissions criteria. Traditional criteria (e.g., SAT scores, high school grades) were designed to admit Euro-American students who attended high schools that offered college preparatory experiences consistent with university requirements. However, these standards were often inappropriate for the evaluation of entering African-American students because most had not been exposed to educational demands as rigorous as those experienced at Euro-American high schools. These students were also less likely to be of middle and upper class socioeconomic status. Given the influence of structural inequities on the educational preparedness of African-American students, many entered Euro-American university environments with comparative academic deficiencies. Mixed reactions to this dilemma were expressed among institutions (e.g., total resistance, waiver of traditional criteria), although many were willing to admit students with the expectation that personal/vocational counseling and academic/tutorial assistance would alleviate academic deficits.

Obvious consequences of poor academic performance were inadequate progression and low retention and graduation rates. The African-American enrollment on predominantly Euro-American college campuses increased substantially between 1960 and 1975. Approximately 75% of all African-American students in college were enrolled on predominantly Euro-American campuses (Blackwell, 1982). However attrition rates were high as well. Almost fifty percent of enrolled African-American students failed to matriculate to degree completion between 1969 and 1974 (Abramowitz, 1976). These exceptionally low persistence rates contributed to increases in empirical research to account for the reasons that African-Americans more than Euro-Americans failed to progress toward degree completion.

Students admitted into these institutions soon discovered, however, that psychosocial and emotional needs were intricately related to successful academic adjustment and performance. Many students appeared for counseling with multiple needs. Gibbs (1973) described five concerns in addition to academic performance that were commonly presented, including: interracial interpersonal relations, autonomy, sexual and aggressive feelings, career planning, and identity issues. Personal and social needs have been found to be as important as academic needs to students whether enrolled in regional, liberal arts, urban, technical, or traditionally African-American institutions (Ragan & Higgins, 1985). An early study conducted by Jones, Harris and Hauck (1971) found that African-American students to report competition with students, inadequate high school education, irrelevant course requirements, campus coldness and hostility, inadequate social experiences and poorly planned counseling and advising as important issues on predominantly Euro-American campuses. Although the expressed concerns of African-American students have changed slightly during the years, many of the early needs that evolved from student-university interactions remain problematic.

Using a stress inventory designed for African-American students, Edmunds (1984) found financial and academic stressors to be of paramount importance to undergraduate African-Americans. Environmentally related stressors (e.g., small numbers of same-race classmates, an absence of same-race student leadership), personal concerns (e.g., decision making/problem solving) and intraracial interpersonal relations (e.g., male/female relations) were cited as well. Peer counselors also report problems for African-American students in areas of study efficiency, academic difficulty, career goals, university system negotiations, campus facilities, and financial assistance (Westbrook & Smith, 1976). Gallagher

(1992) mailed a survey to 1800 randomly selected students at the University of Pittsburgh and found concerns related to career, self-confidence, motivation, fear of failure, anxiety, faculty, depression, life purpose, sexual abuse, and suicide. According to this researcher, "Black students in particular seem to find the college experience stressful and worrisome" (p. 281). African-American undergraduates have also been found to use minority orientation programs more often than Asian, Hispanic or Native American students (Minatoya & King, 1984). Using a mailed needs assessment survey and considering age, gender and race/ethnic status, female minority undergraduates on a private, predominantly Euro-American campus were most likely to perceive a need, whereas older, married Euro-American male graduate students were least likely to perceive a need (Talley, 1985).

The literature on needs with graduate student populations yield similar findings (Rimmer, Lammert & McClain, 1982). Levin and Franklin (1984) administered questionnaires to first and second year medical students at Emory University School of Medicine and found nonwhites to rate their needs as important and unsatisfied more often than did Euro-Americans in regard to money, interpersonal relations, time, and treatment by others as mature and responsible.

A more recent eleven year analysis of African-American students' experiences and services on the same predominantly Euro-American campus reveals concerns in areas related to finances, academic adjustment, living conditions, emotional-psychological well-being, and career-vocational, respectively (June, Curry, & Gear, 1990). The authors attribute the increase in importance to living conditions, finances and emotional-psychological concerns to changes in federal laws related to a reduction in assistance for education, a resurgence in overt and covert campus racism, and concern about the safety and physical aspects of living conditions.

These studies suggest that African-American students perceive a greater number and different set of needs than their Euro-American peers. Yet, the results of some assessments that compare responses of African-Americans and Euro-Americans do not substantially differ. Based on a 74 percent return rate from a stratified random sample of 200 junior and senior undergraduates at the University of Maryland, alienation, financial aid, study skills, residence, negotiating the university system, and discrimination were needs perceived by students, irrespective of racial background (Webster, Sedlacek, & Miyares, 1977). Likewise, Westbrook,

Miyares and Roberts (1978) found few differences in needs of students who attended predominantly Euro-American colleges and those who attended traditionally African-American institutions. Regardless of the campus, African-American students reported greater concerns than Euro-Americans with study efficiency, financial assistance, ethnic unity, and ethnic trust. Issues of ethnic unity and trust were reported as intraracial conflict at traditionally African-American institutions and interracial conflict and low ethnic unity and trust at predominantly Euro-American institutions. Euro-American and African-American students also seem more similar than different in their experience and report of personal problems and help-seeking behavior (Cheatham, Shelton, & Ray, 1987). Needs assessment results that show few racial differences contradict findings from the substantive body of literature on African-American students' experiences and performance on predominantly Euro-American campuses. Overall, the experiences of this student group tend to be of a lower quality than those of their Euro-American peers on the same campuses (Remsik, 1979; Suen, 1983). African-American students have been shown to encounter more difficulties with faculty (Allen, 1988; Aaron & Powell, 1982; Nettles & Johnson, 1987), campus life (Bennett, 1988), interpersonal relations with Euro-American students (Muir, 1989; Boyer, 1990), and in general report feeling a sense of isolation, powerlessness, and meaninglessness (Allen, 1982; Lee, 1982; Loo & Rolison, 1986). When more than one ethnic/racial group is considered, undergraduate and graduate African-Americans also express more problems related to race concerns than do Native Americans, Asian Americans and Hispanic Americans (Carrington & Sedlacek, 1977; Webster, Sedlacek, & Miyares, 1977). Additionally, African-Americans sometimes report different ways to resolve concerns than do Euro-Americans. For example, Cheatham et al. (1987) found African-American students to report that they would be three times more likely to seek help from an academic counselor than their Euro-American peers.

Some of these discrepancies may relate to the way in which the collection of needs assessment data has been approached. Most of the literature on needs assessment for African-American students has followed an outcome perspective. That is, assessors seek to determine actual differences in needs with interracial, intraracial or between campus comparisons. Variables involved in the process of conducting a needs assessment and hypotheses about the possible influence of these factors on obtained outcomes are rarely considered. Although student perceptions provide valuable information, acceptance of these results assumes that the methodological procedures have little or no impact on outcomes. However, assessment studies involve different data collection strategies. For example, the findings of Carrington, et al. (1977), Gallagher (1992), Helwig and Vidales (1988), Ragan and Higgins (1985), and Webster et al. (1977), are derived from responses to mailed needs assessment surveys, whereas the findings of Levin and Franklin (1984), Minatoya and King (1984), Richmond, et al. (1983), and Rimmer, et al. (1982), and Webster, et al. (1978) stem from responses obtained when assessment instruments are directly administered to student groups.

Research literature found under the description "minority retention" also differs in methodological procedures from those that make racial comparisons and used the descriptor "needs assessment." A review of these studies indicates that racial comparisons without the needs assessment descriptor often involve administering questionnaires to student volunteers in a face to face, large group format. The extent to which African-American students respond to needs assessment surveys in a manner consistent with their actual behaviors may also influence the reliability of assessment data. For example, Stabb and Cogdal (1992) found inconsistencies between the needs assessment survey responses of African-American males and their concerns as described in actual counseling records.

Mail survey as a form of data collection, for example, is often employed in college settings and the use of self-report surveys is the most commonly used method to identify student needs. However, studies have shown that African-Americans approach mail survey questionnaires in a way that differs from Euro-Americans. Bachman and O'Malley (1984), for example, found racial differences in response patterns to Likert-type items. Specifically, African-American students were more likely to use extreme response categories than Euro-American students. Survey sponsors also rarely consider the differential ways in which African-Americans and Euro-Americans interpret survey items in relation to the ways in which particular queries are worded (Myers, 1977).

A substantial amount of literature has been conducted to investigate mail survey techniques. This body of literature has both practical and theoretical significance for research (e.g., Backstrom & Hursh-Cesar, 1981; Stinchcombe, Jones & Sheatsley, 1981). Mail survey methodology has been selected for use above other methods for several reasons including: lower survey costs, data from difficult to reach populations, use in various locations, expediency, and less variability with interviewer bias (Cote & Grinnel, 1984; Sudman & Bradburn, 1984). As a result of these benefits, mail survey questionnaires have been frequently used in psychological and educational research (Barrow, Cox, Sepich & Spivak, 1989; Cote & Grinnel, 1984). Despite the many benefits of mail survey questionnaires, non-response is a significant problem with this type of methodology (Kerlinger, 1973). Several efforts have been made to reduce nonresponse bias by increasing response rates. Two important efforts that have been investigated are concurrent techniques and differences between respondents and nonrespondents.

Although several techniques have been found to have some effect on mail surveys, anonymity is the concurrent technique that has been most extensively studied. Studies that show the impact of uncoded or unsigned (anonymous) versus coded or signed (confidential) cover letters on response rates yield varied results. However, these results generally suggest that anonymity is inversely related to nonresponse bias. For example, Andreasen (1970) reported that personalization of cover letters (i.e., decreased anonymity) was associated with decreased response rates. Kerin and Peterson (1976) found that use of a coded (confidential) cover letter accounted for increased response rates. In contrast, King (1970) concluded that response rates did not differ between coded and uncoded questionnaires. Downs and Kerr (1986) summarized the findings by noting that in six of ten studies, researchers concluded that anonymity did not affect response rates. According to these reviewers, sample and questionnaire differences prevent generalization of the results. Thus, "empirical findings often provide strongest evidence that anonymity is a desirable factor to include in mail survey research" (p. 75).

The results of studies that report on the relation between response rates and sociocultural variables have generally shown that respondents have sociocultural characteristics that differ from nonrespondents (Robins, 1963; Sudman & Bradburn, 1984; Wallace, 1954). Different response rates as a function of age, educational level, financial status, and place of dwelling have been noted. Racial background has also been identified as an important factor in nonresponse bias (Bachman & O'Malley, 1984; Downs & Kerr, 1986). However, the impact of this variable has been rarely studied in comparison with other sociocultural characteristics. In spite of these findings, services and programs to assist with African-American college students' adjustment and progress are heavily influenced by mail survey results. Research practices designed to obtain information about the needs of African-Americans without considering possible differences in response patterns may yield inaccurate feedback. Consequently, institutional programs that rely on these data may be ineffective in promoting retention, satisfaction and graduation. Effective student services can only originate from reliable and valid assessment data. Research efforts made without regard for cultural influences on various aspects of the survey process maximize the probability of distorted outcomes. Interracial and intraracial differences observed on survey instruments may reflect cultural patterns of responding rather than actual group differences. For example, an absence of differences found between the counseling center needs of African-American and Euro-American student groups may relate more to the manner in which respondents approach mail survey questionnaires than to actual differences as regards survey content (Bachman & O'Malley, 1984). Failure to respond to self-report surveys can lead to inaccurate population estimates and ineffective counseling center services (Bachman & O'Malley, 1984).

A comprehensive approach to needs assessment should include an examination and evaluation of variables specific to the methodological process to identify factors that could serve as potential biases. Thus, procedures used to collect data in needs assessment research and specific outcomes that originate from racial comparisons deserve consideration. The present research used two studies to examine the effects of anonymity versus confidentiality and presence versus absence of a titled signature of an African-American dean on African-American students' responses to a mailed psychological/mental health services needs assessment survey. Appendices A through G, which can be found at the back of this book, contain copies of the needs assessment materials used in these and related studies (see especially Appendix E).

STUDY I

The purpose of Study 1 was to examine the effects of anonymity (uncoded) and confidentiality (coded) on the response rates of African-American and Euro-American college students to a mailed psychological needs assessment survey.

Method

Participants

Participants were 688 undergraduate, graduate and professional students who received a questionnaire out of the 700 who were sent the questionnaire at a southeastern university of approximately 9500 full-time degree seeking students in residence. Students were randomly drawn by computer in four separate stratified random samples. The first and second general samples consisted of 300 students each and were stratified by race, gender, school, and year in program so that the samples were proportionally representative of the university population. The second two samples consisted of 50 African-American students each and represented approximately 20 percent of the enrolled African-American student population.

Materials

A questionnaire covering a wide range of mental health, counseling and psychological service-related needs was used. The questionnaire included such topics as stress management, career concerns, interpersonal issues, and concerns about coping with various problematic feelings related to the possible life circumstances of a university student.

Participants were asked to rate each item in terms of its current perceived importance to them from 1 (none) to 5 (extremely) and whether they would be likely to seek service for that item by the modality of (a) one-to-one counseling at the service, (b) a small group at the service, or (c) a large group educational presentation elsewhere on campus. The questionnaire was a revised version of one previously used (Talley, Barrow, Fulkerson & Moore, 1983) and took approximately fifteen to twenty minutes to complete.

Each survey was accompanied by a stamped envelope addressed back to the counseling and psychological services center. A cover letter explaining the project and the importance of responding by returning the completed survey was enclosed. The importance of returning the surveys so that student opinion could be incorporated into program and service delivery planning was also emphasized. The cover letter sent to the first general sample and the first sample of African-American students promised anonymity (that is, not even the principle investigators would be able to link responses with a student's name). The cover letter for the second general sample and the second sample of African-American students promised confidentiality (that is, the principle investigators alone could match names with the visible number printed on the questionnaire).

Procedure

All packets including questionnaire, cover letter and return envelope were mailed out on the same day. Three weeks later, a similar follow-up packet was sent out again to all subjects in the "confidential" cover letter condition who had not responded. A follow-up packet was also sent to all participants in both "anonymous" samples because it could not be determined which students had responded. Records were kept concerning completed surveys returned and those that were returned undelivered by the post office due to the student's moving.

Results

The return rate for the African-American anonymous group was 13 (26.53%) of the 49 received by students. For the African-American confidential group 18 (40.91%) were returned of the 44 received by students. The stratified random sample used for the general anonymous group contained 14 African-American students. According to the ethnicity question on the questionnaire, 4 (28.57%) of the 14 students returning the questionnaire were African-American and were therefore dropped from the comparisons leaving a return rate of 137 of 284 (48.24%) non-African-American students who received a questionnaire. The stratified random sample used for the general confidential group initially included 18 African-American students and 5 (27.78%) respondents indicated that they were African-American and were dropped from the comparisons. Thus 133 (46.50%) of 286 non-African-American students receiving a questionnaire returned it.

A Chi-Square comparing the four groups indicated no statistically significant differences between any of the groups ($X^2 = 2.126$, $df = 3$, $p = .145$). Thus, there were no statistically significant differences in return rates due to the effects of race and cover letter (anonymous versus confidential) conditions.

STUDY II

Findings that show African-American students to approach survey questionnaires in a way that differs from Euro-American students may be related to cultural mistrust (Tucker, Chennault, & Mulkerne, 1981). That is, African-Americans may fail to complete and return survey questionnaires because of suspicions about the way in which personal data will be used on predominantly Euro-American campuses. One way to minimize possible mistrust experienced by this student population and increase response rates is to combine anonymous and confidential survey conditions with the signature of a well-known African-American on campus. Thus, Study 2 was conducted to examine the effect of anonymity and confidentiality and presence (cosigned) versus absence (not cosigned) of a titled signature of a well-known African-American College dean on students' response rates to the mailed psychological needs assessment survey described in Study 1.

Method

Participants

Participants were 176 African-American undergraduate students who received a questionnaire out of 200 who were sent one at a southeastern university. They were 18 to 22 years of age, 45% male, 55% female, and equally distributed across the four years of undergraduate education. The sample was computer generated by a program selecting a stratified random sample. The participants represented approximately fifty percent of the entire pool of African-American undergraduates.

Materials

Each participant received by mail a packet including the same sixty-item needs assessment questionnaire described earlier in Study 1. An additional 23 items relating specifically to likely needs of importance to African-American students were included for the African-American student samples. These items were selected by reviewing the literature, meeting with a forum of African-American students and by having African-American Student Affairs personnel rate the relative importance of each item. Accompanying each questionnaire was a stamped envelope addressed to the counseling service for use in returning the questionnaire. Also enclosed was a cover letter emphasizing the importance of the survey in determining the type of services offered and thus the need for all students to respond because minority opinion needed to be especially attended to in planning as it may be underreported. However, the cover letters varied according to whether "confidentiality" was promised and visibly coded questionnaires used or "anonymity" promised and uncoded questionnaires used. Further, the cover letters also varied with regard to whether they were cosigned (endorsed) by a well-known African-American dean on campus or not. Thus four cover letter conditions existed as follows: (1) coded/cosigned; (2) coded/not cosigned; (3) uncoded/cosigned; and (4) uncoded/not cosigned.

Procedure

Having been randomly selected, the 200 participants were systematically assigned to one of the four conditions such that the first, second, third, and fourth participants were assigned to the corresponding (1–4) as described above. This assignment pattern was repeated until the entire sample was assigned to a cover letter condition. All letters were mailed out on the same day. Three weeks later, a similar follow-up mailout was done for all anonymous participants and all confidential (coded) participants who did not respond to the first mailing. Records were kept regarding completed surveys returned as well as those returned unable to be delivered by the postal service as the student had moved. The cover letter condition of anonymous (uncoded) questionnaires that were returned was identifiable by the postage stamp picture on the envelope used to return the questionnaire as a different postage stamp had been selected for the accompanying return envelope for each of the four experimental conditions.

Results

Return figures for each group were as follows: anonymous/cosigned, 4 returned undelivered, 15 of 46 (32.61%) returned; anonymous/not cosigned, 5 returned undelivered, 11 of 45 (24.44%) returned; confidential/cosigned, 7 returned undelivered, 16 of 43 (37.21%) returned; confidential/not cosigned, 5 returned undelivered, 17 of 42 (40.48%) returned.

A Chi-Square indicated that there were no statistically significant differences between any of the groups (X^2 = 2.855, df = 3, p = .415). Despite a difference between the anonymous/cosigned and confidential/not cosigned group, the difference was not in the expected direction and was not statistically significant.

DISCUSSION

This research investigated the effects of concurrent techniques on African-American students' response rates as measured by the percentage of completed returned questionnaires. The nonsignificant Chi-Square analyses for the two studies implies that there is no statistically significant difference between African-American and Euro-American students response rates to a mailed psychological needs assessment survey with anonymous or confidential cover letter conditions.

The finding of no difference between African-American and Euro-American students offers some support for the use of traditional methods to obtain responses to needs assessments conducted with mail surveys on college campuses. Standard approaches to this type of data collection procedure have neglected racial/ethnic factors. Only in instances when African-American students have been targeted as the primary response group has race been considered. The decision to request responses to mail surveys without acquiring information related to these background factors assumes that students' response rates are free of cultural influences related to racial/ethnic group membership. The results of the present study offer support for this assumption. However it should be recalled that while this assumption may be useful for some campuses, it is not necessarily true for all colleges. Some student bodies may be more homogeneous than others regardless of race. Nevertheless, the assumption of such homogeneity may be most erroneous with regard to other student bodies. In short, just because African-American students on certain campuses are similar to Euro-Americans does not imply that these similarities hold across different campus environments.

Researchers and theorists have conceptualized these findings by referring to etic (culture general) and emic (culture specific) perspectives. The expectation that response rates would differ for Euro-American and African-American students is consistent with an emic view of behavior. That is, unique characteristics of the African-American worldview and value orientation would be expected to exert influences on students' interpretation of the survey cover letters and the mail survey process to lead to actual behavioral differences in the way the groups responded. An etic perspective, on the other hand, is associated with the expectation that African-American and Euro-American student groups share common-ground universals which exert similar influences that lead to similar behavioral responses as indicated in the expectation of no significant

difference in response patterns. In the present studies, students' responses
to these mail surveys with anonymous and confidential cover letters
appear to follow an etic perspective as evidenced by the absence of
significant differences.

Similar to the lack of interracial differences, study II revealed no
statistically significant differences between the response rates of African-
American students who received anonymous or confidential questionnaires with cover letters endorsed or not endorsed by an African-American
college dean. This finding suggests a unimodal approach to responding
to surveys among African-American students and supports findings of
studies which show similarities in African-American students' responses
to survey instruments. The results of these two studies contradict previous theory on African-Americans' approach to mail survey research
(Bachman & O'Malley, 1984; Myers, 1977).

These findings should be interpreted with caution. Several limitations
are apparent in this study. The respondents were predominantly Euro-
American, although the African-American students surveyed represented
a significant proportion of the African-American student population.
Although the samples were relatively large, the samples were restricted
to one university campus, preventing the generalization of these results
to other student groups. Characteristics of the two African-American
student samples, content of the cover letter, and emphasis of the cover
letter and mail survey method may also have influenced our results.

One explanation for the absence of statistically significant differences
is the consideration of a different social reality within the African-
American student populations sampled. It is possible that among African-
American students, responses to mail survey questionnaires are associated
with cultural characteristics as expressed through their racial identification (Cross, 1971). Within-group psychological differences among the
students sampled may be a better predictor of survey return rates than
race alone. For example, if the majority of the students sampled were in
the Pre-Encounter and Encounter stages of racial identity (i.e., adherence to a Euro-American worldview and rejection of anything Black,
ambivalence and insecurity in being African-American, respectively),
racial differences between the African-American and Euro-American
groups may have been suppressed.

The absence of significant differences among the African-American
sample for anonymity or confidentiality and presence or absence of a
titled signature may also be explained by students' racial identification.

Students' stages of racial identity may have influenced their interpretations of anonymity or confidentiality and the signature of an African-American dean. These different interpretations may have differentially influenced response rates. The nonsignificant but greater percentage of surveys returned under the confidential/not cosigned condition gives some support to this alternative explanation. For example, based upon Cross's (1971) model of racial conversion, students in the Pre-Encounter stage may have interpreted the "cosigned" and "anonymous" conditions in a negative way, thus decreasing the likelihood of returning the surveys for these cover letter conditions. The tendency for students in the Pre-Encounter stage to reject African-American culture and embrace Euro-American culture might have led to low response rates under conditions in which an African-American dean endorsed the cover letters and when students were asked to remain unidentified.

African-American students' response rates may have been influenced by the cover letter request. Students who adhered strongly to an African-American perspective (i.e., Immersion-Emersion Stage) may have interpreted the cover letter request for "minority opinion" as positive for African-American students and therefore chose to respond as a way of expressing commitment to the race. In contrast, students who were in the Pre-Encounter Stage of racial identity may have interpreted the request in an opposing manner.

Finally, the unexpected absence of within and between race differences for the effects of concurrent techniques on mail survey response rates may relate to the type of questionnaire mailed. That is, both Euro-American and African-American students may have approached the questionnaire in a manner consistent with their views and beliefs about psychological assistance and mental health services sponsored by the counseling and psychological services center. Students may have completed and returned the needs assessment questionnaire according to their perceived needs for psychological assistance as opposed to the cover letter conditions. Thus the interactions between content and students' self-evaluations of need for psychological assistance may have been more influential than anonymity/confidentiality or signed/unsigned cover letter conditions, leading to an absence of differences for these techniques.

In summary, using chi-square analysis, the return figures were not found to be significantly different, although Euro-American students returned a higher number of surveys than African-American students. Euro-American students also had a higher (though nonsignificant) return rate for the anonymous cover letter conditions as compared to a higher response rate for the confidential cover letter condition for African-American students. A similar theme was found in study II. Differences among African-American students indicated that both confidential conditions (cosigned and not cosigned) resulted in a higher return rate than the anonymous conditions. Interestingly, the confidential/not cosigned conditions yielded a higher return rate than any of the four cover letter conditions. It was hypothesized, however, that an additive effect of the two variables (anonymity and cosigned) might result in a significantly different increase in students' responses. This hypothesis was based upon the rationale that promised protection of students' identities, in addition to the signature of a well-known same-race dean might result in a greater willingness for African-American students to return the questionnaires as compared to the confidential/not cosigned condition which did not promise protection of students' responses. However, none of the four conditions appeared to affect response rates beyond chance. Nevertheless, these findings may be specific to the survey content, the university campus and student characteristics.

Replication of this study with larger groups, different survey content, diverse college campuses and measures that assess African-American students' stage of racial identification would clarify our findings. Future research is also required to further understand the implications of mail survey methodology for the development of effective student services for African-American students.

REFERENCES

Aaron, R., & Powell, G. (1982). Feedback as a function of teacher and pupil race during reading groups instruction. *Journal of Negro Education, 51,* 50–59.

Abramowitz, E. (1976). *Equal educational opportunity for Blacks in U.S. higher education: An assessment.* Washington, D. C.: Howard University Press.

Akah, R. M. (1990). What Black students need from a tutorial program. *Journal of College Student Development, 31,* 177–178.

Allen, W. (1982). *National Study of Black college students.* Michigan: Department of Sociology.

Allen, W. (1988). The education of Black students on white college campuses: What quality the experience? In M. T. Nettles (Ed.). *Toward black undergraduate student equality in American higher education.* Westport, CT: Greenwood Press.

Andreasen, A. R. (1970). Personalizing mail questionnaire correspondence. *Public Opinion Quarterly, 18,* 40–52.

Bachman, J.G., & O'Malley, P.M. (1984). Yea-saying, nay-saying, and going to extremes: Black-White differences in response styles. *Public Opinion Quarterly, 48,* 491–509.

Backstrom, C. H. & Hursh-Cesar, G. (1981). *Survey Research.* New York: Wiley.

Barrow, J., Cox, P., Speich, R. & Spivak, R. (1989). Student needs assessment surveys: Do they predict student use of services? *Journal of College Student Development, 66,* 164–167.

Bennett, W. J. (1988). Why the West? *National Review, 40,* 37–39.

Blackwell, J. E. (1982). Demographics of desegregation. In R. Wilson (Ed.). *Race and equity in higher education* (pp. 28–70). Washington, D.C.: American Council on Education.

Boyer, E. L. (1990). *Campus life: In search of community.* Princeton, N.J.: Carnegie Foundation for the Advancement of Teaching.

Brown, R. D., Frey, D. H., & Crapo, S. E. (1972). Attitudes of Black junior college students toward counseling services. *Journal of College Student Personnel, 13,* 420–424.

Burrell, L., & Rayder, N. F. (1971). Black and White students' attitudes toward white counselors. *Journal of Negro Education, 40,* 48–52.

Carey, J. C., Reinat, M., & Fontes, L. (1990). School counselors' perceptions of training needs in multicultural counseling. *Counselor Education and Supervision, 29,* 155–169.

Carrington, C. H., & Sedlacek, W. E. (1975). Characteristics of no-shows accepted for admission at a large university. *Journal of College Student Personnel, 15,* 504–507.

Chau, K. L. (1992). Needs assessment for group work with people of color: A conceptual formulation. *Social Work with Groups, 15,* 53–66.

Cheatham, H. E., Shelton, T. O., & Ray, W. J. (1987). Race, sex, causal attribution, and help-seeking behavior. *Journal of College Student Personnel, 28,* 559–568.

Cote, L. S., & Grinnell, R. E. (1984). *The much-maligned mail survey reexamined: A comparative analysis of procedures and techniques to increase response rates.* Paper presented at the annual meeting of The Association for the Study of Higher Education, Chicago.

Cross, W. E. (1971). The Negro-to-Black conversion experience. *Black World, 20,* 13–17.

Downs, P. E., & Kerr, J. R. (1986). Recent evidence on the relationship between anonymity and response variables for mail surveys. *Journal of the Academy of Marketing Science, 14,* 72–82.

Edmunds, G. J. (1984). Needs assessment strategy for Black students: An examination of stressors and program implications. *Journal of Nonwhite Concerns in Personnel and Guidance, 12*(2), 48–56.

Farnsworth, D. L., & Oliver, H. K. (1959). Mental health in colleges and universities in the United States of America. *International Social Science Journal, 11,* 54–62.

Ford-Harris, D. Y., Schuerger, J. M., & Harris III, J. J. (1991). Meeting the psychological needs of gifted Black students: A cultural perspective. *Journal of Counseling & Development, 69,* 577–580.

Gallagher, R. P. (1992). Student needs surveys have multiple benefits. *Journal of College Student Development, 33,* 281–282.

Gibbs, J. T. (1973). Black students/white university: Different expectations. *Personnel and Guidance Journal, 51,* 463–469.

Helwig, A. A., & Vidales, J. L. (1988). Minority and White counselor differences on a needs assessment related to career development. *Texas Association for Counseling and Development, 16,* 51–57.

Jones, C. J., Harris, I. J. & Hauck, W. E. (1971). Differences in perceived sources of academic difficulties: Black students in predominantly white colleges. *Journal of Negro Education, 24,* 519–529.

June, L. N., Curry, B. P., & Gear, C. L. (1990). An 11-year analysis of Black students' experience of problems and use of services: Implications for counseling professionals. *Journal of Counseling Psychology, 37,* 178–184.

Kerin, R. A., & Peterson, R. A. (1976). Personalization, respondent anonymity, and response distortion in mail surveys. *Journal of Applied Psychology, 62,* 86–89.

Kerlinger, F. N. (1973). *Foundations of behavioral research* (2nd Ed.). New York: Rinehart and Winston.

King, F. W. (1970). Users and nonusers of marijuana: Some attitudinal and behavioral correlates. *Journal of the American College Health Association, 18,* 213–217.

Lee, C. C. (1982). Black support group: Outreach to the alienated Black college student. *Journal of College Student Personnel, 23,* 271–273.

Levin, R. B., & Franklin, A. W. (1984). Needs assessment and problem identification of first- and second-year medical students. *Journal of Medical Education, 59(11),* 908–910.

Loo, C. M., & Rolison, G. (1986). Alienation of ethnic minority students at a predominantly White university. *Journal of Higher Education, 57,* 58–77.

Miller, M. J., Springer, T. P., Milford, G. & William, J. (1986). Identifying the counseling needs of Black high school students: A field-tested needs assessment questionnaire. *Journal of Multicultural Counseling and Development, 14(2),* 60–64.

Minatoya, L. Y., & King, B. (1984). A systematic approach to assessment and intervention for minority undergraduates. *Journal of College Student Personnel, 25(3),* 272–274.

Muir, D. E. (1989). White attitudes toward Blacks at a deep south university campus: 1966–1986. *Sociology and Social Research, 73,* 84–85.

Myers, V. (1977). Survey methods for minority populations. *Journal of Social Issues, 33,* 11–19.

Nettles, M. T., & Johnson, J. R. (1987). Race, sex, and other factors as determinants of college students' socialization. *Journal of College Student Personnel, 28,* 512–524.

Ragan, D. T., & Higgins, E. B. (1985). The perceived needs of underclass college students from diverse educational institutions. *Journal of College Student Personnel, 26(5),* 444–449.

Ralston, P. A. (1983). Learning needs and efforts of the Black elderly. *International Journal of Aging and Human Development, 17(1),* 75–88.

Remsik, T. (May, 1979). Minority plan has way to go. *Milwaukee Journal.* p. 27.

Richmond, L. J., Johnson, J., Downs, M., & Ellinghaus, A. (1983). Needs of Non-Caucasian students in vocational education: A special minority group. *Journal of Non-White Concerns,* 13–18.

Rimmer, S. M., Lammert, M., & McClain, P. (1982). An assessment of graduate student needs. *College Student Journal, 16(2)*, 187–192.

Robins, L. N. (1963). The reluctant respondent. *Public Opinion Quarterly, 27*, 276–286.

Shifman, L., Scott, C. S., Fawcett, N. & Orr, L. (1986). Utilizing a game for both needs assessment and learning in adolescent sexuality education. *Social Work with Groups, 9(2)*, 41–56.

Stabb, S. D., & Cogdal, P. A. (1992). Black college men in personal counseling: A five-year archival investigation. *Journal of College Student Psychotherapy, 7(1)*, 73–86.

Stinchcombe, A. L., Jones, C., & Sheatsley, P. (1981). Nonresponse bias for attitude questions. *Public Opinion Quarterly, 45*, 359–375.

Sudman, S., & Bradburn, N. (1984). Improving mailed questionnaire design. In D. C. Lockhart (Ed.), *New directions for program evaluation: Making effective use of mailed questionnaires.* (pp. 33–47). San Francisco: Jossey-Bass.

Suen, H. K. (1983). Alienation and attrition of Black college students on a predominantly white campus. *Journal of College Student Personnel, 26*, 117–121.

Talley, J. E. (1985). Psychological needs reported by students not seeking services. In J. E. Talley, & W. J. K. Rockwell (Eds.). *Counseling and psychotherapy services for university students* (pp. 18–30). Springfield, IL: Charles C Thomas.

Talley, J. E., Barrow, J. C., Fulkerson, K. F., & Moore, C. A. (1983). Conducting a needs assessment of university psychological services: A campaign of telephone and mail strategies. *Journal of American College Health, 32*, 101–103.

Tucker, C. M., Chennault, S. A., & Mulkerne, D. J. (1981). Barriers to effective counseling with Blacks and therapeutic strategies for overcoming them. *Journal of Non-White Concerns, 9*, 68–76.

Wallace, D. (1954). A case for and against mail questionnaires. *Public Opinion Quarterly, 18*, 40–52.

Webster, D. W., Sedlacek, W. E., & Miyares, J. (1979). A comparison of problems perceived by minority and white university students. *Journal of College Student Personnel, 20*, 165–170.

Westbrook, F. D., Miyares, J., & Roberts, J. H. (1978). Perceived problem areas by Black and White students and hints about comparative counseling needs. *Journal of Counseling Psychology, 25(2)*, 119–123.

Westbrook, F. D. & Smith, J. B. (1976). Assisting Black resident students at a predominantly White institution: A paraprofessional approach. *Journal of College Student Personnel, 17*, 205–209.

Chapter 5

NEEDS ASSESSMENT WITH HISPANIC STUDENTS

Susan L. Prieto

College and university campuses have become increasingly diverse, a trend that will likely continue in the years to come. Due to the increase in diversity, campuses have begun to look at the needs of different student groups in an attempt to guide programming and services offered by student affairs professionals. The fastest growing minority group in the United States is the Hispanic population. This chapter will briefly review topics in mental health needs and services with Hispanics, issues in needs assessment research, both in general and when conducted with Hispanic populations, and conclude by offering recommendations and suggestions for further needs assessments with this particular population. Supplemental readings are also included following the chapter references.

CHARACTERISTICS OF THE
HISPANIC POPULATION IN THE U.S.

"Hispanic" is the term that is replacing "Latino" to define those individuals in the United States whose ancestry is from Mexico, Puerto Rico, Cuba, El Salvador and other Latin American countries. Though the term "Hispanic" is not accepted by all groups that it refers to, it will be used throughout this chapter to indicate the common background of Spanish language and customs that peoples from the Latin American countries share.

Sue and Sue (1990) note that, according to the U.S. Census, Hispanics at that time comprised at least 14.6 million people in this country. Of these 14.6 million, it is estimated that 9 million are of Mexican descent, 3 million are Puerto Rican, 1 million are from Cuba, and the rest are from other Latin American countries. Given that the census traditionally underrepresents Hispanics, it is likely that the actual total of that population is closer to between 17 and 20 million.

This group of people is diverse and heterogeneous, in spite of the fact that they are at the same time a fairly coherent cultural group. Aspects that Hispanics share in common include language, religion, values and customs. Within these realms there are also large differences between groups of Hispanics, so that one must look both at the commonalities and differences when thinking about this group of people.

One of the easiest ways to understand the interplay of similarities and differences among Hispanics is to quickly review history. Wright (1987) notes that from 711–1492, Spain was both ruled and influenced by Moorish North Africa, a culture that contributed to Spaniards' developments in science, language, and architecture, among other areas. When Christopher Columbus then crossed the Atlantic in 1492, and came in contact with highly developed American indigenous groups, factors from these cultures were also incorporated into modern Hispanic cultures. Present day variations among Hispanics in language, physical appearance, cultural expressions, food, art and social structures all illustrate the influences that Spanish, American indigenous groups, and Africans from many tribes (who were sent forcibly to the Caribbean during times of the slave trade) have had on the group of people now known as Hispanics. Thus, Hispanics today are black, white, Asian American, American Indian, or a mixture of any of these four groups, and it is difficult to make generalizations about race or any other characteristic related to this group. In spite of this variety, racial discrimination toward Hispanics in the U.S. continues to be strong and is an issue that needs ongoing attention.

Various Hispanic groups have their own distinct profiles, including their perceptions of themselves, of other Hispanic groups, of their place in the United States, and of their country of origin. For example, for Mexican-Americans and Puerto Ricans, U.S. citizenship is the result of U.S. expansionist activities, which may influence those particular Hispanic groups' political perspectives regarding their relationship to the United States. Except for individuals who are politicized, most Hispanics use their specific nationalities when they are identifying themselves, and it is important to be sensitive to the importance that any given individual may place on this, and to understand where it comes from and what the differences between that person's group and other Hispanic groups may be.

Diversity among Hispanics can also be seen in demographic variables such as geographic distribution (Mexican-Americans can be found mainly in the Southwest, Puerto Ricans are heavily represented in New York, and Cubans have tended to settle in Miami and the Southeast), urban versus rural location, level of acculturation, socioeconomic status (SES), gender and age. It should be noted that diversity among Hispanics can also be mediated by generational status, language preference (monolingual or bilingual), and political status (immigrant versus native), or any combination of these three. Thus, when dealing with Hispanic students, it is important to have information about all of these background areas in order to assess the influences that any of these factors may have on that particular student.

General characteristics of Hispanics today include the following, according to Sue and Sue (1990). First, Hispanics are a very young population relative to other groups in the U.S. One implication of this is that we may see, then, a growing number of Hispanic youngsters of college age. The emphasis commonly found on religion, particularly Roman Catholic religion, can be seen in the importance placed on large families and youth in a community. Most Hispanics live in or near metropolitan areas in the U.S. and tend to be overrepresented among the poor, with high unemployment rates and lower incomes than other groups. Many Hispanics are blue collar workers in semiskilled or unskilled occupations. Also, Hispanics are a significantly undereducated group in the U.S. and have historically not done well in public schools. Sue and Sue (1990) note, for example, that Puerto Ricans have the highest dropout rates among Hispanics, who as a whole have the highest dropout rate of any group in this country. It is not uncommon to find that second-generation Hispanics are bilingual, but prefer Spanish and have limited command of the English language. Given different levels of proficiency in English, some educational difficulties are not unexpected, but need to continue to be addressed in an effort to provide an avenue for access to more and better resources for this population. Knowing about these factors may help understand why Hispanics are not currently very well represented in colleges and universities, and may encounter academic and adjustment difficulties once they do take the plunge into secondary education.

Family tradition is an important aspect of life in many Hispanic groups. Family unity, respect for the family, and loyalty are commonly stressed. In general, cooperation tends to be more important than competition, and individuation or independence (as known in Anglo-American culture) may not be strongly valued. Interpersonal relationships are maintained and nurtured in the context of a large network for many Hispanics, and extended family is seen as a resource, so that help is generally sought in these networks first, and outside sources of help (i.e., counselors) are resorted to with the advice or blessing of family and existing networks of close friends.

There are large differences in acculturation among Hispanic groups. For example, many Cubans who emigrated to the U.S. at the time that Fidel Castro took over Cuba were well educated people with economic resources who wanted to leave their mother land. When they settled in the U.S., then, many adopted English readily, and attempted to seek education and adopt the ways of the U.S. Many of these individuals became acculturated faster than others who may not have had economic means and/or may have found themselves in the U.S. for very different reasons (i.e., Mexican-Americans and Puerto Ricans, who were in the U.S. as a result of expansionism, not necessarily by choice). In general, it is important to remember that most Hispanics are bicultural in the sense that they are open, to some degree, to both Hispanic and Anglo cultures and can function in both worlds. For many, Hispanic and Anglo cultures coexist in relative harmony, and in this sense, many Hispanics could be said to be acculturated though not assimilated. Traditional values of the Hispanic culture may interact in a complex way with values of the Anglo culture, with its emphasis on success, work, and the acquisition and accumulation of material goods. It is important to assess the degree of preference and comfort in both cultures for any particular student, and the way that aspects of either culture may be impinging on each other, as difficulties encountered may stem from either culture or from an inter-play between the two.

As is evident, when dealing with Hispanics it is important to note both the differences between groups and the commonalities that exist, and that set Hispanics apart from other groups in the U.S. In spite of the variety mentioned previously, U.S. Hispanics themselves recognize a common, defineable Hispanic culture that exists in the U.S., and respond to being recognized as distinct from other groups, with differences between each other.

HISPANIC CULTURE AND MENTAL HEALTH

There is some agreement among theorists and clinicians that Hispanics' common cultural background causes them to be sufficiently different from non-Hispanics to warrant looking at their mental health needs differently in some ways than those of the general population. Though many of the same principles may apply when dealing with Hispanics' mental health needs, the different variables mentioned previously could mediate these needs, as well as how they are addressed in ways that are culturally sensitive, respectful, and effective.

It is clear that culture can influence the development and expression of mental disorders and personal/emotional difficulties, what is considered acceptable behavior, as well as how one addresses problems when they do arise. As seen previously, it is important for therapists and student affairs professionals to appropriately take culture into account when working with a Hispanic student, avoiding applying stereotypic notions that may not be accurate for the particular client being dealt with, while at the same time being sensitive to differences from the general population that that student may exhibit. If practitioners are to be successful in helping Hispanic students advance, they must be aware of, understand, and appreciate the cultural, economic, social and political backgrounds that Hispanic students bring with them to college campuses, as well as how these may prove to be areas of strength and resources to be tapped, and of difficulties.

Contrary to popular belief, Hispanics in the U.S. may not as a whole hold unfavorable attitudes toward psychologists and/or therapy. Hispanics do tend to see physical and emotional concerns as intertwined, as opposed to the Anglo differentiation between the two. Thus, Hispanics might be more amenable to interventions that address the interrelationship between the mind and the body when seeking help, and might benefit most from a holistic approach to health and illness.

In addition, it would be important to look at the cultural context of the family when dealing with a student in distress (Comas-Diaz, 1989). It is essential to explore the student's experiences and values regarding the emphasis of interdependence over independence, affiliation over confrontation, and cooperation over competition, and to note when these values may be different from those of the dominant Anglo society and/or from the student's cultural group. These areas need to be assessed before intervening, and the family can also be seen as a source of help and support that can be tapped for a student, as well as an area for possible intervention and education that may help the student resolve his/her conflicts.

To the extent that the traditional hierarchy of the Hispanic family, with the special authority given to the elderly, parents and males, and clearly delineated sex roles may be important in a student's background, there may be implications for how the student might view relationships to authority figures and how s/he might relate to professors and others on campus. There could be difficulties in being assertive in ways expected of students in general and differences in ways that a student might go about seeking services. It is important to consider all of these, and to gather information from the student that would be helpful in fully understanding problems, as well as tapping sources of family and social support for addressing them and areas for possible strategic intervention.

Another of the possible sources of difficulty for Hispanic students in colleges and universities is the conflict that can occur between family members at different levels of acculturation. A student seeking higher education may be facing difficulty maintaining family and cultural values, while at the same time not feeling like they belong to the dominant culture on college campuses. These possible internal conflicts may emerge in the form of academic and/or career concerns, as well as adjustment and emotional difficulties that a student may experience while at school. Again, it is extremely important to know about the student's background, as well as to be aware of the cultural values and demographic variables that have formed that student's value system in order to be able to develop an intervention that is strategic and respectful of the student.

Given the expected developmental tasks around relationships with a traditional college-age student population, one of the areas that Hispanic students might show some difficulty in would be that of male-female relationships and sex-role conflicts. Sue and Sue (1990) note that Hispanic men are traditionally expected to be strong, dominant and the providers for family, while women have been expected to be nurturant, submissive to males, and self-sacrificing. The changes in family structure that may have been experienced by Hispanics facing employment difficulties in the U.S. may produce stress and strain in these role expectations, which may then be further tested by a student's further exposure to the majority culture while at college. Possible areas in which males could exhibit these sex-role conflicts include: submissiveness or assertion regarding authority figures; feelings of isolation and depression because of the need to be strong, while at the same time feeling conflicts and pressures related to academics and his role in the college setting; conflicts over the need to be consistent in his role, while needing nurturance and support; and anxiety over questions of sexual relationships and interactions with young women while at college, some of whom may have very different perceptions of the relationship between men and women.

Hispanic young women, on the other hand, might have conflicts over the expectations they perceive from family and their home community to meet the requirements of them mentioned previously, while also being encouraged to be more independent and assertive by the dominant culture. In addition, these students may experience anxiety and/or depression when they are unable to live up to these standards, and when they see the differences between themselves and family members (i.e., father and mother) growing, and do not have a way to bridge these differences comfortably. Another possible area of difficulty for Hispanic young women may be when they feel an inability to act out feelings of anger, which may be discouraged by values and role expectations they have seen in their home communities. These conflicts clearly may arise as Hispanic young women date on college campuses, as well as when Hispanic males and females interact with each other and watch each other interact with members of other groups on campus. It should be noted that the double standard just described for Hispanic men and women does appear to be diminishing fairly rapidly in the urban settings, and may not be as strong a factor as it has been in the past, but is still an area to be assessed.

Another cultural value to be considered and assessed when working with a Hispanic student is the belief that some things are meant to happen regardless of the individual's intervention. This belief reflects an external locus of control, and may relate to SES and ethnic identity. According to Comas-Diaz (1989), the lower the SES, the more likely the Hispanic individual will hold this belief, and the belief may be more related to those individuals of Mexican-American identity, possibly as a result of religious beliefs interacting with political and historical factors.

It is important to examine the extent to which a Hispanic student may be acculturated, and to remember that these students are bicultural to some degree, so that different strategies may be employed in helping students at different levels of acculturation. The degree of acculturation may in fact influence the possible types of problems faced by a Hispanic client, the way these problems are interpreted by the student and by the professional dealing with the student, and the appropriate process and goals for dealing with them. Several theorists note that cultural identification in bilingual Hispanics (and we can assume that most Hispanic students in colleges and universities are bilingual) may be situational, so that they may respond differently depending on the group that they are dealing with.

The important question raised by these cultural issues discussed, how they may affect mental health needs, and implications for possible intervention strategies for Hispanics, is how a professional should decide on a balanced bicultural program or intervention, so that this intervention would respond to the needs of the particular Hispanic client. This question is being addressed more and more by colleges and universities, and implies being able to assess the needs of this group of students, who both share many commonalities and have distinct differences between them.

ISSUES IN NEEDS ASSESSMENT

Sue (1983) reviewed research conducted in psychology with respect to minority populations and found several conflicts in the way that this research has been conducted to date. An overall criticism that Sue (1983) and other researchers have of this body of investigation is that this type of research has suffered from a lack of a conceptual or theoretical framework to guide it, overemphasizing simplistic variables and disregarding psychosocial variables within and outside of the culture that impact on minority group individuals.

Another criticism is that psychological research has traditionally opted for an etic approach, that is an approach that looks at the core similarities in all humans. Kunkel (1990) puts it nicely when he describes the etic-emic dilemma as being one of whether people are fundamentally alike, or whether personality, interpersonal relations, and criteria for mental health vary predictably along ethnic dimensions. The etic perspective is universalistic, while the emic perspective is culture-specific. Sue (1983) advocates using both the emic and etic approaches in researching mental health with minority populations, since both are valid and can provide useful data and information. It is important not to disregard intracultural or within-group differences with minority populations, as concentrating on differences between cultural groups may inadvertently foster stereotyping. By the same token, it is necessary to refrain from "overculturalizing," and to look at aspects of the counseling process and mental health needs that transcend culture and are not bound by it (Ponterrotto, 1988).

Three general themes in ethnic minority research are summarized by

Sue (1983) and offer an understanding of the evolution of the field, as well as suggestions for future development. The first theme is characterized by the assumption that most ethnic minorities have potential problems involving self-identity and self-esteem because of cultural conflicts and negative social stereotypes. He calls this the inferiority model, which researches social factors, the effects of racism on personality and mental health, the adequacy of social services to these groups, and the influence of institutional policies and practices. The second theme is the deficit model, where prejudice and discrimination are presumed to lead to stress and decreased opportunities. Research out of this model neglected strengths, competencies, and skills found in ethnic families, communities, and cultures. The third and last theme is the bicultural or multicultural model, which attempts to conceptualize the influences of different cultures that interact with, and are influenced by, one another. This model tends to emphasize understanding ethnic minority groups in their own terms, and is concerned about with-in group variations and individual differences, allowing for the fact that members of an ethnic minority group show considerable differences in acculturation, assimilation, language proficiency, customs, values, and perceptions of racism.

It is commonly held that an accurate assessment of needs will lead to an increased likelihood that activities and programs can be more efficiently mounted, that students' needs will be satisfied, and that an improvement in student behavior and degree of satisfaction will be seen (Kuh, 1982). In general, a needs assessment program is a research and planning activity designed to determine the needs and utilization patterns of any given community or group of people. One of the purposes for conducting needs assessments has been so that agencies can examine more closely and objectively their existing services, and plan new ones that might be more effective.

The primary objective of a needs assessment is to identify unsatisfactory conditions or challenging situations, according to Kuh (1982). He also notes that there have been two prevalent definitions of "need" in this context. The first is the democratic need, that is, a change that is desired by the majority of some group, and the second is the discrepancy need, which is the difference between any present state and the ideal or acceptable level of functioning. More recent definitions of need for the purpose of needs assessments consider it to be a combination of the level of necessity and the discrepancy on some dimension.

Historically, needs assessments have relied primarily on measures of the prevalence and incidence of psychopathology in any given population, and have involved two steps: the compilation of community needs data, and an analysis and interpretation of the data obtained to ascertain the most salient needs as well as to arrive at some direction for community planning. Milord (1976) summarizes nicely the common approaches typically used in needs assessments, including descriptive statistics about a group, community survey techniques, and non-survey techniques such as the community impressions approach. Each of these approaches has its advantages and disadvantages which limit the generalizability of the results when only one technique is applied at a time. Milord (1978), Kuh (1982) and Evans (1985) all advocate the use of several techniques when conducting a needs assessment, in order to cover the various areas of weakness that each particular method has, as well to tap into the different information that it can offer. For example, the paper-and-pencil survey is quite commonly used in needs assessment because it can be administered efficiently, yields uniform, quantifiable responses, and is relatively inexpensive. The drawbacks, however, are that this objective instrument may reflect assumptions and biases that influence the results and limit the range and depth of responses, and that it may not be accurate when dealing with individuals who may not be fluent in English and/or may not be well educated. In addition, researchers need to be cautious about surveying small samples and overgeneralizing the results.

Evans (1985) attempted to address these issues as applied to a student population by comparing four types of instruments: an objective, theory-based instrument; an objective, empirically-based instrument; a semi-structured, theory-based interview; and a semi-structured, general interview. For the paper-and-pencil questionnaires, she found that items on the theory-based survey were more relevant to students than those on the empirically-based survey. The interviews identified generally the same concerns but responses to the theory-based interview were more comprehensive and meaningful, thus leading to the conclusion that the construction of interview questions based on theory leads to clearer, more comprehensive coverage of developmental concerns that students might have. The theory-based questionnaire seemed to identify issues more specifically within broad categories, while interviews yielded much richer data, but also may reflect a reluctance on the part of the student to admit certain needs. Evans (1985) concludes by stating that self-report techniques provide a report of only those needs that are felt by the student, and that behavioral observation and knowledge of developmental theory should augment student reports to provide an accurate picture of student needs.

Barrow et al. (1989) conducted a needs assessment of college students utilizing paper-and-pencil surveys, but found that there was no evidence to suggest that the results of needs surveys actually predict the students' use of group and workshop services over the following four years. However, with minority groups, it is useful in determining the students' sense of their needs, in itself helpful information, both because student affairs programming has often come out of the interests of student affairs staff, requests made by the vocal students in any particular group and/or political considerations and expediency, and because in the process of conducting a needs assessment a relationship can be fostered or solidified with the group involved, so that the needs assessment becomes both a process and a powerful intervention. This is particularly true in the case of Hispanic students, whose experience may have been one of being small in numbers, relatively distanced from administration and feeling on the fringe of life on campus.

Both of these studies provide information that is extremely helpful when looking at assessing the needs of a college-aged student, but not sufficient in addressing needs for minority populations. In looking at developmental needs for Hispanic students it would be imperative to also consider cultural values and norms that may impinge on the presumed developmental needs, as well as on how a student may experience and/or express this need. Humm-Delgado and Delgado (1983) state clearly that they feel that culture-specific needs assessment methodologies are necessary in order to obtain accurate, valid and reliable information. They go as far as to recommend the field survey approach as the preferred method for obtaining data from Hispanic communities, and note that one of the main issues in this type of research with these communities is gaining entry into, and support from, the community. Other areas to pay attention to in needs assessments with Hispanics, as with other groups, include: defining the research questions and the population; selecting the sample, as well as the instruments; selecting and training staff; and interpreting, presenting, and disseminating findings.

Another common approach to needs assessment is to conduct interviews. This approach is more suitable for the identification of problem areas, results are less likely to be systematically influenced, and there is an opportunity to clarify answers and elicit in-depth responses. This data, however, is difficult to synthesize, is time consuming to gather, and is relatively expensive to obtain.

The key informant technique has also been useful with minority populations. This method involves accessing people who have key positions in the community targeted, and who are willing to share the information that they have access to. Like the field survey approach, this technique calls for working to gain trust from community members, who will support the researchers' efforts. One of the main advantages of this technique is that it is easy to conduct and can bring providers together to share valuable information. On the other hand, one needs to ascertain that community members are well linked with the key informants being tapped, or the information obtained may not truly reflect the needs felt by the community.

Yet another helpful technique is the community forum approach, where members of the community are encouraged to attend an open meeting to discuss their perceptions of community needs. If effective, this method encourages all members of the community to express their needs, thus accessing large numbers of individuals and bypassing the "middle man" in the key informant technique. However, in this method there is no guarantee that the minority community will attend, in large part because of the experiences many minority communities have had, where members have not been heard by providers and develop a sense of wariness and lack of trust in the system. The issue of gaining entry into, credibility with, and support from the community is again crucial in this technique.

Skibbe (1986) describes the nominal group technique as an assessment method that is well suited for college counselors for several reasons. This technique involves a structured, small-group activity led by two trained facilitators. In this small group setting, a question or solution can be explored, or a program can be designed, in anywhere from 45 minutes to 1½ hours. Because the process is structured, graduate and undergraduate students can be taught to conduct these groups, permitting the use of Hispanic facilitators, as needed. It can be relatively easy to assemble a small group of students for this technique, the needs tend to emerge from the participants themselves, and the members can enjoy the process and feel valued as part of a solution. Some of the drawbacks to this method are that data derived are not easily quantified or statistically analyzed, and that the data generally do not come from a statistically representative sample. In the case of Hispanic students, however, when there may not be large groups available for study, this technique could be quite useful in making sure that their needs are not being buried in the statistical averages for the overall campus student body.

There have been a few studies that specifically examine the needs that Hispanic students on college campuses may experience. According to Madrazo-Peterson and Rodriguez (1978) it was not uncommon for universities at that time to have paid very little attention, if any, to special needs of minority students. Most environmental assessment conducted with ethnic minority students had focused on African-Americans, but there were a few that attempted to conduct environmental assessments with Chicano or Mexican-American students. They report that Garza and Nelson (1973) found that Chicano students experienced more discomfort with the campus environment than did Anglo students, while Widlak and Garza (1975) found that Chicanos held more favorable perceptions of the university community. Clearly, results were not consistent or conclusive. Madrazo-Peterson and Rodriguez (1978) conducted a study exploring Chicano, African-American and Native American students' perceptions of a university environment, and found that there were no significant differences between ethnic groups on any of the scales on the College Student Questionnaire, while African-American students reported feeling more isolated than Chicano or Native American students (according to one item of the Environmental Satisfaction Questionnaire). Their overall findings were that: the degree to which social isolation created stress for minority students was unexpected; all reported experiences of racism, prejudice and discrimination on campus; and they all perceived that university activities were directed toward Anglo-Americans, and this belief resulted in feelings of frustration, anger and helplessness on the part of the minority groups sampled. They found that students tended to respond to this stress by withdrawing, associating primarily with other minority students, leaving the university, or immersion in the educational process. In addition, they found that female students tended to experience significantly more stress than the men in the minority groups studied, a finding consistent with previous environmental research conducted.

Wright (1987) observes that Hispanic college students are faced with the challenge of making a decision regarding how to adapt to increased interactions with the dominant U.S. culture, and that two choices faced are: assimilation (implies giving up one's cultural identity and moving into the larger society) and integration (the individual values moving toward becoming an integral part of the larger society, while at the same time maintaining one's cultural identity). Comas-Diaz (1989) also notes that it is important to examine the degree of acculturation that an individual may feel. In the first level, low acculturation, the person has limited contact with the dominant U.S. culture, while in the second level (high acculturation and assimilation) the person may deny their Hispanic identity. In the third level, what she terms the "cultural schizophrenic" model, the Hispanic individual can operate within both cultures, and at times this is a bridge, while at other times it may be a confused state to be in because of the conflicting values that the person may be faced with. Although the choice of responses belongs to each individual student, both authors seem to believe that students need to be in an environment that is sensitive to this process and issues imbedded in it, and that provides students with the information conducive to working this decision through. This implies knowledge and awareness on the part of student affairs professionals about Hispanic students' culture(s) and about the process of cultural identity development.

Pomales and Williams (1989), Kunkel (1990), and Roll, Millen, and Martinez (1980) all talk about the lack of participation of Hispanics in available counseling services. Roll et al. (1980) observe that the under-utilization of therapy by Mexican-Americans is related most to the faulty assumption mentioned previously that this culture and therapy are incompatible. They look at errors in therapy of Mexican-American clients, and propose two major types of errors: errors leading to the exclusion of this population from treatment, and errors in treatment when they do come for services. All of these authors refer to others' work, as well as their own, indicating the need to look at level of acculturation and individual differences when thinking about how best to approach a Hispanic client. There is very little in the culture that would indicate that Hispanics would not be amenable to counseling services, but the cultural factors mentioned previously in this chapter should be taken into consideration as well when developing services for this population.

As seen, previous studies have taken various tacts when attempting to examine the types of needs that Hispanics on campus might feel. When these tacts are combined with the previous discussion about advantages and disadvantages of different techniques for needs assessment, one can find a sense of direction. It is important to take into consideration what one's relationship with the Hispanic student community on campus is, and to strengthen that, if necessary. After that, it would be helpful to learn as much as possible about the particular group of Hispanics, in order to be able to take into account differences between those students and to pose the research question meaningfully, as well as to design an assessment method that would offer information about the similarities and differences that Hispanics from different nationalities might feel. This type of information is as helpful as information about the differences between Hispanic and non-Hispanic students. If an accurate needs assessment is conducted, we can expect to open a dialogue between Hispanic and non-Hispanic students, faculty and staff, and thus begin to appreciate each other's points of view better. In addition, we might see more participation on the part of Hispanic students in programs and services that could be helpful in fostering their development.

REFERENCES

Barrow, J., Cox, P., Sepich, R., & Spivak, R. (1989). Student needs assessment surveys: Do they predict use of student services? *Journal of College Student Development, 30*, 77–82.

Comas-Diaz, L. (1989). Culturally relevant issues and treatment implications for Hispanics. In Koslow, D.R. & Salett, E.P. (Eds.). *Crossing cultures in mental health.* Washington, D.C.: SIETAR, International.

Evans, N.J. (1985). Needs assessment methodology: A comparison of the results. *Journal of College Student Personnel, 26*(2), 107–114.

Humm-Delgado, D. & Delgado, M. (1983). Assessing Hispanic mental health needs: Issues and recommendations. *Journal of Community Psychology, 11*, 363–375.

Kuh, G.D. (1982). Purposes and principles for needs assessment in student affairs. *Journal of College Student Personnel, 23*, 202–209.

Kunkel, M.A. (1990). Expectations about counseling in relation to acculturation in Mexican-American and Anglo-American student samples. *Journal of Counseling Psychology, 37*(3), 286–292.

Madrazo-Peterson, R. & Rodriguez, M. (1978). Minority students' perceptions of a university environment. *Journal of College Student Personnel, 19*, 259–263.

Milord, J.T. (1976). Human service needs assessment: Three non-epidemiological approaches. *Psychologie Canadienne, 17*(4), 260–269.

Pomales, J. & Williams, V. (1989). Effects of level of acculturation and counseling style on Hispanic perceptions of counseling. *Journal of Counseling Psychology, 36*(1), 79–83.

Ponterrotto, J.G. (1988). Racial/ethnic minority research in the Journal of Counseling Psychology: A content analysis and methodological critique. *Journal of Counseling Psychology, 35*(4), 410–418.

Roll, S., Millen, L. & Martinez, R. (1980). Common errors in psychotherapy with

Chicanos: Extrapolations from research and clinical experience. *Psychotherapy: Theory, research and practice, 17,* 158–168.

Skibbe, A. (1986). Assessing campus needs with nominal groups. *Journal of Counseling and Development, 64,* 532–533.

Sue, D.W. & Sue, D. (1990). *Counseling the culturally different* (2nd Edition). New York: John Wiley & Sons.

Sue, S. (1983). Ethnic minority issues in psychology: A reexamination. *American Psychologist, 38,* 583–592.

Wright, D.J. (Ed.). (1987). *Responding to the needs of today's minority students.* San Francisco: Jossey-Bass.

Supplemental Readings

Arbona, C. (1990). Career counseling and Hispanics: A review. *The Counseling Psychologist, 18,* 300–323.

Atkinson, D.R., Jennings, G.R. & Liongson, L. (1990). Minority students' reasons for not seeking counseling and suggestions for improving services. *Journal of College Student Development, 31,* 342–350.

Carter, D.J. & Wilson, R. (1989). *Eighth annual status report: Minorities in higher education.* Washington, D.C.: American Council on Education.

Cheatham, H.E., Shelton, T.O. & Ray, W.J. (1987). Race, sex, causal attribution, and help-seeking behavior. *Journal of College Student Personnel, 27,* 559–568.

Dillman, D.A. (1978). *Mail and telephone surveys: The total design method.* New York: John Wiley & Sons.

Garni, K.F. (1980). Counseling centers and student retention: Why the failures? *Journal of College Student Personnel, 21,* 223–228.

Garza, R.T. & Nelson, D.B. (1973). A comparison of Mexican- and Anglo-American perceptions of the university environment. *Journal of College Student Personnel, 14,* 399–401.

Hess, R.S. & Street, E.M. (1991). The effect of acculturation on the relationship of counselor ethnicity and client ratings. *Journal of Counseling Psychology, 38*(1), 71–75.

Kaiser, L.R. (1972). *The ecosystem model: Designing campus environments.* Boulder, CO: Western Interstate Commission on Higher Education.

Lopez, S. & Hernandez, P. (1987). When culture is considered in the evaluation and treatment of Hispanic patients. *Psychotherapy, 24*(1), 120–126.

Marrero, R. (1983). Bilingualism and biculturalism: Issues in psychotherapy with Hispanics. *Psychotherapy in Private Practice, 14,* 57–62.

Mayes, A.N. & McConatha, J. (1982). Surveying student needs: A means of evaluating student services. *Journal of College Student Personnel, 25,* 272–274.

Ruiz, A.S. (1990). Ethnic identity: Crisis and revolution. *Journal of Multicultural Counseling and Development, 18,* 29–40.

Sanchez, A.R. & Atkinson, R. (1983). Mexican-American cultural commitment, preference for counselor ethnicity, and willingness to use counseling. *Journal of Counseling Psychology, 30,* 215.

Szapocznik, J., Scopetta, M.A., Aranalde, M.A. & Kurtines, W. (1978). Cuban value structure: Treatment implications. *Journal of Consulting and Clinical Psychology, 46,* 961–970.

Tryon, G.S. (1980). A review of the literature concerning perceptions of and preferences for counseling center services. *Journal of College Student Personnel, 21,* 304–311.

White, T.J. & Sedlacek, W.E. (1987). White student attitudes towards Blacks and Hispanics: Programming implications. *Journal of Multicultural Counseling and Development, 4,* 171–182.

Widlak, F.W. & Garza, R.T. (1976). Antecedents of Chicano and Anglo student perceptions of the university environment. *Journal of College Student Personnel, 17,* 295–299.

Chapter 6

COLLEGE STUDENT-ATHLETES
AND NEEDS ASSESSMENT

Edward F. Etzel, James W. Pinkney, and J. Scott Hinkle

Collegiate athletics have reached a point where several sources insist on the assessment of the needs of student-athletes. Administrators, parents, and organizations such as the National Collegiate Athletic Association (NCAA) are recognizing the importance of meeting the needs of student-athletes. The implied intent of this process is to begin to find ways not only to meet their normal developmental needs, but also to better understand and address the personal-social and educational-vocational needs of this special on-campus population. A primary reason for considering student-athletes a special population beyond their exceptional sport-related skills and abilities, are the reasonable suspicions that the demands associated with the development and use of these skills and abilities as representatives of their respective schools create special needs unique to student-athletes (Lanning & Toye, 1993).

STUDENT-ATHLETE NEEDS

There is relatively little data regarding the assessment of psychosocial needs and treatment issues associated with college sports participation. Some college student-athletes experience difficulties of a clinical nature, including significant levels of stress, depression, drug abuse and drug dependence, as well as low self-esteem (Beisser, 1967; Bergandi & Wittig, 1984; Lederman, 1988; Tricker, Cook, & McGuire, 1989). Others have observed that student-athletes are vulnerable to and often experience greater psychological pressure and distress than non-athletes (Bergandi & Wittig, 1984; Etzel, 1989; Ferrante & Etzel, 1991; Pinkerton, Hinz, & Barrow, 1987). As they progress through university life, student-athletes' experiences can become progressively characteristic of developmental crises and psychosocial distress (Pinkerton, et al., 1987; Wittmer, Bostic,

Phillips & Waters, 1981). These issues are especially true for athletes involved in college revenue producing sports.

Further, Sowa and Gressard (1983) found that student-athletes have unique needs in career planning, time management, peer relationships, and academic performance. They suggest that these unique needs are directly attributable to participation in intercollegiate athletics. Blann (1985) reported that student-athletes who competed in highly competitive athletics developed less mature career and educational plans than non-athletes. Rehabilitation from injury and coping with disability are major concerns and sources of distress for many student-athletes (Tunick, Etzel, & Leard, 1991). Time constraints, the physical and psychological demands of training and competition, the highly competitive values system, and the reward structure all contribute to an educational experience far removed from that of students who do not participate in intercollegiate athletics. Most student-athletes cannot be considered regular students. Rather, they "are [more] like staff members whom the university hires on the basis of their skills to do particular jobs" (Sperber, 1990, p. 208).

Athletes are constantly caught in a struggle between balancing realistic life expectations and idealistic goals (Smallman, Sowa, & Young, 1991). Not only must they satisfy themselves, but student-athletes perceive that parents, peers, and coaches also require attention. Relatedly, many student-athletes have the belief that universities and coaches have not prepared them well for life following college (Boone & Walker, 1987).

The combination of these various struggles often results in the student-athletes exhibiting psychosocial symptoms. Unfortunately, a limited number of student-athletes (as with the remainder of the population) are predisposed biologically to some degree of clinical symptomatology. Sports counselors, psychologists, and other should be prepared to meet the needs of the athlete experiencing emotional difficulties. Professionals working with athletes need to be aware of the importance of recognizing clinical problems, providing coping skills training, and making counseling referrals for the troubled student-athlete (Bunker & McGuire, 1985; Butt, 1987). "Front-line" professionals often make the initial assessments concerning the conflicts of student-athletes. Unfortunately, not all professionals are sensitive to the unique needs of athletes and the impact sport has on their college life and everyday living.

There is currently a growing demand for counseling, psychology, and sports medicine professionals sensitive to the problems of individuals involved in collegiate sports and athletics. Student-athletes will benefit from integrated programs provided by sport psychologists, sports counselors, sports medicine professionals and athletic administrators that focus on assessment, diagnosis, and effective interventions (Hinkle, in press). Colleges and universities also need to develop broad assessment programs to assist athletes with the barriers to the treatment of psychosocial problems.

Depression and Anxiety

Proficiency in needs assessment, diagnosis, and intervention on behalf of athletes is an important responsibility of helping professionals, including sports counselors and psychologists, working with student-athletes (Hinkle, 1990). Specifically, it is particularly important for helping professionals to be aware of the symptoms associated with clinical or major depression and anxiety. A decline in sports performance will typically be one of the first observations/assessments to be made when an athlete is depressed and/or anxious.

Similarly, failure to succeed in the classroom may lead to personal stress and potentially threatens psychological functioning among student-athletes (Ferrante & Etzel, 1991). Concomitant failure in athletic performance also jeopardizes mental well-being. Student-athletes often experience cognitive and somatic anxiety when competition approaches (Begel, 1992; Swain, Jones, & Cale, 1990), as well as within the context of their nonathletic lives. In addition, student-athletes' behaviors are scrutinized both on and off the playing field (Ferrante & Etzel, 1991). Such daily pressures often lead to anxious behaviors. Anxiety resulting from the threat of evaluation by others, lack of self-confidence, and unreasonable expectations from coaches are but a few of the psychosocial difficulties experienced by athletes. Anxiety associated with competition can become progressively exacerbated and develop into more serious symptoms. Student-athletes may encounter a variety of psychosocial and emotional difficulties as a function of participation in sports. Moreover, continuous anxiety and depressive mood may lead to substance abuse as an attempt to self-medicate and alleviate distress.

Substance Abuse

Substance abuse and dependence also may arise out of a sense of helplessness and hopelessness. Consequently, timely assessments and treatment for drug problems is a must. Sports counselors and psychologists need to develop effective programs that will provide athletes with helpful drug and alcohol education and treatment. Although alcohol, marijuana, cocaine and stimulants are the most popular drugs, other substances may also be abused by student-athletes. Alcohol has been reported to be the major drug abuse problem among student-athletes (Gay, Minelli, Tripp, & Keilitz, 1990). Reported abuse of alcohol has ranged from about 30% (Murphy, et al., 1985) to 88% (Anderson & McKeag, 1985). Relatedly, Duda (1986) has estimated that over one million athletes in the United States use anabolic steroids. Reports of steroid abuse among student-athletes have ranged from a minimum of approximately 4% (Murphy et al., 1985) to 20% (Dezelsky, Toohey, & Shaw, 1985; Toohey, 1978). Amphetamine abuse has been consistently reported among student-athletes in the 2–9% range (Anderson & McKeag, 1985; Murphy et al., 1985).

Ultimately, no drug should be minimized when assessing student-athletes. For example, heavy marijuana use can result in sexual dysfunction and impotence and can interfere with normal ovulation (George, 1990), all of which can contribute to depressed or anxious mood, and subsequently, diminished academic and athletic performance. Likewise, the effects of cocaine use are usually followed by some degree of depression, irritability and nervousness (George, 1990), which certainly inhibit athletic ability. Moreover, college athletes encounter many stressors that other students do not. Thus, from a logical standpoint, if stress results in drug abuse and dependence, student-athletes may at times be more prone to use drugs than non-athletes (Damm, 1991). Substance abuse and/or dependence should always be assessed if student-athletes complain of gastrointestinal difficulties such as stomach pains, liver problems, and pancreas difficulty; clinical problems such as anxiety and depression; and repeated physical injuries (George, 1990). A collateral interview with someone who knows the student-athlete is an important step in the substance use assessment process (Damm, 1991). Social expectations and the need for social approval and support should not be ignored when assessing substance abuse among student-athletes. Social facilitation and group compliance, along with potential susceptibility to influence from others, also should be considered in substance abuse assessment and treatment.

It is questionable how well drug testing assesses and reduces the incidence of drug abuse among student-athletes (Benson, 1988). Some universities implement drug testing as a face-saving procedure, rather than developing genuine programs with a concerned focus on the needs and welfare of the student-athlete. Furthermore, Damm (1991) has stated that drug testing programs can only be as good as their intentions. Rather than drug-testing, what is needed is ongoing needs assessment of student-athletes and personal support interventions (Marcello, Danish, & Stolberg, 1989).

PROVIDING ASSISTANCE TO STUDENT-ATHLETES IN NEED

Not surprisingly, high percentages of student-athletes have reported a need for counseling assistance from their coaches (Selby, Weinstein, & Bird, 1990). Unfortunately, as a group, student-athletes tend to not seek assistance for these concerns (Pinkerton, et al., 1987). As a result, psychosocial issues among student-athletes can no longer be ignored. Sport psychologists and counselors should be aware, that at times, there may be a tendency to idealize student-athletes, creating a barrier to the recognition and assessment of psychosocial problems (Begel, 1992).

While educational information can be disseminated by informed sports psychologists and helping professionals, most problems of a clinical nature will require clinical counseling and potentially extended treatment. Unfortunately, there is not a systematic body of knowledge in counseling, psychology, or psychiatry which focuses on the psychosocial problems of athletes (Begel, 1992; Hinkle, 1990). There is a need for additional case studies and research about assessing and treating athletes experiencing such distress (Begel, 1992). Although sports counseling is in an embryonic stage (Hinkle, 1990), effective interventions are being developed and implemented.

Many of the personal, interpersonal, and career-planning problems encountered by student-athletes will not necessarily require unique psychological techniques or therapeutic competencies (Chartrand & Lent, 1987). What is needed, however, are theoretical models that increase the use of existing needs assessments aimed at interventions with athletes and the integration of counseling and sport psychology programs and services (Hinkle, in press).

New and innovative models specifically developed for the prevention and treatment of clinical distress among student-athletes would be beneficial. For example, a problem-solving and decision-making counseling format circumscribed in a *discover, uncover, recover* continuum could be easily utilized by athletes when guided by helping professionals (Hinkle, 1993). Included in the model are goal setting, exploring alternatives, decision making, and personal psychological resources.

POTENTIAL BARRIERS TO THE
NEEDS ASSESSMENT FOR STUDENT-ATHLETES

Brooks, Etzel, and Ostrow (1987) found that the helping professionals available to student-athletes at the NCAA Division I level tended to be ex-student-athletes who primarily focused their efforts on maintaining academic eligibility and sport performance enhancement. Over 62% of their counseling time was invested in these areas. Chartrand and Lent (1987) add that the role of athletic counselors often involves assisting athletes who get themselves into trouble. Obviously, student-athletes can face almost any problem that non-participating students have, but this subgroup appears to receive restricted attention that appears to ignore many needs.

At this point in time the reasons for why athletic department counselors may restrict their helping efforts to just three areas is conjectural, but there must exist a void for meeting other needs that student-athletes have. The present situation regarding student-athletes' needs and the apparent lack of information about those needs may indicate some barriers to needs assessment for this group.

Several barriers come to mind that might limit or prevent the process of needs assessments for student-athletes. The arena of athletic competition, the athletic department, institutional assumptions or needs, and the student-athletes themselves have the potential to prevent normal or typical needs assessment. Intercollegiate athletics has been described as a "closed system" within the institution (Ferrante & Etzel, 1991); outsider involvement for any purpose may be difficult. Needs assessment in particular may appear to be a threat to this closed and seemingly self-sufficient system.

The Arena of Athletic Competition

Athletic competition is concerned with the thrill of victory, the agony of defeat and often making money for participating institutions. Needs that do not contribute to this simple reality are usually viewed as either trivial, irrelevant, or both. Most of the people involved in athletic competition accept the outcome of the competition as all-important and resist activities that do not relate to that outcome. Given the high stakes often involved, needs assessment may appear to be far removed from other, more important "stakes" involved. Indeed, we have observed that many athletic staff do not focus their attention on the personal-social, developmental or academic needs of student-athletes unless they are somehow negatively influencing the quality of play or eligibility of their athletes. For athletic administrators, coaches and other staff, there are many other more pressing priorities to address within the arena of intercollegiate athletics.

This barrier to needs assessment has some problematic realities. The hierarchy of competition has coaches and star athletes at the top. Either of these groups can effectively sabotage a needs assessment effort. Both groups have a great deal of leadership within the competitive arena. Resistance, if offered, is likely to be pervasive and extend throughout the entire system.

A related barrier concerns status within the arena: coaches and athletes have the most power to lose if the rules of the arena change. They may choose to defend the status quo. Attempts to conduct needs assessments also can be undermined by coaches and athletes because they do not understand the potential usefulness of information obtained or because change is perceived as a threat to the existent system.

For example, one author (E.E.) who is involved in the conduct of annual research on the needs and perceptions of exiting student-athletes, has encountered only mixed interest and cooperation from coaches and student-athletes. Despite an NCAA requirement for all graduating or departing student-athletes to participate in an exit survey, moderately low response rates were obtained.

The Athletic Department

Athletic departments, as closed systems, often attempt to handle all aspects of their student-athletes' lives from housing and eating to academic registration and survival. External needs assessments could easily be interpreted as a potential negative evaluation of how the department is taking care of student-athletes. A department also may conclude that it has the most experience with student-athletes, therefore, the way it is working with its student-athletes is the best way.

Closely related to this barrier, assuming overall responsibility for student-athletes has a reverse side—being highly autonomous within the institutional climate. This autonomy may be highly prized and easily threatened by needs assessment. Given the amount of money and power that may be involved, an athletic department has a ready rationale for protecting its autonomy and information about its affairs and members' needs.

Athletics departments are far more likely to be attacked by outsiders than praised. Needs assessment could be interpreted as looking for tools to use against the department or for coattails the uninitiated do-gooder can use to get something from the department. Unsolicited involvement can be quite suspicious to an autonomous athletic department that has experienced outside criticism.

Finally, athletic department staff typically do not come from backgrounds that foster an awareness and sensitivity to the usefulness of understanding and addressing student-athlete needs. Indeed, very few have training in psychology, counseling or student services. Most come from physical education, education, sports medicine or business backgrounds. Although many are concerned about the development and welfare of their student-athletes, their responsibilities often do not involve assisting these young people with personal-social or educational-vocational concerns. They are not trained in how to assess needs or how to use such information to benefit student-athletes.

Institutional Assumptions

Another potential barrier related to the athletic department are the assumptions its parent institution is making about that department. An overview of the department's administrative structure might appear to exhaustively cover possible needs, in light of coaches, trainers, sports medicine, consultants, tutors, and counselors availabilities to the student-athlete. The institution may conclude that no additional resources are needed.

If the athletic program is successful, the institution may assume that intervention will create adverse reactions from students, alumni, and fans. On the other hand, if the athletic program is unsuccessful, the institution may assume that it is best to distance itself administratively and adopt a hands-off policy of divorce from a negative situation. In either case, a barrier exists to outside needs assessment.

Another assumption with adverse implications for needs assessment is when the institution decides that involvement will be interpreted as pampering or protecting the student-athletes from normal academic expectations of students. Remer, Tongate, and Watson (1978) point out that student-athletes are perceived by some as an overprivileged minority. Faculty especially may perceive student-athletes as getting preferential treatment in registration, excused absences, and tutoring support.

Student-Athletes Themselves

Student-athletes often function from a "macho" point of view where self-reliance and willingness to suffer for the team are virtues and expressions of need are a weakness (Ferrante & Etzel, 1991). They can form a barrier to needs assessment by refusing to reveal needs and avoiding identified services that deal with meeting needs. In fact, it has been observed that student-athletes as a group tend to underutilize helping services (Pinkerton, et al. 1987). Given the reward system in which they function, admitting to needs could conceivably damage their chances to succeed by reducing playing time or weakening the coach's confidence in their ability to perform.

Given the focus on winning in athletics, student-athletes often assume that if they are performing well in competition, then any problems or needs will be taken care of as part of that success. This faith in the system can lead them to assume that needs are trivial and do not require attention or action. Why report or mention something that is trivial and likely to be taken care of anyway? Why reveal anything that powerful others (e.g., coaches) often do not attend to or encourage student-athletes to discuss or seek assistance for?

Student-athletes also attract a social life based on their athletic status. Given a long exposure to being sought out and valued, they may expect others to solve their problems as part of the relationships that athletic participation creates. They have supporting evidence in such benefits as readily available tutors, easy social access, and a built-in peer group in the form of their team.

These barriers to the needs assessment of student-athletes are not exhaustive but representative. This suggests that normal approaches to needs assessment must be carefully thought out and carefully presented to all of the involved or impacted subgroups (Ferrante, Etzel, & Pinkney, 1991).

METHODS FOR ASSESSING THE
NEEDS OF COLLEGE STUDENT-ATHLETES

The uniquely complex nature of the student-athlete's collegiate experience and the barriers mentioned above both argue for caution in determining the methodology of needs assessment for college student-athletes. In the often regimented and highstakes world of collegiate athletics student-athletes may have trouble making their needs known. They may be asked about needs related to successful performance, but not about needs related to other issues with little or no apparent connection to sport (i.e., their development as independent, competent people). In such a situation, student-athletes may assume that those other needs are unimportant and can be ignored.

Several approaches to needs assessment would suffer from this differential evaluation of the importance or relevance of needs. Miller and Hustedde (1987) present a concise and informative summary of various approaches to needs assessment. Their critique of each approach clarifies this problem of differential evaluation for strategies such as jury workshops, nominal groups, and public hearings. A needs assessment for student-athletes would have to be responsive to this issue of differential evaluation as well as to the barriers mentioned above. This is especially so if differential evaluation is based solely on a highly specific basis such as future athletic success.

And yet, the input of student-athletes is vital to any needs assessment that directly concerns them. The closed nature of the student-athlete's world, the high stakes involved and the growing interest in this subgroup of college students all indicate that those involved have strong personal investments in the issue of needs assessment for student-athletes. Groups such as coaches, student support personal, counseling professionals, and sport psychologists can all claim to be experts about student-athletes. Each of these groups also has a vested interest in what the needs assessment may find and, to some extent, has a biased view of what is best for student-athletes. The reason for this biased view is simply that a needs assessment has major implications for these experts' own future relationships with student-athletes.

Kellerman (1987) points out that even in a democracy there exists a hierarchy of ability to get needs noticed and addressed by various groups. At the same time, Gaventa (1980) pointed out that responses to issues or needs are unlikely to occur unless there is some opportunity for participation in bringing those issues or needs to conscious awareness. Both of these points argue for student-athlete input into a needs awareness methodology. The athletic arena is usually not a democracy and does not focus on needs other than success.

Formal and Informal Methods of Assessment

Information about student-athlete needs and development can be assessed using either formal or informal methods. Formal assessment methods may include objective measures such as standardized inventories, scales or surveys designed to investigate student-athlete needs, opinions or attitudes. More subjective approaches may include structured or unstructured interviews, self-report inventories, questionnaires or systematic observations of behavior (Miller, 1982). Formal methods have the potential benefits of being conducted in a more systematic manner, being applicable to specific groups and using known standardized scoring procedures: characteristics which typically produce more valid and reliable data (King, 1990).

An example of a formal approach to student-athlete needs assessment was a self-report survey administered to a stratified random sample of the general student population and a subsample of student-athletes on the campus of a private southern university (Etzel & Barrow, 1992). The needs assessment questionnaire, developed by a group from the staff of the university counseling and psychological services center, consisted of 54 Likert format items administered to all participants inquiring about a variety of personal-social and educational-vocational concerns. Ten additional items designed to assess concerns associated with student-athletes (e.g., stress of practice and competition, relationships with coaches and teammates, effects of injury) were administered to the student-athlete sample.

Informal methods of obtaining information about student-athlete needs may also be quite fruitful. Although informally obtained information may not be as valid and reliable as data produced through formal assessment procedures, it can provide cost-effective insight over time from a number of sources and across situations. Student-athletes may share things about themselves in conversations (private or public), interactions with others, or other observed behavior that can help to formulate impressions about student-athletes' needs.

An example of an informal method of sampling are impressions about student-athletes' needs gleaned over time from the content of counseling sessions with student-athletes. More specifically, clinical work over the years tends to support the notion that student-athletes experience considerable life stress, from the multiple demands placed upon them to be successful both academically and athletically, while at the same time attempting to cope with developmental concerns.

There are some potential problems for either formal or informal methods of needs assessment with active student-athletes. Beyond the barriers already mentioned, both methods seem to fit Voss, Tordella and Brown's (1987) definition of secondary data when conducting a needs assessment. They define secondary data as information gathered for another purpose but related to the needs assessment.

For example, counseling sessions with student-athletes may offer valuable clues to various needs. However, the purpose of those counseling sessions was likely the resolution of immediate, strongly felt needs experienced as problematic. The counseling session is a suggestive source of secondary data, but necessarily limited by its purpose in providing a comprehensive overview of the needs of student-athletes in general.

This issue exists even when student-athletes identify an on-campus resource person and advertise his or her skills among themselves. Student-athletes may limit their referrals to those teammates with similar needs that they themselves found help for and not realize that the resource person may have an extensive network of additional resources.

Formal assessment methods can be skewed by student-athlete bias against owning needs, considering needs unrelated to competition as trivial, simple disinterest in the assessment, or lack of encouragement from coaches and teammates to fully and honestly participate in the assessment. The active student-athlete may consider formal assessment unimportant or secondary to his or her competitive needs and weaken the reliability of the data collected.

A Modified Delphi Approach for
Needs Assessment of Student Athletes

A needs assessment approach that appears to offer a resolution to the barriers and issues presented would be a modified Delphi method. Linstone and Turoff (1975) suggest the Delphi method utilizes expert judgment while avoiding the interpersonal effects of face-to-face involvement and allows each expert to consider and incorporate feedback from other experts to refine his or her subsequent judgments.

Lottes (1991) reported a traditional Delphi study of the needs of college student-athletes using a panel of ten experts—counselors, educators, and sport psychologists actively working with student-athletes. The experts were asked to report their individual perceptions on resources for student-athletes in the form of Likert scales from "not important" to "essential." For example, "Help with academic major selection," "Tutorial assistance," and "Counseling for drug users" are representative of the academic and personal/social components of the Delphi study. Means for each resource were then obtained and the experts were asked to again do the scaling task in light of the feedback from the other experts. At this point the experts were also asked to assess the feasibility of implementing each resource at their respective institutions.

However, the true experts on the needs of student-athletes should be the student-athletes who actually experience the competitive world of intercollegiate athletics. Unfortunately, two additional concerns make student-athlete input somewhat suspect. First, the active student-athlete has a number of constraints to deal with as mentioned above—for example, personal investment in the status quo, long term deference to coaches, financial rewards from scholarships, and the pervasive "macho" atmosphere in which he or she operates.

Second, the wide diversity in success level and in institutional commitment to athletics means very different levels of resource availability and willingness to consider new resources for student-athletes. Those institutions with large, successful programs may have vastly more money and personnel available to the athletic department compared to smaller, or less successful programs. Student-athletes in less successful programs may have a pessimistic view of anything changing unless they first start winning.

Lottes' (1991) experts have some limitations for the needs assessment of student-athletes. While knowledgeable about student-athletes, they are relatively rare and limited in their experience with different institutions. This may limit the relevance of their judgements to a specific institution's situation. They also see a restricted picture of student-athletes' needs, either through their area of expertise or their perceived role by coaches and student-athletes. Finally, the experts have a formalized point of view about student-athletes and use it in their needs assessment.

A methodology that addresses these issues would be a modification of the Lottes study. Since expert opinion has been obtained on the resources needed for student-athletes (and the feasibility of those resources), a modification to assess the relevance of those resources would be to continue the Delphi process but with a new group of "experts." This new group of experts would be an institution's own retired student-athletes who have completed their collegiate eligibility.

For example, an institution could take a sample of its student-athletes who completed their eligibility within the last three years and have them continue the Delphi process based on their own recent experience as a student-athlete. This would base the needs assessment on the judgments of student-athletes with experience in that particular institution's environment. The student-athletes could evaluate the resources considered essential on the basis of their personal experience.

Retired student-athletes should be able to be more objective since they are no longer active in the competitive environment. At the same time, they have competed in that environment and may be the most qualified experts available on what is truly needed for the student-athletes who are still competing. Their objectivity would also be enhanced by not having a coaching staff, pressure from teammates to conform, or other constraints that go along with collegiate competition.

An asset for this approach to needs assessment for student-athletes is that it allows the Delphi process to be specific to an institution. Since each institution has a unique relationship with its student-athletes, this avoids the possibility of irrelevant generalization. Depending on the institution's interest and commitment, subgroups of student-athletes could participate in the modified Delphi process. Women's athletic programs may feel they have a different environment than the men's programs. Non-revenue sports might also feel that their student-athletes are treated differently than the revenue sports' student-athletes.

There are some suggestions in the literature that minority student-athletes have an even more unique collegiate experience than student-athletes in general. Scales (1991) reported indications that African-

American student-athletes go through a very different socialization process within their home communities. For example, athletic success often equals conquering hero status within the African-American community. His suggestion that attempting to compete at the professional sport level receives more support in the minority community than elsewhere would easily affect the minority student-athlete's perceived needs.

CONCLUSIONS

Needs assessment for student-athletes is an issue with numerous complications, both for the initiation of the needs assessment and for the integrity of the process after it is initiated. A potential solution to these complications is to tailor various needs assessment processes to an institution. Certainly, the arena is complicated enough to make generalizing across institutions, and categories like gender, revenue status, and minorities, a very challenging task. A modified Delphi approach for the assessment of student-athletes needs is recommended given the limitations of other formal and informal approaches.

REFERENCES

Anderson, W. A., & McKeag, D. B. (1985). *The substance use and abuse habits of college student-athletes.* East Lansing, MI: College of Human Medicine, Michigan State University.

Begel, D. (1992). An overview of sport psychiatry. *American Journal of Psychiatry, 149,* 606–614.

Beisser, A. R. (1967). *The madness in sports.* New York: Appleton, Century Crofts.

Benson, D. C. (1988). A perspective on drug testing. *The Physician and Sportsmedicine, 16,* 151.

Bergandi, T. A., & Wittig, A. F. (1984). Availability of and attitudes toward counseling services for the college athlete. *Journal of College Student Personnel, 25,* 557–558.

Blann, W. (1985). Intercollegiate athletic competition and students' educational and career plans. *Journal of College Student Personnel, 26,* 115–118.

Boone, J. N., & Walker, H., Jr. (1987, February). *Ungraduated college athletes: Stereotype and reality.* Paper presented at the Annual Meeting of the Association for the Study of Higher Education, San Diego, CA.

Brooks, D. D., Etzel, E. F., & Ostrow, A. C. (1987). Job responsibilities and backgrounds of NCAA Division I athletic advisors and counselors. *The Sport Psychologist, 1,* 201–207.

Bunker, L. K., & McGuire, R. T. (1985). Give sport psychology to sport. In L. K.

Bunker, R. J. Rotella, & A. S. Reilly (Eds.). *Sport Psychology* (pp. 3–14). Ann Arbor, MI: McNaughton & Gunn.

Butt, D. S. (1987). *Psychology of sport.* New York: Van Nostrand Reinhold.

Chartrand, J., & Lent, R. (1987). Sports counseling: Enhancing the development of the student-athlete. *Journal of Counseling and Development, 66,* 164–167.

Damm, J. (1991). Drugs and the college student-athlete. In E. F. Etzel, A. P. Ferrante, & J. W. Pinkney (Eds.). *Counseling college student athletes: Issues and interventions* (pp. 151–174). Morgantown, WV: Fitness Information Technology.

Dezelsky, Y., Toohey, J., & Shaw, R. (1985). Non-medical drug use behavior at five United States universities: A nine-year study. *Bulletin on Narcotics, 37,* 49–53.

Duda, M. (1986). Do anabolic steroids pose an ethical dilemma for U.S. physicians? *The Physician and Sports Medicine, 14,* 124–132.

Etzel, E. (1989). *Life stress, locus of control and competition anxiety patterns of college student-athletes.* Unpublished doctoral dissertation. West Virginia University, Morgantown.

Etzel, E. & Barrow, J. (1992). College student-athletes: A needs assessment. Unpublished manuscript.

Ferrante, A. P., & Etzel, E. (1991). Counseling college student-athletes: The problem, the need. In E. F. Etzel, A. P. Ferrante, & J. W. Pinkney (Eds.). *Counseling college student-athletes: Issues and interventions* (pp. 1–17). Morgantown, WV: Fitness Information Technology.

Ferrante, A., & Etzel, E., & Pinkney, J. (1991). A model for accessing student-athletes with student affairs resources. In E. F. Etzel, A. P. Ferrante, & J. W. Pinkney (Eds.). *Counseling college student-athletes: Issues and interventions* (pp. 19–30). Morgantown, WV: Fitness Information Technology.

Gaventa, J. (1980). *Power and powerlessness: Quiescence and rebellion in an Appalachian valley.* Urbana, IL.: University of Illinois Press.

Gay, J. E., Minelli, M. J., Tripp, D., & Keilitz, D. (1990). Alcohol and the athlete: A university's response. *Journal of Alcohol and Education, 35,* 81–86.

George, R. L. (1990). *Counseling the chemically dependent.* Englewood Cliffs, NJ: Prentice Hall.

Hinkle, J. S. (1990, April). Sport psychology and sports counseling: Educational programs, research, and an agenda for the 1990s. In J. S. Hinkle, (Chair), *Sport psychology and sports counseling: Developmental programming, education, and research.* Symposium conducted at the 36th Annual Meeting of the Southeastern Psychological Association, Atlanta, GA.

Hinkle, J. S. (1993). Problem solving and decision making: Life skills for student athletes. In S. V. Kirk, & W. D. Kirk (Eds.), *Student athletes: Shattering the myths and sharing the realities.* Alexandria, VA: American Counseling Association.

Hinkle, J. S. (In press). Integrating sport psychology and sports counseling: programming, education, and research. *Journal of Sport Behavior.*

Kellerman, B. (1987). Foreword. In D. E. Johnson, L. R. Meiller, L. C. Miller, & G. F. Summers, (Eds.). *Needs assessment: Theory and methods* (pp. xii–ix). Ames, IA: Iowa State University Press.

King, P. (1990). Assessing development from a cognitive developmental perspective.

In D. G. Creamer & associates (Eds.). College student development: *Theory and practice for the 1990s* (pp. 81–98). Alexandria, VA: American College Personnel Association.

Lanning, W., & Toye, P. (1993). Counseling athletes in higher education. In W. D. Kirk, & S. V. Kirk (Eds.). *Student-athletes: Shattering the myths and sharing the realities* (pp. 61–70). Alexandria, VA: American Counseling Association.

Lederman, D. (1988, December 7). Players spend more time on sports than on studies, an NCAA survey of major college athletes finds. *The Chronicle of Higher Education,* pp. A33–A38.

Linstone, H. A., & Turoff, M. (Eds., 1975). *The Delphi method: Techniques and applications.* Reading, MA: Addison-Wesley.

Lottes, C. (1991). A "whole-istic" model of counseling student-athletes on academic, athletic, and personal-social issues. In E. F., Etzel, A. P. Ferrante, & J. W. Pinkney, (Eds.). *Counseling college student-athletes: Issues and interventions* (pp. 31–49). Morgantown, WV: Fitness Information Technology.

Marcello, R. J., Danish, S. J., & Stolberg, A. L. (1989). An evaluation of strategies developed to prevent substance abuse among student-athletes. *The Sport Psychologist, 3,* 196–211.

Miller, T. (1982). Student development assessment: A rationale. In G. Hanson, (Ed.). *Measuring student development* (pp. 516). San Francisco: Jossey-Bass.

Miller, L. C., & Hustedde, R. J. (1987). Group approaches. In D. E. Johnson, L. R. Meiller, L. C. Miller, & G. F. Summers, (Eds.). *Needs assessment: Theory and methods* (pp. 91–125). Ames, IA: Iowa State University Press.

Murphy, R. J., Baezinger, J., Dutcher, J., Gikas, P., Idel-Morse, K., Miller, D., & Underwood, C. (1985). *Big ten intercollegiate conference: Awareness committee on alcohol and drug abuse.* Unpublished survey, The Ohio State University.

Pinkerton, R., Hinz, L., & Barrow, J. (1987). The college student athlete: Psychological considerations and interventions. *Journal of American College Health, 37,* 218–226.

Remer, R., Tongate, F., & Watson, J. (1978). Athletes: Counseling the overprivileged minority. *Personnel and Guidance Journal, 56,* 626–629.

Scales, J. E. (1991). African-American student-athletes: An example of minority exploitation in collegiate athletics. In E. F. Etzel, A. P. Ferrante, & J. W. Pinkney, (Eds.). *Counseling college student-athletes: Issues and interventions* (pp. 71–99). Morgantown, WV: Fitness Information Technology.

Selby, R., Weinstein, H. M., & Bird, T. S. (1990). The health of university athletes: Attitudes, behaviors, and stressors. *Journal of American College Health, 39,* 11–18.

Smallman, E., Sowa, C. J., & Young, B. D. (1991). Ethnic and gender differences in student athletes' responses to stressful life events. *Journal of College Student Development, 32,* 230.

Sowa, C., & Gressard, C. (1983). Athletic participation: Its relationship to student development. *Journal of College Personnel, 24,* 236–239.

Sperber, M. (1990). *College sports inc.: The athletic department vs the university.* New York: Henry Holt.

Swain, A., Jones, G., & Cale, A. (1990). Interrelationships among multidimensional competitive state anxiety components as function of the proximity of competition. *Perceptual and Motor Skills, 71,* 1111–1114.

Toohey, J. (1978). Non-medical drug use among intercollegiate athletes at five American universities. *Bulletin on Narcotics, 30,* 61–65.

Tricker, R., Cook, D. L., & McGuire, R. (1989). Issues related to drug abuse in college athletics: Athletes at risk. *Sport Psychologist, 3,* 155–165.

Tunick, R., Etzel, E., & Leard, J. (1991). Counseling injured and disabled student-athletes: A guide for understanding and intervention. In E. F. Etzel, A. P. Ferrante, & J. Pinkney (Eds.). *Counseling college student-athletes: Issues and interventions* (pp. 199–220). Morgantown, WV: Fitness Information Technology.

Voss, P. R., Tordella, J. A., & Brown, D. L. (1987). *Role of secondary data.* In D. E. Johnson, L. R. Meiller, L. C. Miller & G. F. Summers (Eds.). *Needs assessment: Theory and methods* (pp. 156–170). Ames, IA: Iowa State University Press.

Wittmer, J., Bostic, D., Philips, T. D., & Waters, W. (1981). The personal, academic, and career problems of college student athletes: Some possible answers. *The Personnel and Guidance Journal, 59,* 52–55.

Chapter 7

GAY, LESBIAN, AND BISEXUAL STUDENT NEEDS

Robin A. Buhrke and Sally D. Stabb

This chapter examines the needs of lesbian, gay, and bisexual students, and how needs assessment with these students might best be conducted. Three broad areas are covered: background information including minority group status, homophobia, and heterosexism; the psychological needs of lesbian, gay, and bisexual students; and special issues involved in conducting needs assessments with this population. The chapter concludes with a summary and recommendations.

BACKGROUND INFORMATION: MINORITY GROUP STATUS, HOMOPHOBIA, AND HETEROSEXISM

Many of the needs of lesbian, gay, and bisexual students stem from being members of an oppressed minority. Being lesbian, gay, or bisexual in a homophobic and heterosexist environment creates stresses analogous to those experienced by students of color and women in racist and sexist environments.

Minority Group Status

As a minority group, lesbians, gay men, and bisexuals are subject to many of the pressures and processes of other minorities—stigmatization, in-group/out-group dynamics, and prejudice. Their minority status may not be obvious, and indeed this group has been referred to as the "hidden minority" (cf, Fassinger, 1991). Although it has been estimated that lesbians and gay men comprise approximately 10% of the population, and that as many as nearly one-third of the population has experienced some degree of attraction to or physical contact with members of their own gender (Kinsey, Pomeroy, & Martin, 1948; Kinsey, Pomeroy, Martin, & Gebhard, 1953), it is impossible to unequivocally determine the proportion of the population who are lesbian, gay, or bisexual. Furthermore, it is not possible to "detect" via stereotypes who is and is not lesbian, gay, or bisexual (Berger, Hank, Rauzi, & Simkins, 1987).

Stigma is a central feature of minority status. Stigma refers to over-generalized, negative assumptions based on minority membership (Hammersmith, 1987). In essence, minority status becomes a lens through which all information is seen and interpreted. For the lesbian, gay, or bisexual student, this means that sexual orientation is the filter through which all judgments are made. Hammersmith suggests that the consequences of stigma for lesbian, gay, and bisexual students include stereotypic and global interpretations; social rejection, distancing and discrimination; "passing" (that is, active or passive attempts to appear heterosexual); altered self-concept; and development of a subculture.

DeMonteflores (1986) describes four categories of reactions to stigma: assimilation, confrontation, ghettoization, and specialization. Assimilation, synonymous with passing, refers to adopting mainstream (i.e., heterosexual) ways, often at the cost of a sense of self-betrayal. Many lesbian, gay, and bisexual individuals assimilate selectively—that is, they assimilate in some contexts (e.g., at work) and not in others (e.g., at home). Confrontation refers to actively becoming visible to oneself and to others (e.g., appearing in lesbian, gay, and bisexual pride marches, wearing lesbian-, gay-, and bisexual-affirmative buttons or paraphernalia). Ghettoization refers to remaining within certain geographical or psychological confines, a process that provides a close group and/or community, but may limit exposure to others (e.g., living, working, and/or socializing only with lesbian, gay, or bisexual others). Specialization refers to viewing one's sexual orientation and/or group as particularly exotic, unique, or as "chosen."

Minority status also involves in-group versus out-group processes. Membership in a group generates strong feelings of cohesion, forms a base of identity and esteem, and may be actively protected. It is not uncommon for group members to exhibit pride in their group, to promote the in-group way of life, to have low tolerance for dissent among insiders, and to devalue out-group members (Tajfel, 1981). These processes occur for heterosexual groups and lesbian, gay, and bisexual groups alike, regardless of which is designated "in" or "out." However, because minorities are usually in a lower power position relative to majority members, these processes may have a particularly negative impact on lesbian, gay, and bisexual persons.

Although student attitudes toward lesbians and gay men in the United States are negative (D'Augelli & Rose, 1990) and the campus environment is often described as hostile by gay students (Reynolds, 1989), these prejudicial views of lesbian, gay, and bisexual behavior and lifestyle are culture-bound and of relatively recent origin. Historically and cross-culturally, there is ample evidence that same-sex behavior has been viewed as "normal" for at least some portion of the population in more cultures than not (Blumenfeld & Raymond, 1988; Ford & Beach, 1951; Ross, Paulsen, & Stalstrom, 1988). The United States has been described as "one of the more homophobic of the world's cultures" (Hammersmith, 1987, p. 174).

Prejudicial attitudes are compounded for lesbians, gays, and bisexuals of color. The sequelae of multiple oppression is exacerbated when one cultural group does not value another. African-American (Loiacano, 1989), Asian-American (Chan, 1989), and Japanese-American (Wooden, Kawasaki, & Mayeda, 1983) lesbians and gay men often experience racism from the lesbian, gay, and bisexual community and homophobia from their ethnic communities. The more orthodox the religious beliefs of a given culture, the more conflict that is created between sexual orientation and ethnic identities (Falco, 1991).

Homophobia

Homophobia is defined as the irrational fear and hatred of lesbian, gay, and bisexual people (Weinberg, 1972). *Internalized homophobia* is the term used to describe negative attitudes toward or fears about same-sex feelings and behaviors by lesbian, gay, and bisexual people. Homophobia can be found operating on four levels: the personal, the interpersonal, the institutional, and the cultural (Blumenfeld, 1992). *Personal homophobia* is the personal prejudice against lesbian, gay, and bisexual people. *Interpersonal homophobia* is the discrimination that occurs when personal homophobia is acted on. "Jokes," verbal harassment, and physical violence are all examples of interpersonal homophobia. While the incidence of violence against lesbians, gay men, and bisexuals has risen dramatically in recent years (Herek & Berrill, 1992), only 30 of the 50 United States and the District of Columbia have enacted hate crimes legislation, and only 15 of those include sexual orientation. This lack of governmental protection for lesbians, gay men, and bisexuals is an example of *institutional homophobia.* Institutional homophobia describes discrimination based on sexual orientation by governments, businesses, and organizations. The U. S. military ban on service by lesbians, gay men, and bisexuals is another example of institutional homophobia. *Cultural homophobia* refers to the social norms or codes of behavior that work within society to oppress lesbians, gay men, and bisexuals.

Homophobia hurts everyone in several ways, regardless of sexual orientation (Elze, 1992). First, homophobia "forces" people to have heterosexual sex to prove their heterosexuality. Second, it "forces" people into rigid gender roles—men in traditionally female roles and women in traditionally male roles violate traditional gender roles and risk being stigmatized as lesbian, gay, or bisexual. Finally, homophobia stifles physical and emotional intimacy between same-sex friends. Physical affection and emotional vulnerability are avoided for fear of being "misunderstood."

According to Herek (1984), people holding homophobic attitudes are characterized by the following:

- they are less likely to have had personal contact with lesbians or gay men,
- they are less likely to report having engaged in homosexual behaviors or to identify as lesbian or gay,
- they are more likely to perceive their peers as manifesting negative attitudes, especially if the respondents are male,
- they are more likely to have resided in areas where negative attitudes are the norm (e.g., the midwestern and southern United States, the Canadian prairies, and in rural areas or small towns), especially during adolescence,
- they are more likely to be older and less well-educated,
- they are more likely to be religious, to attend church frequently, and to subscribe to a conservative religious ideology,
- they are more likely to express traditional, restrictive attitudes about sex roles,
- they are less permissive sexually or manifest more guilt or negativity about sexuality,
- they are more likely to manifest high levels of authoritarianism and related personality characteristics.

In addition, heterosexuals tend to hold more negative, homophobic attitudes towards members of their own gender (Herek, 1984).

Homophobia is manifest in stereotypes of lesbians, gay men, and bisexuals. It is often assumed that all lesbians are alike, all gay men are alike, and all bisexuals are alike (Krajeski, 1986). More pernicious stereotypes and myths of lesbians, gay men, and bisexuals as promiscuous, unstable, dangerous around children, and "sick" can have a profound effect on lesbians, gay men, and bisexuals. Even the more subtle assumption that if lesbians, gay men, and bisexuals have problems of any kind, it is because of their sexual orientation (Buhrke & Douce, 1991; Dulaney & Kelly, 1982; Fassinger, 1991; Garnets, Hancock, Cochran, Goodchilds, & Peplau, 1991; Nuerhing, Fein, & Tyler, 1974) or the related underestimation of the degree to which prejudice and discrimination affect lesbians, gay men, and bisexuals form a cultural and social context which must continually be monitored and "handled."

Internalized homophobia can be manifest in a number of ways. These include a fear of discovery; discomfort with those who are obviously or openly lesbian, gay, or bisexual; limiting contact or expression of lesbian, gay or bisexual sexual orientation by having short or inappropriate relationships; or a reactive need to reject and denigrate all heterosexuals and to feel superior to them (Falco, 1991).

Heterosexism

Heterosexism, closely related to homophobia, refers to the assumption or belief that heterosexuality is the only acceptable or viable life option (Blumenfeld & Raymond, 1988). The lesbian, gay, and bisexual experience is seen as insignificant or inferior (Iasenza, 1989) and heterosexuality is viewed as more "normal" or "natural" (Fassinger, 1991). Heterosexism tends to be more subtle, indirect, and difficult to detect than homophobia. Heterosexism is manifest in a lack of knowledge, legal institutionalization, bias in research, and language.

Lack of Knowledge

Most people have little knowledge of lesbian, gay, and bisexual culture. Few know of the roles lesbian, gay, and bisexual people have played throughout history (Katz, 1976), or even the background of the lesbian, gay, and bisexual liberation movement in the United States since 1969 (Silverstein, 1991). There is a general lack of knowledge about lesbian, gay, and bisexual identity development; a lack of awareness of the depth and effects of discrimination and prejudice against lesbians, gay men, and bisexuals; a failure to recognize the diversity between individuals who identify as lesbian, gay, or bisexual; and a lack of knowledge about the variety of lesbian, gay, and bisexual lifestyles, relationships, and family structures (Garnets et al., 1991).

In addition to these general deficits, the training programs of most student service professionals have failed to incorporate material on lesbian, gay, and bisexual students, much less teach appropriate skills for interaction and intervention (Buhrke, 1989a; Dulaney & Kelly, 1982; Graham, Rawlings, Halpern, & Hermes, 1984; Silverstein, 1991; Thompson & Fishburn, 1977). Heterosexism is reflected in the lack of consideration of lesbian, gay, and bisexual issues in theories about individual human development, about group processes, about career development, and in assessment instruments (Buhrke, 1989b).

Legal Institutionalization

In addition to a lack of accurate information, lesbians, gay men, and bisexuals face institutional heterosexism as well. There is no federal civil rights legislation protecting lesbians, gay men, and bisexuals, and only a handful of state and local jurisdictions have enacted anti-discrimination policies which include sexual orientation (Buhrke, 1993). Many of those jurisdictions which do protect lesbian, gay, and bisexual citizens are facing ballot initiatives designed to remove these protections. In most jurisdictions in the United States, it is legal for lesbians, gay men, or bisexuals to be denied housing, custody of their own children, adoption privileges, and employment based on sexual orientation. Lesbians, gay men, and bisexuals are not allowed to marry, and therefore are unable to file joint income tax returns, are unable to claim certain kinds of insurance benefits, and are unable to enter into certain kinds of legal agreements. Same-sex partners, necessarily unmarried, are not "next of kin" and may be denied hospital access to their sick or injured partners.

Heterosexual Bias in Research

Lesbians, gay men, and bisexuals are invisible in most of the psychological literature. Research participants are presumed to be heterosexual, and research questions and questionnaires are formulated based upon this presumption. Participants are rarely asked their sexual orientation, even in studies of lesbian, gay, and bisexual populations (Buhrke, Ben-Ezra, Hurley, & Ruprecht, 1992). There is no reason to believe that lesbians, gay men, and bisexuals don't comprise some proportion of every research sample.

Herek, Kimmel, Amaro, and Melton (1991) have devised guidelines for evaluating heterosexist bias in existing research and for avoiding heterosexist bias in prospective research. These guidelines, detailed in Appendix H, make recommendations regarding formulating research questions, sampling, research design and procedures, protection of participants, and interpreting and reporting results. These guidelines should be carefully consulted in needs assessment design and planning.

In a review of the counseling psychology research literature on lesbian and gay issues, Buhrke et al. (1992) made similar recommendations. In addition, it was recommended that researchers not equate lesbian and gay male populations, not assume the sexual orientation of participants, increase the use of observable, behaviorally anchored outcomes, and avoid the use of heterosexual paradigms in conducted research on lesbian-, gay-, or bisexual-related issues.

Heterosexist Language

Heterosexism is expressed in many ways through language. The mental health professions, the lesbian, gay, and bisexual communities, and concerned others struggle with evolving terminology and conflicting preferences for terms. For example, the term "straight," used to denote heterosexuals, implies that lesbian, gay, or bisexual people are somehow "crooked" and deviant. Likewise, comparisons of lesbian, gay, and bisexual samples and "normal" samples implies abnormality. The Committee on Lesbian and Gay Concerns (CLGC) of the American Psychological Association developed suggestions for avoiding the use of heterosexual language (CLGC, 1991). In brief, the term *sexual orientation* is preferred to sexual preference, the terms *lesbian and gay male* are preferred to homosexual, the terms *same-gender sexual behavior, male-male sexual behavior, and female-female sexual behavior* are preferred to homosexual or lesbian, gay, or bisexual sex, the terms *bisexual women and men, bisexual persons, or bisexual* are preferred to describe those who relate sexually and affectionally to women and men, the term *heterosexual* is preferred to straight, and the term *gender* is preferred to the term sex when differentiating between sexual orientation and gender. (Note: Copyright © 1991 by the American Psychological Association. Adapted by permission. This article presents *suggestions* from the Committee on Gay and Lesbian Concerns on avoiding heterosexual bias in language and are not *guidelines* adopted by the American Psychological Association.)

In addition to this specific terminology related to sexual orientation, broader uses of language are also important (CLGC, 1991). Many terms reflect a heterosexist view of the world. For example, using terms like marital status and sexual intercourse to denote relationship status and sexual behavior excludes the experiences of lesbians, gay men, and bisexuals. Thus, the use of heterosexist language contributes to the invisibility encountered by lesbians, gay men, and bisexuals.

PSYCHOLOGICAL NEEDS OF GAY, LESBIAN, AND BISEXUAL STUDENTS

The literature assessing the needs of lesbian, gay, and bisexual students is nascent at best, and the preponderance is psychological in nature. Given the preliminary status of this literature, it is best to view the findings as a starting point. In addition, while some needs are universal, others are context specific. Each student service worker will need to determine the degree to which a given situation reflects universal or context-specific needs. Four need areas will be presented: needs common among lesbian, gay, and bisexual students, and needs unique to each of these three groups.

Needs Common Among Gay, Lesbian, and Bisexual Students

Lesbian, gay, and bisexual students all share certain common concerns. These include lesbian, gay, or bisexual identity development, the experience of certain stressors inherent in the stigmatized nature of non-heterosexual sexual orientation, and the need for information, resources, and networks.

Identity Development

The formation of a positive lesbian, gay, or bisexual identity is important for psychological adjustment (Miranda & Storms, 1989). Several models of lesbian, gay, or bisexual identity development have been proposed (e.g., Cass, 1979; Chapman & Brannock, 1987; Coleman, 1982; Lewis, 1984; McCarn & Fassinger, 1990; Minton & McDonald, 1984; Sophie, 1988). Most are developmental in nature, consisting of a sequence of events, experiences, thoughts, feelings, or behaviors that occur over time. Key to each model is the "coming out" process—the process of identifying, acknowledging, and disclosing one's sexual orientation. This process occurs with a great deal of temporal variation—some students "come out" very quickly, and others take a relatively long time (months or even years, in some cases).

There is a great deal of diversity in the models. Cass' (1979) classic model of identity development consists of six, fairly detailed, stages. The first stage, *Identity Confusion,* is marked by feelings of turmoil and by questioning of previously held assumptions about one's sexual orientation. Stage two, *Identity Comparison,* is characterized by feelings of alienation during which one accepts the possibility of being lesbian, gay or bisexual, and becomes isolated from heterosexual others. *Identity Tolerance,* stage three, is marked by feelings of ambivalence, during which one seeks out other lesbians, gay men, and bisexuals, while maintaining separate public and private images. In stage four, *Identity Acceptance,* selective disclosure occurs, in which one begins to legitimize (publicly and private-ly) one's sexual orientation. In the fifth stage, *Identity Pride,* one ex-periences anger, pride, and activism, becomes immersed in the lesbian, gay, and bisexual subculture, and rejects heterosexual people, institutions, and values. The final stage of *Identity Synthesis* is characterized by clarity and acceptance. The person at this stage moves beyond a dichotomized worldview and incorporates his or her sexual orientation as one aspect of a more integrated identity.

At the other end of the spectrum, Schneider (1991) conceptualizes identity formation as simply a two-step process in which identity first shifts from heterosexual to lesbian, gay, or bisexual, and then the evalua-tion of the non-heterosexual sexual orientation shifts from negative to positive. Others note that the identity development process may not necessarily be linear; students may oscillate between stages, or recycle through the process under varying conditions (DeMonteflores, 1986; Dillon, 1986; McCarn & Fassinger, 1990). Many identity models fail to take into account variables such as gender, racial/ethnic background, and differences in individual versus group identity formation.

Regardless of the differences in conceptualizations, lesbian, gay, and bisexual students have needs that vary significantly depending on the stage of identity development in which they find themselves (Buhrke & Douce, 1991; Dillon, 1986; Falco, 1991). Understanding and acceptance by others facilitate development at each stage. Early stages focus more on exploration and understanding of feelings and beliefs, as well as of the effects of socialization. Lesbian, gay, and bisexual students need support during the coming out process. Disclosure of sexual orientation is greatly facilitated by knowing the recipient of the information will be accepting, by strong beliefs by the individual in the right to be oneself, by the sense of confidence and pride, and by the desire to be free of the burden of hiding (Falco, 1991). The primary inhibitors of disclosure are related to nonacceptance—fears that disclosure would make others uncomfortable, fears of repercussions socially and occupationally, and hearing prejudicial jokes and comments from family, coworkers, and friends. In later stages, the focus shifts to developing competencies for interpersonal relationships and negotiating the broader context of social interaction, both within lesbian, gay, or bisexual subculture and within the majority heterosexual culture.

Psychological and Psychosocial Stressors.

The hostile sociocultural environment in which lesbian, gay, and bisexual students find themselves contributes to a variety of psychological reactions and interpersonal difficulties. Again, these problems are *not* due to sexual orientation, but to the unsupportive, punitive, and hostile attitudes and behaviors of family, friends, co-workers, community, and society at large.

There are numerous psychological and psychosocial concerns of lesbian, gay, and bisexual students. Lesbian, gay, and bisexual students may experience feelings of fear, loneliness, anxiety, guilt, shame, anger, self-hate, betrayal, and depression because of societal values regarding their sexual orientation. Some studies report that suicidal ideation and suicide attempts are higher among adolescent and young adult lesbian, gay, and bisexual students than among their heterosexual counterparts, but these studies are controversial and have been criticized on methodological grounds. Feelings of isolation are real and common, especially at earlier developmental stages. Rates of drug and alcohol abuse are higher than in comparable heterosexual samples (Glaus, 1988). It is difficult to maintain self-esteem as a member of a discredited and devalued subculture. Some grieve for the loss of mainstream, heterosexual privilege, and experience conflicts about religion and spirituality. These trends have been identified by a number of authors (Carl, 1990; Coleman, 1987a; Dillon, 1986; Forstein, 1986; Hammersmith, 1987; Lourea, 1985; Paroski, 1987; Schneider, 1991).

In the domains of school, career choice, and interpersonal relationships, additional issues arise. Social withdrawal is common, especially in the early stages of development. Lesbian, gay, and bisexual students face unique concerns in choosing careers, and may need special assistance

(Hetherington, Hillerbrand, & Etringer, 1989; Hetherington & Orzek, 1989). Identifying which career options are more or less repressive, dealing with negative stereotypes of "gay" careers, employment discrimination, and limited role models are all issues with which the lesbian, gay, or bisexual student must contend. Students may experience academic difficulties as a result of turmoil created by the threat of or actual disclosure of one's sexual orientation to classmates, roommates, and faculty. Romantic relationships bring additional stressors. Inquiries from heterosexual friends and gestures from would-be heterosexual partners must be handled. Same-sex dating has its own difficulties: knowing where and how to meet people and what the norms are for social interaction may be unknown or problematic. Many lesbian, gay, and bisexual students have only heterosexual dating norms and traditional male-female roles to go by. Again, a variety of researchers have noted these themes (Buhrke & Douce, 1991; Carl, 1990; Coleman, 1987a; Dillon, 1986; Hammersmith, 1987; Lourea, 1985; Paroski, 1987; Schneider, 1991).

Family issues are another area of concern. This includes both the lesbian, gay, or bisexual student's family of origin, as well as decisions about future roles as spouse and/or parent. When an individual comes out to his or her family, there are often repercussions, and the entire family may need assistance in dealing with their reactions. The same is true for the husband or wife to whom a partner's same-sex orientation is revealed. Legalized marriage is not available to same-sex partners, few jurisdictions allow same-sex couples to adopt children, and "biological" parenting options are constricted (Carl, 1990; Coleman, 1987a; Dillon, 1986; Dulaney & Kelley, 1982; Garnets, et al., 1991; Hammersmith, 1987; Hays & Samuels, 1989; Savin-Williams, 1989; Strommer, 1989).

Finally, the AIDS crisis has been a concern for lesbians, gay men, and bisexuals alike. While it is clear that AIDS is more prevalent in the gay male and bisexual communities, it has had an impact on the entire lesbian, gay, and bisexual community. Even if one is not personally infected, many lesbians, gay men, and bisexuals have friends, colleagues, or loved ones who are. And, although the prevalence of HIV infection is lower in the lesbian community, they are not immune. Lesbians who are infected may take a back seat when treatment interventions are designed for gay and bisexual men. Accurate information and social support is needed by all involved. Student service professionals must be prepared to be involved with the special needs of students who are HIV infected and who have AIDS (Coleman, 1987a; Edelman, 1986; Nichols, 1986; Shernoff, 1991).

Information, Resources, and Networks

The need for information, resources, and networks has been identified regularly in the literature on lesbian, gay, and bisexual groups (Dillon, 1986; Dulaney & Kelley, 1982; Paroski, 1987). Accurate information is as important for these students themselves as it is for the student service professional. Information may be needed on any or all aspects of the lesbian, gay, or bisexual experience. Student service professionals should also develop lists of resources to serve the special needs of these students, including health care, mental health care, clergy, and other campus staffs as well as social and recreational facilities. Lesbian, gay, and bisexual community and campus organizations should be contacted to develop a support network.

Needs Unique to Lesbian Women

Many of the needs unique to lesbian women stem from being raised in a sexist culture which places women in a double bind. Women are seen as unhealthy if they fulfill their traditional roles (e.g., caregiver) and inappropriate if they step outside traditional gender-role expectations. Lesbians, by virtue of being women-identified, violate traditional heterosexual roles and are subject to homophobia and societal disapproval. Many lesbians' coming out has been facilitated by the feminist movement, where there they find support for nontraditional aspects of their identity (DeMonteflores & Schultz, 1978). Faderman (1984) suggests that women, because of the feminist movement, develop a lesbian identity via a process which may be reversed for gay men: (1) dominant social norms are critically evaluated, (2) stigma and internalized homophobia are encountered, and (3) sexuality is experienced.

Lesbian women often come out within the context of a romantic relationship (Fassinger, 1991). This results in the simultaneous negotiation of both intimacy and identity tasks, making coming out more complicated. In addition, because lesbians are often more relationship oriented by dint of their female socialization, coming out to others may be more stressful.

A common dynamic in lesbian relationships is "merger" (Browning, Reynolds, & Dworkin, 1991; Burch, 1986; Falco, 1991). Merger refers to the fusion of boundaries between two individuals that results in heightened closeness and intimacy, and sometimes results in oppressive, emotional enmeshment. The process varies among couples, and may or may not be problematic. A primary factor contributing to merger is women's socialization and gender roles. Women are taught to be interpersonally sensitive, nurturing, compromising, attentive to interpersonal process, to base self-esteem on relationships, and to subjugate individual needs to the good of the relationship and/or partner. Thus, two women in a relationship may "compete" to "out-care" for each other. Anger and distancing are likely to result in guilt or anxiety. Another contributor to the development of merger is the hostile environment of a heterosexist culture. This occurs as lesbian couples seek solace from an unaccepting world primarily within their relationship. Many lesbian couples, therefore, need to pay special attention to issues of privacy, to "space" within the relationship, and to negotiating boundaries (Browning et al., 1991; Falco, 1991).

There are unique needs for lesbian women with regards to questions of family and children. Our culture supports a "motherhood hierarchy," in which married, heterosexual women are seen as the most appropriate mothers, and single, lesbian women as the least acceptable mothers (DiLapi, 1989). In addition to those concerns common to all mothers regardless of sexual orientation, lesbians contemplating children or raising children have additional considerations. A great deal of planning and decision making must go into the decision to have a child. Decisions must be made about such concerns as method of conception or adoption, role of the non-biological mother, coming out (e.g., to children, child care, medical, and school personnel), and the reactions of the community.

Finally, lesbians have unique needs in terms of health care (Edelman, 1986). Lesbian women may not obtain proper gynecological services since routine visits for birth control are not needed, and due to personal discomfort with medical providers who assume all women are heterosexual.

Needs Unique to Gay Men

Like lesbians, gay men progress through identity development tasks and relationships with a unique twist generated by gender role socialization (Carl, 1990; Fassinger, 1991; Forstein, 1986; Friedman, 1991; Schwartz & Harstein, 1986; Shannon & Woods, 1991). Gender role socialization has taught men to be autonomous, powerful, competitive, controlling, and to value separation over interdependence. These roles, especially if they have been strongly internalized, may lead to difficulties in gay men's relationships. There may be difficulty in attaining or maintaining intimacy, power struggles, or a tendency to exit the relationship by distancing or leaving. Many gay men have internalized negative stereotypes about their relationships which get in the way of forming close attachments.

Family issues are of concern to many gay men. Gay men who have children may fear loss of custody or visitation because of their sexual orientation. Gay men wanting children have limited options. Although gay fathers value their children as highly as do heterosexual fathers, gay fathers may have difficulty in gaining acceptance from both the gay community and from the heterosexual community (Bigner & Jacobson, 1989a, 1989b; Bozzett, 1989).

An issue of great concern within the gay community is AIDS (Nichols, 1986). Not only are there medical aspects of the disease to cope with, but profound psychological concerns as well: death and dying, spirituality, and finding meaning in living with a chronic illness. Feelings may run the gamut of depression, anger, guilt, self-pity, and isolation. AIDS has impacted relationship patterns for many gay men, as well. Early partnering, decreased sexual experimentation, and increased anxiety are not uncommon. As the illness progresses, it is not uncommon for individuals to lose their jobs, incomes, homes, and sometimes their friends and families. Along with his own internal reactions and those of close friends and family, the gay man with AIDS suffers from increased societal stigma and homophobia as a result of the illness.

Needs Unique to Bisexual Women and Men

Bisexual women and men are often invisible within the "hidden" minority of lesbians and gay men. Bisexuals are omitted when sexual orientation is dichotomized into heterosexual and lesbian/gay categories (CLGC, 1991). Their same-gender relationships may experience many of the uniquenesses already presented. Their heterosexual relationships may experience the stresses unique to heterosexual relationships. In addition, bisexual women and men experience concerns unique to bisexuals.

Bisexuals experience a coming out process as do lesbians and gay men, but it may be complicated by an even greater lack of acceptance. Bisexuals are often not accepted by lesbians and gay men for having heterosexual relationships, and are not accepted by heterosexuals for having lesbian or gay relationships. They are marginalized within an already marginalized group.

Many bisexuals experience confusion as a part of their bisexual identity development (Lourea, 1985). Many lesbians, gay men, and heterosexuals assume that this confusion is related to difficulty negotiating the process of coming out as a lesbian or gay man. This may be partly because many lesbians and gay men, in the course of their own coming out process, have temporarily described themselves as bisexual. Some lesbians and gay men use the term "bisexual" when transitioning between their heterosexual identity and their lesbian or gay identity. However, confusion in bisexual identity is related to the struggle to accept oneself as bisexual.

Bisexuals may experience having to hide their sexual orientation to lesbians, gay men, and heterosexuals alike. Bisexuals may only be able to get support and affirmation for their heterosexual relationships if their same-gender relationships remain hidden. The converse may be true for gaining support and affirmation for their lesbian or gay relationships. Thus, bisexuals may have more limited opportunities for validation and support.

NEEDS ASSESSMENT WITH GAY, LESBIAN, AND BISEXUAL STUDENTS

A review of the needs of lesbian, gay, and bisexual students, while helpful as a starting point, cannot substitute for a needs assessment of your students on your campus or in your community. Although you may eventually identify many of the needs mentioned, your own needs assessment will allow you to tailor interventions to your unique context and setting. The sections that follow provide guidelines for planning and conducting a needs assessment specifically focused on lesbian, gay, and bisexual students. Thus, it is intended to highlight aspects that will need special attention, rather than to provide a complete review of needs assessment procedures. The reader is referred to the chapter on needs assessment methodologies for an in-depth treatment of general needs assessment procedures. This section describes the lesbian, gay, and bisexual student culture, reviews the methodology and findings of prior needs assessments with these populations, and makes specific recommendations for conducting needs assessments with lesbian, gay, and bisexual students.

Gay, Lesbian, and Bisexual Student Culture

Very little has been written about lesbian, gay, and bisexual student cultures per se. Dillon (1986) suggests that, in many ways, the college campus reflects society-at-large. There are, in all likelihood, students, faculty, and staff who are lesbian, gay, or bisexual. Some lesbian, gay, and bisexual students, faculty, and staff will be open about their sexual orientation and others will not. The environment is likely to be homophobic and heterosexist.

The lesbian, gay, and bisexual campus community has both formal and informal structure. Campus lesbian, gay, and bisexual student groups usually form the basis of the formal structure. These groups serve several functions: they foster a sense of lesbian, gay, and bisexual pride and dignity; they offer an opportunity to socialize and to organize politically; and they offer the opportunity to improve relationships with and attitudes of heterosexuals (Nuehring et al., 1974). The informal structure consists of friendship networks; group norms, language, and fashion; as well as a sophisticated and complex web of contacts and connections complicated by varying degrees of openness regarding sexual orientation.

Prior Needs Assessments with Gay, Lesbian, and Bisexual Populations

There is a dearth of published literature in which needs assessments per se have been conducted with lesbian, gay, and bisexual groups. The methodology and results of the relatively few studies which have been published will be reviewed.

Neuhring et al. (1974) held informal discussions with gay student organizations to get ideas about the needs of lesbian, gay, and bisexual students on campus. Recommendations for student service professionals included increasing the awareness of and comfort level with sexual orientation issues, being direct about sexual orientation in therapy, making special assurances about confidentiality, offering support groups, using lesbian, gay, and bisexual students in paraprofessional roles, and referring students to the broader lesbian, gay, and bisexual community.

Edelman (1986) conducted an informal needs assessment of lesbians' health care needs. Discussions were held with lesbian members of various lesbian, gay, and bisexual student groups, and women's organizations. Respondents described concerns regarding a tendency for lesbian students not to seek health care services and not to disclose their sexual orientation to health care providers. Students identified needs for more sensitive and non-heterosexist health care treatment and more regard for the lesbian couple as a legal entity in the minds and policies of the medical profession. As a result, a lesbian health workshop was created to address these needs.

Three needs assessments conducted within the community rather than on campus are worthy of review. In order to improve mental health services for lesbian, gay, and bisexual clients, Rabin, Keefe, and Burton (1986) surveyed 160 staff members about their perceptions of staff attitudes and competency to serve lesbian, gay, and bisexual clients. The survey included such questions as "Do you feel there are enough staff . . . who are comfortable and competent in serving lesbian, gay male, and bisexual clients?" and "If you were a gay male, lesbian, or bisexual, would you be open about it in our agency?" Because the study targeted agency staff and not the lesbian, gay, and bisexual community, results were only able to identify attitudes of the staff, which in this case were neutral to negative. The specific needs of the lesbian, gay, and bisexual clientele they hoped to serve were not addressed. However, as a result, it was recommended that lesbian, gay, or bisexual practitioners be hired, that staff receive training on lesbian, gay, and bisexual concerns, and that contacts within the lesbian, gay, and bisexual community be developed.

Paroski (1987) assessed the health care concerns of lesbian and gay adolescents in a New York City clinic operated by and for the lesbian and gay community. Participants, 89 gay male and 32 lesbian adolescents, completed a questionnaire during their first visit to the clinic. Six areas were addressed: participant's stereotypes of the lesbians, gay men, and bisexuals; the process of accepting one's sexual identity; how the adolescent learned about lesbian and gay lifestyles; how the adolescent learned to hide his or her sexual orientation; coping mechanisms for dealing with peers, school, and family; and any specific concerns of and recommendations by the respondent. Results indicated that males were most concerned about identifying their sexual orientation, subsequent humiliation, and receiving non-judgmental care from their health care provider. Females were more concerned with the provider's gentleness in dealing with their bodies. Both groups expressed concern that health care providers have specific knowledge of the health care needs of lesbians and gay men. One interesting finding was that males wanted to be seen by lesbian or gay health care providers and females wanted to be seen by women regardless of sexual orientation. Participants' concerns and rec-ommendations included health care providers not assuming that all adolescents are heterosexual, a desire for greater availability of peer support groups, a wish for more open lesbian and gay role models, a need for greater availability of resource materials and persons, and a need for having a supportive person available to talk about non-medical concerns.

In an effort to develop services for lesbian and gay adolescents in Toronto, Schneider (1991) interviewed 30 self-identified lesbian and 30 self-identified gay male adolescents. Participants were contacted from a variety of sources: through friendship networks, via word-of-mouth, through various groups and organizations, and via a notice in a newsletter. A guided interview methodology was employed and response themes and categories were examined. Results indicated the need for services that address the by-products of early stages of coming out (e.g., depression, withdrawal, isolation, loneliness, anxiety, school problems, substance abuse) and the importance of having knowledgeable and affirming mental health providers.

This overview of the lesbian, gay, and bisexual campus environment and of previous needs assessments sets a context for the recommendations that follow. The overview gives many clues about how to obtain access to the lesbian, gay, and bisexual population as well as the methods to assess their needs.

Planning the Needs Assessment

Purpose and Rationale

Assessing the needs of lesbian, gay, and bisexual students can serve a variety of purposes (Kuh, 1982). Needs assessments might be used to explore and monitor the perceptions about the general condition of lesbian, gay, and bisexual students on campus. They can also be used to determine if present services are sufficient and/or to collect support for additional programs. Needs assessments also allow lesbian, gay, and bisexual students to become actively involved in determining the services and/or policies relevant to them. Finally, needs assessments can be used as a vehicle for political and social change (e.g., Schneider, 1991). Regardless of your reasons, it is crucial to specify your purposes in conducting your needs assessment. Many of the decisions you will make regarding participants, methodology, and question content will be guided by your goal for utilizing the results. Failure to specify your goals or purposes may lead to results which do not serve your needs.

Specific rationales for assessing the needs of lesbian, gay, and bisexual students include ethical mandates to accommodate diversity in existing or developing programs, to provide services to this traditionally under-served group of students, and to facilitate the development of a more accepting campus environment. Elaboration on the rationale may be needed to convince colleagues and funding sources of the necessity of your needs assessment.

Research Method and Tools

Choosing your research method, design, and instrumentation is a large task. Typically, a primary researcher or a small core team will coordinate planning. Lesbian, gay, and bisexual students themselves should be included in the process, along with key members of the campus community. Everyone who has some stake in the outcome should be represented.

Although there may be times when a traditional, purely quantitative methodology may be selected, the use of mixed qualitative/quantitative methods are recommended here. By using both methods, the strengths and weaknesses of each approach complement each other (Jick, 1983; Polkinghorne, 1991; Smith, 1986).

In choosing your needs assessment tools, there are a number of considerations. First, any standardized instruments you use should have adequate reliability and validity. In particular, pay attention to the norm groups, and determine whether it has ever been used with lesbian, gay, or bisexual students. Certainly most standard assessments have not been specifically normed with this population. Instruments should be examined for heterosexist language and bias.

If you are developing a survey or structured interview, literature reviews and professional networking may be useful for locating existing needs assessment instruments which may be modified for your use with lesbian, gay, and bisexual students. No matter what the final form of your survey or interview, it is important to ask not only what needs exist, but to assess the relative importance of those needs, as well as what types of services or programs to remedy those needs students would actually be willing to use.

Be sure to assess sexual orientation per se (Buhrke et al., 1992). Do not rely on your sampling strategy to insure the sexual orientation of your participants. It is not safe to assume that all members of a lesbian, gay, and bisexual student group, all respondents to a call for participation, or all participants in a lesbian, gay, or bisexual event are indeed lesbian, gay, or bisexual. Also, consider the impact of your conceptualization of sexual orientation.

Defining sexual orientation, or more precisely, determining who is and who is not lesbian, gay, or bisexual, is very controversial (Gonsiorek & Weinrich, 1991). Kinsey et al. (1948, 1953) conceptualized sexual orientation as sexual behavior and sexual fantasy falling on a 7-point continuum from exclusively heterosexual to exclusively homosexual. Shively and DeCecco (1977) expanded this conceptualization suggesting that two scales, one for homosexuality and one for heterosexuality, provide a more comprehensive categorization. More recently, Klein, Sepekoff, and Wolf (1985) have added a third component—affective orientation. Affective orientation refers to the gender with whom an individual prefers to relate on an intimate or emotional level. Coleman (1987b) goes even further in describing nine dimensions: current relationship status, self-identification identity, ideal self-identification identity, global acceptance of current sexual orientation identity, physical identity, gender identity, sex-role identity, sexual orientation identity as measured by behavior, fantasies, and emotional attachments, and past and present perception of sexual identity compared to idealized future. Gonsiorek and Weinrich (1991) suggest that it may be most useful to assess people on at least three dimensions: sexual behavior, sexual fantasy, and affectional orientation. The important consideration is whether your definition "matches" your purpose. If you choose to assess sexual orientation using self-identification on a bipolar scale, you may obtain a different sample than if you assess sexual orientation via a multidimensional, more inclusive technique. The degree of sample diversity you desire will determine the scope of your definitional scheme.

At this point, it is crucial to get input from lesbian, gay, and bisexual students, faculty, and staff if at all possible. They can assist in developing questions that reflect the uniqueness of your particular campus, and to help fill in gaps in knowledge. A good place to locate students is in lesbian, gay, or bisexual student organizations. If no such organizations exist on your campus, you may need to search the broader community for input. It is crucial that your assessment have good face validity. It is recommended that a pilot-test of your assessment be conducted with a small group of lesbian, gay, and bisexual students in order to determine if the items are clear and make sense, to get feedback on what items to include, and to determine administration time. At the very least, involving members of the lesbian, gay, and bisexual student community will facilitate your data collection later on.

Data Collection

A traditional approach to needs assessment would involve taking a survey or a structured interview, randomly sampling your population, and administering your instruments. Random sampling is extremely difficult, if not impossible, with lesbian, gay, and bisexual student populations for several reasons. First, the number of students involved is relatively small to begin with—10% of the student body, on average. Second, a great many potential participants are not identifiable: many lesbian, gay, and bisexual students may be unwilling to disclose their sexual orientation to anyone, let alone an "unknown" researcher. The only way to get a random sample would be to select a random sample of all students, ask all students their sexual orientation, ask all students about their needs relative to their sexual orientation, and only utilize the data from self-identified lesbians, gay men, and bisexuals. It is possible that if no students are openly lesbian, gay, or bisexual on your campus, this alternative might be necessary. However, even then it is unlikely that the forces contributing to students remaining hidden would be overcome sufficiently within a needs assessment setting to insure honest participation.

To obtain data from lesbian, gay, and bisexual students, needs assessors must first gain access to this community. Crucial to gaining access is having researchers who are familiar with, sensitive to, and affirming of these students. Also critical is having good contacts within the lesbian, gay, and bisexual community. Researchers should consider including lesbian, gay, and bisexual students in the process—from inception and data collection, through data analysis and interpreting the results.

The best and most realistic strategy for sampling is "purposeful" sampling (Patton, 1990). Purposeful sampling, based on logical or theoretical, rather than statistical, grounds involves utilizing a number of techniques, all of which assume an available entry point. One suggested strategy is to start with key informants who give in-depth interviews, or with a small group interview with active lesbian, gay, and bisexual students. Research participants may be selected because they represent a typical case, an atypical case, or the diversity of the population. Students who are open and willing to participate may then be willing to assist in distributing questionnaires to others who are less open. This "snowball" or "chain" sampling, where participants tell their friends, who tell their friends, and so on can provide a more efficient means of collecting data. Other methods, such as participant observation, in which a researcher becomes involved in the day to day workings of a lesbian, gay, or bisexual student group, can also provide useful data. There are a wide variety of data collection methods available, and while it is important to utilize a combination of strategies, it is critical that they be implemented in a planful way.

Data collection with lesbian, gay, and bisexual populations invokes a number of ethical considerations. Confidentially must be completely and vigorously assured (Buhrke & Douce, 1991; Krajeski, 1986). While some students may not be concerned about being publicly identified as lesbian, gay, or bisexual, many students will desire complete anonymity. The repercussions for lesbian, gay, and bisexual students whose identities become known can be very real and very serious, ranging from harassment, violence, discrimination in the classroom, to loss of current or future employment. Also, if the lesbian, gay, and bisexual community learns that you, as a researcher, do not protect their privacy, you will have a great deal of difficulty finding students to participate in your research. Thus, every effort should be made to protect participants.

Data collection techniques require careful consideration. For example, asking lesbian, gay, or bisexual students to drop off a survey at a student service office, even if the survey is discrete, can be seen as a violation of confidentiality. Information collected in interviews or on surveys should be obtained without the use of identifying information, such as names and addresses if at all possible. Lesbian, gay, and bisexual students should be asked to participate only under conditions of informed consent. They should be made aware of all possible uses of the data—to whom the results might be given and in what form. If a researcher wishes to become a participant observer in a lesbian, gay, or student group, permission should be obtained from all members, not just from the students with whom the researcher made the initial contact. Confidentiality concerns may also affect the viability of mail surveys.

While it is impossible to identify and assess the needs of lesbian, gay, and bisexual students who are not open about their sexual orientation, they do have needs. Those who are open may be able to give retrospective information, and literature on the developmental process of coming out may assist in determining the needs of these even more hidden students.

Data Analysis and Interpretation

Qualitative data supports and enhances quantitative findings. Case material provides context and breathes life into numbers, and numbers can strengthen arguments based on descriptive data. Quantitative and qualitative data need to be analyzed in an appropriate fashion. Quantitative statistical analysis is relatively straightforward: usually frequencies, percentages, and means are the mainstay of needs assessments. However, researchers should not make comparisons between heterosexual and lesbian, gay, or bisexual student groups. Such a practice implies that differences are deficits from the "norm."

Qualitative data often involves content or theme analysis of interviews. In such cases, care must be taken not to impose biases and categorizations. Verifying interpretations with independent raters and with actual participants where possible is necessary for insuring quality control. Bias can also be lessened by presenting interview or open-ended questionnaire responses verbatim, thereby allowing the participants' own words to speak for themselves. In all cases, attention must be given to avoiding heterosexist language.

Use of Results

Results should be distributed to all interested parties: administrators, funding sources, student service professionals, and, of course, to the participants themselves. Presentation of results may be tailored to a particular audience as long as data are not misrepresented or withheld. Just as in data collection, distribution of results to lesbian, gay, and bisexual students may be an involved process of networking. However, this does not absolve the researcher of the obligation to follow through in this way.

Obviously, the primary use of needs assessment results is to know which services are satisfactory, which need to be modified, and which need to be developed. In developing new programs, it is very useful to continue collaborating with members of the lesbian, gay, and bisexual community. It may be useful to view the needs assessment as an early step in the process of developing an ongoing relationship with the lesbian, gay, and bisexual student population.

SUMMARY AND RECOMMENDATIONS

This chapter has described many of the issues facing lesbian, gay, and bisexual students, and recommended strategies for assessing the needs of this population. It is clear that these students remain at risk for harassment and discrimination on campus and in society-at-large.

There are common threads in the needs of lesbian, gay, and bisexual students: the need to manage the coming out process and positive identity development, the need for accurate and accessible information, and help with a host of stressors that result from stigmatized minority status. Internal turmoil and external lack of acceptance can combine to disrupt ability to function at tasks and relationships, and can undermine self-esteem. Legal restrictions and social norms may limit opportunities. Gender role socialization contributes to unique same-sex relationship dynamics which must be negotiated. Differences among lesbians, gay men, and bisexuals have yet to be adequately explored.

Needs assessment with lesbian, gay, and bisexual students demands special attention to issues such as confidentiality, sampling, and heterosexist bias in theory, instrumentation, and data interpretation. It provides challenges to develop services affirmative to lesbian, gay, and bisexual students.

In conclusion, we offer three recommendations. First, review and follow the guidelines outlined by Herek et al. (1991) for avoiding heterosexist bias in research. These guidelines should be the starting point for any research conducted on lesbian, gay, and bisexual issues (See Appendix H).

Second, use a variety of methods in assessing the needs of lesbian, gay, and bisexual students. Combinations of quantitative and qualitative methods are likely to give the best coverage of needs. Pay special attention to the unique constraints that research with these students requires—an accepting and knowledgeable working relationship, utmost concern with ethics, and an ever-vigilant stance with regard to heterosexist bias.

Finally, if there is one over-arching need for lesbian, gay, and bisexual students, it is the need for the creation of a lesbian-, gay-, and bisexual-affirming environment. The transformation of a typical repressive-to-ambivalent academic community to one that is supportive and accepting will not be an easy or quick process. It begins with personal examination by student service professionals—and all other staff and faculty—of their experiences, values, attitudes, and beliefs. It continues with education and consciousness-raising activities. Attention to heterosexist policies (e.g., married student housing policies) and procedures (e.g., demographic survey inclusion of indicators for same-sex partnerships as "marital status") is a beginning step for making the campus community more open and inclusive for its lesbian, gay, and bisexual students. Most universities hold a vision of creating an environment that fosters the growth of all its members. Lesbian, gay, and bisexual students must not be left out of this vision.

REFERENCES

Berger, G., Hank, L., Rauzi, T., & Simkins, L. (1987). Detection of sexual orientation by heterosexuals and homosexuals. *Journal of Homosexuality, 13,* 83–100.

Bigner, J. J. & Jacobsen, R. B. (1989a). The value of children to gay and heterosexual fathers. In F. W. Bozett (Ed.). *Homosexuality and the Family* (pp. 163–172). Harrington Park Press: Binghamton, NY.

Bigner, J. J. & Jacobsen, R. B. (1989b). Parenting behaviors of homosexual and heterosexual fathers. In F. W. Bozett (Ed.). *Homosexuality and the Family* (pp. 173–186). Harrington Park Press: Binghamton, NY.

Blumenfeld, W. J. (Ed.). (1992). *Homophobia: How we all pay the price.* Beacon: Boston.

Blumenfeld, W. J. & Raymond, D. (1988). *Looking at gay and lesbian life.* Beacon: Boston.

Bozett, F. W. (1989). Gay fathers: A review of the literature. In F. W. Bozett (Ed.). *Homosexuality and the Family* (pp. 152–159). Harrington Park Press: Binghamton, NY.

Browning, C., Reynolds, A. L. & Dworkin, S. H. (1991). Affirmative psychotherapy for lesbian women. *The Counseling Psychologist, 19,* 177–196.

Buhrke, R. A. (1989a). Female student perspectives on training in lesbian and gay issues. *The Counseling Psychologist, 17,* 629–636.

Buhrke, R. A. (1989b). Incorporating lesbian and gay issues into counselor training: A resource guide. *Journal of Counseling and Development, 68,* 77–80.

Buhrke, R. A. (1993). *Professionals advocating on lesbian and gay public policy: A call to action.* Presented at the Lesbian and Gay Public Policy Institute for Behavioral and Social Scientists and Mental Health Providers, sponsored by the American Psychological Association, Washington, D.C., April 23.

Buhrke, R. A., Ben-Ezra, L. A., Hurley, M. E. & Ruprecht, L. J. (1992). Content analysis and methodological critique of articles concerning lesbian and gay male issues in counseling journals. *Journal of Counseling Psychology, 39,* 91–99.

Buhrke, R. A. & Douce, L. A. (1991). Training issues for counseling psychologists in working with lesbian women and gay men. *The Counseling Psychologist, 19,* 216–234.

Burch, B. (1986). Psychotherapy and the dynamics of merger in lesbian couples. In T. S. Stein & C. J. Cohen (Eds.). *Contemporary Perspectives on Psychotherapy with Lesbians and Gay Men.* (pp. 57–72). Plenum: New York.

Carl, D. (1990). *Counseling Same-sex Couples.* W.W. Norton: New York.

Cass, V. C. (1979). Homosexual identity formation: A theoretical model. *Journal of Homosexuality, 4,* 219–235.

Chan, C. S. (1989). Issues of identity development among Asian-American lesbians and gay men. *Journal of Counseling and Development, 68,* 16–20.

Chapman, B. E., & Brannock, J. C. (1987). Proposed model of lesbian identity development: An empirical examination. *Journal of Homosexuality, 14,* 68–80.

Coleman, E. (1982). Developmental stages of the coming out process. *Journal of Homosexuality, 8,* 31–43.

Coleman, E. (1987a). Psychotherapy with homosexual men and women: Integrated identity approaches for clinical practice—Introduction. *Journal of Homosexuality, 14,* 1–8.

Coleman, E. (1987b). Assessment of sexual orientation. *Journal of Homosexuality, 14,* 9–24.

Committee on Gay and Lesbian Concerns. (1991). Avoiding heterosexual bias in language. *American Psychological Association:* Washington, D.C.

D'Augelli, A. R. & Rose, M. L. (1990). Homophobia in a university community: Attitudes and experiences of heterosexual freshmen. *Journal of College Student Development, 31,* 484–491.

DeMonteflores, C. (1986). Notes on the management of difference. In T. S. Stein & C. J. Cohen (Eds.). *Contemporary Perspectives on Psychotherapy with Lesbians and Gay Men.* (pp. 73–102). Plenum: New York.

DeMonteflores, C. & Schultz, S. J. (1978). Coming out: Similarities and differences for lesbians and gay men. *Journal of Social Issues, 34,* 59–72.

DiLapi, E. M. (1989). Lesbian mothers and the motherhood hierarchy. In F. W. Bozett (Ed.). *Homosexuality and the Family* (pp. 101–121). Harrington Park Press: Binghamton, NY.

Dillon, C. (1986). Preparing college health professionals to deliver gay-affirmative services. *Journal of American College Health, 35,* 36–40.

Dulaney, D. D. & Kelly, J. (1982). Improving services to gay and lesbian clients. *Social Work, 27,* 178–183.

Edelman, D. (1986). University health services sponsoring lesbian health workshops: Implications and accessibility. *Journal of American College Health, 35,* 44–45.

Elze, D. (1992). "It has nothing to do with me." In W. J. Blumenfeld (Ed.). *Homophobia: How we all pay the price.* pp. 95–113. Beacon: Boston.

Faderman, L. (1984). The "new gay" lesbians. *Journal of Homosexuality, 10,* 85–95.

Falco, K. L. (1991). *Psychotherapy with Lesbian Clients: Theory into Practice.* Brunner/Mazel, Inc.: NY.

Fassinger, R. E. (1991). The hidden minority: Issues and challenges in working with lesbian women and gay men. *The Counseling Psychologist, 19,* 157–176.

Ford, C. S., & Beach, F. A. (1951). *Patterns of sexual behavior.* Harper: New York.

Forstein, M. (1986). Psychodynamic psychotherapy with gay male couples. In T. S. Stein & C. J. Cohen (Eds.). *Contemporary Perspectives on Psychotherapy with Lesbians and Gay Men.* (pp. 103–138). Plenum: New York.

Friedman, R. C. (1991). Couple therapy with gay couples. *Psychiatric Annals, 21,* 485–490.

Garnets, L., Hancock, K. A., Cochran, S. D., Goodchilds, J. & Peplau, L. A. (1991). Issues in psychotherapy with lesbians and gay men: A survey of psychologists. *American Psychologist, 46,* 964–972.

Glaus, K. O. (1988). Alcoholism, chemical dependency, and the lesbian client. *Women and Therapy, 8,* 131–144.

Gonsiorek, J. C., & Weinrich, J. D. (1991). The definition and scope of sexual orientation. In J. C. Gonsiorek & J. D. Weinrich (Eds.). *Homosexuality: Research implications for public policy.* Sage: Newbury Park, CA.

Graham, D. L., Rawlings, E. I., Halpern, H. S., & Hermes, J. (1984). Therapists' needs for training in counseling lesbians and gay men. *Professional Psychology: Research and Practice, 15,* 482–496.

Hammersmith, S. K. (1987). A sociological approach to counseling homosexual clients and their families. *Journal of Homosexuality, 14,* 173–190.

Hays, D. H. & Samuels, A. (1989). Heterosexual women's perceptions of their marriages to bisexual or homosexual men. In F. W. Bozett (Ed.). *Homosexuality and the Family* (pp. 81–100). Harrington Park Press, Inc.: Binghamton, NY.

Herek, G. M. (1984). Beyond "homophobia": A social psychological perspective on attitudes toward lesbians and gay men. *Journal of Homosexuality, 10,* 1–21.

Herek, G. M., & Berrill, K. T. (1992). *Hate crimes: Confronting violence against lesbians and gay men.* Sage: Newbury Park, CA.

Herek, G. M., Kimmel, D. C., Amaro, H. & Melton, G. B. (1991). Avoiding heterosexist bias in psychological research. *American Psychologist, 46,* 957–963.

Hetherington, C., Hillerbrand, E., & Etringer, B. D. (1989). Career counseling with gay men: Issues and recommendations for research. *Journal of Counseling and Development, 67,* 452–454.

Hetherington, C., & Orzek, A. (1989). Career counseling and life planning with lesbian women. *Journal of Counseling and Development, 68,* 52–57.

Iasenza, S. (1989). Some challenges of integrating sexual orientations into counselor training and research. *Journal of Counseling and Development, 68,* 73–76.

Jick, T. D. (1983). Mixing qualitative and quantitative methods: Triangulation in action. In J. Van Maanen (Ed.). *Qualitative Methodology.* (pp. 135–148). Sage: Beverly Hills, CA.

Katz, J. (1976). *Gay American history: Lesbians and gay men in the U.S.A.* Avon: New York.

Kinsey, A. C., Pomeroy, W. B., & Martin, C. E. (1948). *Sexual behavior in the human male.* Saunders: Philadelphia.

Kinsey, A. C., Pomeroy, W. B., Martin, C. E., & Gebhard, P. H. (1953). *Sexual behavior in the human female.* Saunders: Philadelphia.

Klein, F., Sepekoff, B., & Wolf, T. (1985). Sexual orientation: A multi-variable dynamic process. *Journal of Homosexuality, 12,* 35–49.

Krajeski, J. P. (1986). Psychotherapy with gay men and lesbians: A history of controversy. In T. S. Stein & C. J. Cohen (Eds.). *Contemporary Perspectives on Psychotherapy with Lesbians and Gay Men.* (pp. 9–26). Plenum: New York.

Kuh, G. D. (1982). Purposes and principles for needs assessment in student affairs. *Journal of College Student Personnel, 23*, 202–209.

Lewis, L. A. (1984). The coming out process for lesbians: Integrating a stable identity. *Social Work, Sept–Oct,* 464–469.

Loiacano, D. K. (1989). Gay identity issues among Black Americans: Racism, homophobia, and the need for validation. *Journal of Counseling and Development, 68*, 21–25.

Lourea, D. N. (1985). Psycho-social issues related to counseling bisexuals. *Journal of Homosexuality, 11*, 51–62.

McCarn, S. R., & Fassinger, R. E. (1990). *Development of a model of sexual minority identity development.* Unpublished manuscript, University of Maryland.

Minton, H. L., & McDonald, G. J. (1984). Homosexual identity formation as a developmental process. *Journal of Homosexuality, 9*, 91–104.

Miranda, J., & Storms, M. (1989). Psychological adjustment of lesbians and gay men. *Journal of Counseling and Development, 68*, 41–45.

Nichols, S. E. (1986). Psychotherapy and AIDS. In T. S. Stein & C. J. Cohen (Eds.). *Contemporary Perspectives on Psychotherapy with Lesbians and Gay Men.* (pp. 209–240). Plenum: New York.

Nuehring, E. M., Fein, S. B. & Tyler, M. (1974). The gay college student: Perspectives for mental health professionals. *The Counseling Psychologist, 4*, 64–73.

Paroski, P. A. (1987). Health care delivery and the concerns of gay and lesbian adolescents. *Journal of Adolescent Health Care, 8*, 188–192.

Patton, M. Q. (1990). *Qualitative evaluation and research methods.* Sage: Newbury Park, CA.

Polkinghorne, D. E. (1991). Two conflicting calls for methodological reform. *The Counseling Psychologist, 19*, 103–114.

Rabin, J., Keefe, K. & Burton, M. (1986). Enhancing services for sexual minority clients: A community mental health approach. *Social Work, 31*, 294–298.

Reynolds, A. J. (1989). Social environmental conceptions of male homosexual behavior: A university climate analysis. *Journal of College Student Development, 30*, 62–69.

Ross, M. W., Paulsen, J. A. & Stalstrom, O. W. (1988). Homosexuality and mental health: A cross-cultural review. *Journal of Homosexuality, 15*, 131–152.

Savin-Williams, R. C. (1989). Coming out to parents and self esteem among gay and lesbian youths. In F. W. Bozett (Ed.). *Homosexuality and the Family* (pp. 1–36). Harrington Park Press: Binghamton, NY.

Schneider, M. (1991). Developing services for lesbian and gay adolescents. *Canadian Journal of Community Mental Health, 10*, 133–151.

Schwartz, R. & Hartstein, N. (1986). Group psychotherapy with gay men. In T. S. Stein & C. J. Cohen (Eds.). *Contemporary Perspectives on Psychotherapy with Lesbians and Gay Men.* (pp. 157–177). Plenum: New York.

Shannon, J. W., & Woods, W. J. (1991). Affirmative psychotherapy for gay men. *The Counseling Psychologist, 19*, 197–215.

Shernoff, M. (1991). Eight years of working with people with HIV: The impact upon a therapist. In C. Silverstein (Ed.). *Gays, Lesbians, and Their Therapists.* (pp. 227–239) W.W. Norton: New York.

Shively, M. G., & De Cecco, J. P. (1977). Components of sexual identity: *Journal of Homosexuality, 3,* 41–48.

Silverstein, C. (1991). Psychotherapy and psychotherapists: A History. In C. Silverstein, (Ed). *Gays, Lesbians, and Their Therapists.* (pp. 1–14). W.W. Norton: New York.

Smith, M. L. (1986). The whole is greater: Combining qualitative and quantitative approaches in evaluation studies. In D. D. Williams (Ed.). *Naturalistic Evaluation: New Directions for Program Evaluation, No. 30.* (pp. 37–54). Jossey-Bass: San Francisco.

Sophie, J. (1988). Counseling lesbians. In D. R. Atkinson & G. Hackett (Eds.). *Counseling Non-ethnic American Minorities.* pp. 307–318. Charles C Thomas: Springfield, IL.

Strommer, E. F. (1989). "You're a what?": Family member reactions to the disclosure of homosexuality. In F. W. Bozett (Ed.). *Homosexuality and the Family* (pp. 37–58). Harrington Park Press: Binghamton, NY.

Tajfel, H. (1981). *Human groups and social categories.* Cambridge University Press: Cambridge, MA.

Thompson, G. H., & Fishburn, W. R. (1977). Attitudes toward homosexuality among graduate counseling students. *Counselor Education and Supervision, 17,* 121–130.

Weinberg, G. (1972). *Society and the healthy homosexual.* New York: Anchor.

Wooden, W. S., Kawasaki, H. & Mayeda, R. (1983). Lifestyles and identity maintenance among gay Japanese-American males. *Alternative Lifestyles, 5,* 236–243.

Chapter 8

INTERNATIONAL STUDENT POPULATIONS
AND NEEDS ASSESSMENT

Susan Lynn Prieto

International students are an increasingly important population in
institutions of higher education in the United States, as these have
become ever more dependent on these students, particularly in the
sciences. Most international students are in engineering, business or
management, mathematics and computer sciences, or the physical and
life sciences. According to Pedersen (1991), in 1989 26.1% of new Ph.D.
recipients were students not from the U.S., considerably higher than the
12.2% in 1960.

Pedersen (1991) generally describes the international student population at that time in the following manner. He notes that more than half of
the international student population was from Asia and this proportion
continues to increase. In addition, about one-third of the international
student population at present is comprised of women. Most are in
four-year institutions and about two-thirds are in public schools.

Clearly, international students continue to have an impact on colleges
and universities across the United States, an impact that is increasing in
magnitude. Because of this, it becomes ever more important to understand this subpopulation of students on our campuses, and to be able to
assess and address their needs. This chapter will discuss common issues
facing international students and make recommendations for further
research. A list of supplemental readings is also included following the
chapter references. For specific discussion of needs assessment methodology as applied to non-majority groups please refer to Chapters Two and
Three. Because of the negative connotations associated with the word
"foreign," the population of students in question will be referred to
throughout the chapter as "international" students.

INTERNATIONAL STUDENT ADJUSTMENT
TO COLLEGES & UNIVERSITIES

Schram and Lauver (1988) assert that international students can feel more severe alienation from university life than non-international students. This is of concern to professionals on college and university campuses because of the possible effect of this phenomenon on the retention of these students, on their academic success, and satisfaction with their time spent in the United States. Specifically, international students are more likely to have positive academic and nonacademic experiences if they enjoy satisfying contact with the host culture, and the successful achievement of the educational goals that bring them to the U.S. is more likely to occur if the emotional and social atmosphere are pleasant and relatively stress-free. Host nationals benefit from international students' presence through social interaction with them, enrichment of the learning environment due to the addition of international students' experiences and perspectives, and the establishment of long-term commercial, trade and diplomatic links with other countries.

Pedersen (1991) has a very nice review of the current literature on research regarding international students and their adjustment and experiences in the U.S. He notes that there is not much coherence or consistency in this area of research because the research is quite varied, divergent, and unrelated in its approaches. Also, the goals of this body of research have not been conceptually defined and the theoretical formulations that have been proposed have not to date been validated. Thus, it is evident that this area of research is in a young stage of development, leaving much room for continued work.

Common theories to describe or explain the process of adjustment that international students experience rely on the ideas of curves and stages, culture shock, a focus on situational or background factors, social interaction and its effect on the adjustment process, and personality traits and typologies. Culture shock is one of the most common theories and the term implies three phases of acculturation. The first of the three stages is the contact stage, which is followed by conflict and adaptation. This theory relied on the U-curve concept of adaptation, indicating that the international student will initially feel excited and happy to be in the host culture. This will be followed by a period of feeling depressed, anxious, upset, confused, and angry. The last stage is characterized by the individual feeling more comfortable in the host culture, not as upset, anxious or depressed. This idea has been modified to resemble a W-curve as professionals have become more aware of the process that the international student undergoes upon re-entry into his/her home country, which also entails some period of adjustment. Although this theory has been useful to counselors and professionals dealing with international students, it has been difficult to do research on it as it encompasses many factors or variables.

Another theory addresses the process of adjustment that an international student faces from the point of view of two basic questions that the student is faced with. The first of these questions is "Is my cultural identity of value and to be retained?" and the second is "Are positive relations with the dominant society to be sought?" (Pedersen, 1991). Authors and theorists espousing this point of view indicate that the way that a student answers these two questions will help determine whether the individual experiences assimilation (giving up his/her cultural identity and moving into that of the larger society), integration (the individual maintains his/her cultural identity while also becoming part of the larger society), rejection (withdrawal and segregation from the host culture), or deculturation (feeling alienation, a loss of identity, high levels of acculturative stress and loss of contact with both the home and host cultures).

Yet a third research area, which comes from a variety of theoretical perspectives, takes a look at cognitive strategies that people use to develop their perception of in-groups and out-groups. Some of the research has focused on a number of different personality characteristics (such as empathy, interest in the local culture, flexibility, tolerance, and technical skill) that have been identified as important for adjustment in other cultures. The difficulty with this research is that it is difficult to define and measure these characteristics.

Hull (1978; cited in Schram & Lauver, 1988) found that the quality of contact and relationships between international students and host culture members is important in the adjustment of international students and in how satisfied they feel with their experience in the U.S. Burbach (1972; cited in Schram & Lauver, 1988) focused on feelings of alienation that international students sometimes experience, and noted that alienation seems to include feelings of powerlessness, meaninglessness, and loneliness. In this study, he examines variables that might be predictive of alienation among international students, and concluded that international students who have a high amount of social contact with host

country nationals are apt to report more satisfaction. There is controversy among theorists about whether a lot of contact with co-nationals
hinders international students' adjustment to the new country. In fact,
some argue that contact with co-nationals may be soothing and encouraging when they first come to the U.S. Some authors indicate that there is
no evidence for any relationship between gender and degree of alienation,
while others suggest that female international students may be more apt
to report more difficulty adjusting to life abroad than males. This still
needs to be clarified. Younger students and undergraduates tend to
adjust better to the host culture, but older students and graduates report
more academic and personal satisfaction with their stay abroad (Pedersen,
1991). Based on the literature surveyed, international students who experience less feelings of alienation are likely to be those who have extensive
social contact with Americans, live with a spouse, are older, are in
graduate studies, are male, come from Europe, are from an urban
background, and have been in the U.S. for a relatively longer period of
time. These findings offer service providers some direction when exploring areas of functioning with students, and to identify students who may
be more at risk.

Mallinckrodt and Leong (1992) tried to identify international students'
perceptions of their own adaptation to a new social and academic
environment, as well as to analyze the students' interactions in the host
culture as a way of examining and clarifying the nature of these students'
adjustment. They found that students identified the following as principal areas that required adaptation and adjustment for them: language
skills (particularly the mastery of formal as well as conversational English),
academic issues (mastering a new educational system and performing
well), cultural differences, racial discrimination, and social interactions
with host culture members. The two groups these authors looked at were
African and Chinese international students. They found that the Asian
students reported the most serious problems with language, the African
students in general had the least difficulty adjusting to the new academic
system, and both groups commented on the difference in male-female
relationships, as well as on feeling insecure and unwelcomed when faced
with instances of discrimination. In addition, Asian students who were
isolated reported more problems related to cultural, academic and social
adjustment, which is consistent with Hull's theory, mentioned previously.

Another study by Penn and Durham (1978) examined the levels of
cross-cultural interaction between American and international students,

the barriers to successful interaction, and ways in which to increase and improve interactions between the two groups. They found significant differences among American and international students in regards to the amount of contact they had with each other, with the amount of formal contact members of each group had with each other being less than the amount of informal contact. For international students, barriers to interaction included difficulty understanding the language and unfamiliarity with American customs. For American students, discomforts related to unfamiliarity with foreign customs and misinterpretations of actions, dislike of particular national groups or personal characteristics, and lack of common interests were the most common barriers. Specifically, they found that American students in liberal arts preferred increased contact with international students, as did American students who had traveled in various parts of the U.S. and abroad, and those who had attended institutions outside of the state. The authors thus found that interaction and friendship between American and international students are related to similarity in interests and academic field, the opportunity and willingness to participate in campus activities, the extent of previous travel, and previous experience in a number of different college settings. Stereotypes, preconceived views of other cultures, and different concepts of friendship were barriers to interaction between members of the two groups.

For both American and international individuals, whether student or faculty and staff, the skill of adapting to cultural diversity will become an increasingly important resource for facilitating learning about other people and themselves in this society that is becoming increasingly multicultural in nature. As seen previously, the research on international students seems to indicate that environmental and social factors are important in successful adjustment, thus we must be aware of the social supports that the international student has left behind and those that they do or do not have available to them in the U.S. In addition, it is important to examine the student's interpersonal skills, the extent of his/her involvement with host culture members and co-nationals, and assess and emphasize self-confidence, self-esteem and empathy, as higher levels of these will facilitate the learning of coping responses and adaptive behavior (Pedersen, 1991).

HEALTH CARE AND THE INTERNATIONAL STUDENT

One of the main areas in which assessing the needs of international students has been examined is in regards to the provision of health care services on college and university campuses. Ebbin and Blankenship (1986) comment that international students tend to utilize health services frequently, though Ogbudimpka, Cresswell, Lambert, and Kingston (1988) argue that they in fact underutilize these services. Regardless of the exact rate at which international students may avail themselves of health services, given the nature of the concerns and problems that may arise it is likely that health centers will at some point come into close contact with this student population. These students may come to the United States with different health values, belief systems, and attitudes about health, all of which need to be taken into consideration when designing services for this population.

Many services available to international students through health centers are less utilized than they might otherwise be due to a variety of barriers these students experience. Ebbin and Blankenship (1988) indicate that the most common barriers to health care noted by the majority of their respondents were language, health beliefs and attitudes, nutrition, sanitation, financial concerns, and reluctance to accept mental health counseling referrals. These were in contrast to the domestic students they examined, for whom the most common health care barriers were peer pressure and noncompliance. Vogel (1986) also notes language difficulties as a barrier, and indicated that for some international students unfamiliarity with the role of nurse practitioners, feeling overwhelmed by our insurance system, and concerns about whether medication might fit their bodies were also difficulties to overcome when thinking about seeking health care on campus. Ogbudimpka et al. (1988) found that, at their institution, families from Middle East countries reported having the most difficulty with language and that those international students who had little or no difficulty with language were more satisfied with their health care.

Vogel (1986) addresses the issue of language as a barrier, and also notes that sometimes what may be labelled as a language problem is really a problem of cross-cultural communication. Specifically, it is possible that an international student might understand the words, but not the meaning, which usually comes from the social context or interpersonal relationship. If the student is not familiar with either of these it will be difficult for him or her to understand what is actually being expressed. In addition, how something is communicated may vary greatly from culture to culture, and contribute to misunderstanding if there is not an awareness of these possible differences. For example, some cultures (like the Japanese) value silent understanding and indirect communication, while we value clarity of expression, asking for wants and needs directly, and negotiating openly and honestly. As providers of services (health care or others), it is incumbent upon us to be aware of these differences and find ways of communicating to the international student how our systems work, as well as designing ways that we can minimize some of these barriers for these students.

Several studies address the "foreign student syndrome," which is characterized by vague physical complaints that may bring an international student into the health services. Allen and Cole (1987) indicate that the theory behind this is that international students may somatize their problems because they feel that complaining of anxiety, loneliness, or distress and seeking psychotherapy for psychological symptoms of culture shock would entail loss of face (Ward, 1967; cited in Allen & Cole, 1987). They note that evidence for this syndrome came largely from case history material, and more rigorously examined the rate of attendance of international students to their health services, as well as the diagnoses received. They found no evidence for this "foreign student syndrome," but are also careful to note that this finding does not deny the very real problems that some international students have to deal with when coping with adjusting to a new culture.

What these authors do recommend is increased awareness in health service providers of possible communication difficulties, better preparation of international students for dealing with the needs of everyday life in the new country, and the issuance of a phrase book with basic medical questions that the student can then refer to in an attempt to improve understanding between health care professional and the international student. Other authors suggest printing written materials to be offered in health services in a number of different languages, and developing programming for international students on issues including exercise, nutrition, and stress reduction. It might also be helpful to have other faculty, staff or students who could be used as interpreters when necessary, and to ask the student what they might do or how they might be treated if they had these symptoms at home. This would help clarify their experiences with and beliefs about health care, as well as their expectations. As much as possible, both the diagnosis and treatment need to be discussed and negotiated with the international student according to his/her belief system. This might help the student's understanding of his/her concerns, decrease fears about the difficulty and/or its treatment, and increase chances for their compliance with treatment.

PSYCHOLOGICAL CONCERNS
AND THE INTERNATIONAL STUDENT

From the previous discussion, it comes as no surprise that international students often are seen at health service agencies on campus for concerns that may be more psychological in nature. International students seem less intimidated and/or stigmatized by seeking help from a medical rather than a psychological service. This section will review literature on adjustment difficulties of international students and the variables that seem to be influential in their obtaining psychological help.

Adjusting to a new country and lifestyle can be quite painful for international students. When they arrive, new circumstances suddenly impose a variety of competing roles and demands. The student must learn these quickly at the same time that they are attempting to settle into a new academic environment. Pedersen (1991) notes that when requirements are realistically perceived and effectively learned, the experience in the new culture becomes successful. However, when roles are not accommodated, the student may experience identity confusion and conflict in roles and may have difficulty with his/her sense of well-being. If this is not dealt with, it may present serious obstacles to the achievement of the student's educational goals.

International students, like other students in the U.S., must make educational/vocational decisions while in college. In addition, however, they need to acquire language skills (both in formal/professional arenas and in the informal/social setting), cope with possible differences in daily living skills, integrate new values, and adapt socially. Added stressors may surface if the student's home country is in political or social turmoil, or if there are emergencies in the family. Leong (1984; cited in Boyer & Sedlacek, 1986) identified three realms in which international students may have adjustment problems. The first are problems that are common to all students in a university setting, and that may have to do with developmental tasks, such as separation/individuation and relationship issues. Second are problems typically encountered by individuals who live outside of their home country for an extended period, including culture shock, culture fatigue, and role shock. The last realm of problems are those associated with being a student in another country, and include financial difficulties that need to be negotiated from a long distance, and immigration problems.

Many authors note that it is important to conceptualize the adjustment process for international students as ongoing, beginning with the preparations to leave and the actual departure from the home country to the time that the student returns home and attempts to reintegrate. Difficulties in this period of adjustment, and the stress associated with it, may be characterized by feeling the following: vulnerability, loneliness, a loss of identity, helplessness, wanting to depend on someone, fear, confusion, alienation and hostility (Schram and Lauver, 1988). The greater the cultural differences between the student's home culture and the host culture, the more complicated their adjustment is likely to be. Triandis (1991) refers to Murdock's cultural regions in the context of looking at how a student's culture compares to the home culture, and notes as well that the student's difficulty may show up differently because of the situation that is eliciting the student's response. Specifically, he reports that one can expect a student to have the most trouble when a similar situation calls for a very different response than they may be used to, whereas less difficulty may be experienced when the student faces a very different situation and needs to learn a different response. Thus, to the degree that similarity in cultures also extends to similarity in responses to situations, the student may have less difficulty adjusting. However, if similar situations call for very different responses, we can expect that the amount of difficulty experienced by the student will increase.

Triandis, Kashima, Shimada and Villareal (1986; cited in Triandis, 1991), described changes that can occur during acculturation, and note that sometimes people will change in the direction of the host culture. Others will become more like the host culture than the average member of that culture might be, while yet others may become ultranationalistic, affirming the "correctness" of their own culture. They hypothesize that individuals may take any one of these directions in different areas of their life. For example, it is possible that on things that are highly visible, such as clothing, an individual might take the second strategy and become more like the host culture than the nationals, while on items that are less visibly linked to behavior the individual might take the third strategy and show more ethnic affirmation.

It is important to both recognize that many of the issues an international student may face are similar to those of other students we deal with and that there are issues that may arise with international students that are related to their status as an individual coming to the United States from another country. In addition, each individual is unique, and this needs to be acknowledged to avoid stereotyping a student due to their status as an international student, and to be aware of resources that this particular student brings as well as difficulties that they may be experiencing because of their individual history, background, and personality.

Clark Oropeza, Fitzgibbon, and Baron (1991) discuss the types of stressors that can be important in precipitating mental health crises in international students, and identify six key areas. The first of these is culture shock, which can be exhibited in a number of ways, most of which can be seen as symptoms of depression and anxiety. The most difficult period in the culture shock process seems to come sometime between the third and twelfth month after arrival, and the timing and intensity of this low point may be affected by the degree of cultural difference between the student's home culture and the host culture, personality factors (including maturity, tolerance for ambiguity, flexibility and emotional stability), the student's preparation for the host culture, and how satisfied the student was in his/her home culture.

Changes in social status are the second factor that Clark Oropeza et al. (1991) discuss. These changes can be social and/or economic, and are particularly difficult when the student has enjoyed a high status at home or has had a career that they are now leaving in order to come to the U.S. to study. If a student's financial or social status is threatened upon coming to the U.S., feelings of loss, grief, and resentment may result as the student struggles to adjust to his/her new situation.

The third factor has to do with expectations about academic performance. In the past, international students tended to be the "cream of the crop" among students in their home country. Although this is no longer necessarily the case given some countries' increased resources for sending students overseas for studies, a student's expectations about their academic performance in a new and alien educational system may be unrealistically high. This can be particularly true at the beginning of their stay in the U.S. and if their educational system was very different from the system in the U.S. In addition, scholarships and other forms of financial aid can create increased pressure to perform. For some cultures, the student may feel additional pressure to perform well from feelings of family loyalty and pride. Last, if the student is not academically gifted, there may be some pressure that they could encounter as they face academic demands that they are not prepared to meet.

Feelings or experiences of isolation, alienation and discrimination may be another factor precipitating mental health difficulties in international students. Clark Oropeza et al. (1991) cite Heikinheimo and Shute's (1986) study that suggests that students who have language difficulties, who do not actively learn about the new culture, and who perceive themselves as targets of discrimination have more difficulty adjusting.

Family-related pressures are the fifth category of stressors that Clark Oropeza et al. (1991) discuss. These relate to international students who come to the U.S. with a spouse and/or children. The magnitude and scope of adjustment problems can become magnified when there are family members trying to adjust to the new culture as well. It is important to look at and be aware of differences in the rate of acculturation across family members as these may cause intrafamily tension and alienation among family members, possibly leading to disintegration of the family system. For example, it is not uncommon to find that children may become acculturated much quicker than their parents, which can cause tension as the parents struggle with how to instill and maintain their own cultural ways and values. In addition, the parent who is the student may acculturate at a different rate as well, as s/he has the structure of being a student to fall back on and more contact with American students. The spouse may feel isolated and alone, and have the most difficulty acculturating, particularly if s/he is not involved in activities that promote contact with others (co-nationals and/or other international students and Americans).

The last group of stressors that Clark Oropeza et al. (1991) discuss is really a miscellaneous category. These stressors may come from: political or social upheaval in the home country, as mentioned previously; cultural differences in male-female relationships; unrealistic fears about immigration authorities and possible deportation; emergencies, such as death or illness among friends or family at home; and deciding where to live after graduation or dealing with the anxiety of returning home, which can come from the conflict between loyalty to family and country, and the individual's acculturation to American mores and customs. It is important to be aware of these as possible precipitating stressors when faced with an international student experiencing symptoms of depression and/or anxiety.

As is evident, international students face adjustments in a lot of different arenas when they come to the United States to study, and may experience stress and tension in a variety of ways. In spite of this, these students may be generally reluctant to initiate a counseling relationship (Sue & Sue, 1977; cited in Boyer & Sedlacek, 1986). Dadfar and Friedlander (1982) note that international students who are inexperienced with professional help see it as a nontrustworthy, inappropriate way to address personal difficulties. They also report that Pedersen (1975; cited in Dadfar & Friedlander, 1982) found that international students tend to turn to fellow countrymen for help with personal problems. Students' preferences for sources of help have been studied in different groups of American students, and Dadfar and Friedlander (1982) undertook this question in international students. They found that, when dealing with an educational/vocational difficulty, international students preferred to turn to a faculty advisor, a parent, an older friend, or a fellow student, while American students would turn to faculty, relatives, or a counselor. As for emotional/social problems, they found that international students were less likely than Americans to turn to a friend, and more likely to look to faculty/advisors, counselors, and psychologists or physicians. They would also be likely to turn to parents or an older student. Overall, the study found that international students would be more likely to turn to formal sources of help, while American students seemed to prefer informal sources of help for emotional/social difficulties. If this is so, it would be important to provide international students with information about various formal sources of help during their orientation, so that they might avail themselves of these, if needed, until they develop more informal networks of help and support.

It has been mentioned previously that health services and medical personnel may be more likely to initially see an international student who needs some psychological attention. Some authors look at other factors that might influence international students' attitudes toward obtaining psychological help. Two areas considered are the differential effects of attitudes toward mental health issues between Western and non-Western societies, and the differential influence of American acculturation across nationalities. Western, including European and Latin-American, attitudes toward therapy seem to be more positive than non-Western (African and Asian) attitudes. Some authors wonder if

Western students may have a more positive attitude toward professional help because of fewer differences on dimensions of authoritarianism, restrictiveness, and acceptability of seeking help outside the family, but these hypotheses have not been tested or verified as of this date. It also seems to make a difference whether the student has sought psychological help previously (either in the U.S. or in their home country). Gender and educational level, on the other hand, have not been found to be predictive of international students' attitudes toward seeking professional help, nor has length of time in the United States or acculturation.

Some research indicates that international students underutilize counseling services, and suggests that there is a low level of awareness among these students about what counseling is and how it might be helpful, as well as low levels of satisfaction with experiences in counseling. Another group of studies indicate that international students use counseling under certain conditions. Specifically, they are most likely to seek counseling for educational and vocational problems. A last, seemingly contradictory, theme in this area of research is that international students use counseling at about the same rate as other students, but it emphasized the importance of counseling style when dealing with a student from another country. Specifically, results preliminarily show that international students tend to prefer direct to indirect methods in counseling, they look for a directive therapist that gives pragmatic information and emphasizes shared counselor-client responsibility, and that one needs to know about the client's specific culture to look for different ways to communicate and to be aware of other issues that may be impacting the student's difficulty.

Ka-Wai Yuen and Tinsley (1981) looked at how four different groups of students differed in their expectations of counseling. They included American, Chinese, African and Iranian students in their sample, and used the Expectancies About Counseling Questionnaire (Tinsley, Workman, & Kass, 1980; cited in Yuen & Tinsley, 1981) to measure these students' expectations about counseling, finding significant differences between the four groups of students on 12 of the 17 expectancy scales. American students expected the counselor to be less concrete, directive, empathic, nurturant, and expert than did international students. These students expect to play a more active role in the counseling relationship and admit more responsibility for the counseling process. The three groups of international students expected the counselor to be an authority figure prescribing more definite and clear-cut solutions to their

problems, and they saw themselves as less active in the process. Interestingly, Iranian and African students did not differ significantly on any
scale. African females had less concern with being emotionally involved
with the counselor, and would thus be expected to be more cognitively
and interpersonally reserved with the counselor. These results suggest
that African and Iranian students might be more receptive to reality-
oriented, directive, behavioral approaches to counseling, should they
seek psychological services.

Like the other two groups of international students, the Chinese
students in this study expected less direct confrontation from the counselor;
less openness, motivation and responsibility in the process of counseling
from themselves; less immediacy and concreteness in the counseling
process; and a less beneficial outcome. These authors suggest that,
behaviorally, these students might be more concerned with whether the
counselor is courteous, respects their privacy, and keeps their relationship distant and smooth. What may appear to be passivity on the student's
part may reflect the appropriate, accepted way of interacting with authority figures in their culture.

Boyer and Sedlacek (1986) addressed incoming international students'
perceptions about counseling, and found that these students indicated
an interest in seeking counseling for various concerns in order to improve
the efficiency of their studying, should anything jeopardize their educational goals. They wanted an advisor who would take an interest in them
and who knows the technical information important to students. As far as
their preferences as clients are concerned, they expected to: see an
experienced counselor; to speak frankly about their problems and the
causes of these; and did not expect to take psychological tests or do
assignments outside of the counseling session. These students expected
the counselor to be a "real" person and to make them feel free to say
whatever they think. This study did not differentiate students from
different cultural regions or groups, so it is not clear how this might
affect the results in terms of looking at differences along these dimensions among international students.

Further research on the help-seeking behavior of international students might look at data about their preferences at different points in
time. As these students go through different stages in their adjustment to
the host culture, their needs of counseling and of the therapist may vary.
Further research could be aimed at delineating and identifying what the
different needs at different stages might be, and how counseling interven-

tions might change accordingly. This research could also further explore cultural and gender differences among international students, and it would be helpful to have more process and outcome research conducted on students' experiences seeking help from various sources on campus.

Overall, Ka-Wai Yuen and Tinsley (1981) suggest that international students clearly need more information about counseling as a helping resource. In addition, counselors should be especially aware when working with international students, that the assumption that they and the student share common assumptions about the process may not hold true. The counselor may also need to remain sensitive to specific cultural differences, and may facilitate the development of a good relationship by finding out how the individual international student perceives the counseling process and that specific relationship, and by letting the client know what is realistic to expect. These suggestions hold true for any professional dealing with international students on a college or university campus.

As authors look at the issue of cross-cultural counseling with international students, several additional suggestions emerge. Siegel (1991) captures the essence when she notes that the key issue for international students is how to make the necessary adaptations to fulfill their educational and personal goals in the U.S., while at the same time figuring out how to hold on to their roots and a sense of cultural integrity. Our challenge as counselors is to figure out what our role is in facilitating this process for the student. Most importantly, it is helpful for professionals to acknowledge with the student that it may be difficult for him/her to solve problems in a way that may go against their values of privacy and independence. This acknowledgement may help the student develop trust in the process. A skilled counselor needs to understand the student's personality dynamics, look at developmental issues that may arise, examine the student's health status (physical and psychological), and be aware of cultural factors and circumstances. Balancing these is what the struggle will be for the therapist.

It is important for the student service professional to be aware of his/her own cultural values, to have respect for cultural diversity, to have (or acquire) knowledge about the particular group that the international student belongs to, and to have a genuine interest in other cultures. For many of us, it is important to be involved in the development of and participation in training and consultation activities that center on issues regarding international students and cross-cultural awareness and knowledge.

When exploring the student's cultural background, find out what the mental health mechanisms in that culture are like, and where the student might go for help, as well as what the structure would be likely to be. The professional must also need to be able to tolerate ambiguity and be creative and flexible in adapting or developing strategies that would be helpful in the client's attempts to cope with the new environment. For example, a counselor needs to have a large repertoire of verbal and non-verbal responses, so that s/he can use them appropriately (given knowledge about the student's cultural group) to communicate more effectively with the student. It is also important that the professional be sensitive to his/her tendency to cultural stereotyping, as well as the tendency to either over- or under-emphasize cultural differences. It can be difficult to understand the complexity facing an international student, trying to sort out what are issues that are specific to the individual and/or normal for that age group, and those issues that are related to being a person from one culture in an entirely different environment.

Pedersen (1991) points out that it is helpful for the professional to realize that "adjustment" means different things to different people, so finding out what the student expects would be essential. In general, it is beneficial to pay attention to the goals in seeking and providing assistance and what these might be for both parties involved in the process. Sometimes it would be in the student's best interests for the professional to serve as an advocate for the student, and to pull in international student advisors, residence hall staff, faculty or other university personnel, as needed, to help address the student's needs. It can be very helpful to teach students how to build support systems in this new culture, as well as to examine environmental factors that can be manipulated to help the student develop or master new skills that they might need to function more effectively in this setting. It may be helpful for counseling centers to develop peer support groups for international students.

CONCLUSIONS

Clearly, the research conducted to date on international students leaves room for improvement. It has, however, offered insights into themes and issues that appear to be important for faculty and staff on university campuses to be sensitive to and aware of as they deal with students who come from other countries and cultures. Given that the world appears to be becoming smaller with respect to interactions with different countries, it would behoove us to continue pursuing research in the areas of adjustment to different cultures, and issues that arise for both the individual entering into a new culture and the host nationals involved. Though this chapter has focused on the international student, it is this author's contention that it is of vital importance for us to spend time and energy on our own awareness and knowledge of, and sensitivity to, issues that may arise for us as we deal with people from cultures different from our own. Lee (1981; cited in Pedersen, 1991), found that the highest ranked barriers to good relationships for international students with U.S. nationals were negative American attitudes toward international students, a lack of sensitivity by Americans to cultural differences, as well as the international students' own isolation as foreigners. These results highlight the need for us to look at both sides of the coin, so to speak, when exploring the experiences of international students on our campuses. It would be exciting to conduct a needs assessment project that could focus on international and American students' needs in their interactions with each other.

It is important for those of us working with international students to be aware of our own cultural self-awareness and sensitivity, as well as of the assumptions we make about the world and the values we hold dear. Along with these, we need to foster openness to, and respect for, different value systems, which may challenge us as we are faced with systems that we find difficult to understand or agree with. In this work, it is also important to be able to tolerate ambiguity, as we are sure to be faced with new issues, ways of thinking and values on a regular basis. As we work with international students, it is helpful to be willing to learn with and from them, and to be able to let our genuine concern for people show through.

International students share a common experience in being away from their native land and living in an unfamiliar culture. In spite of this commonality, it is important to remember that these students represent distinct cultural groups as well, and that the degree to which any individual student is able to successfully adapt to their new environment depends on various factors, including the student's individual ability, motivation, background, and previous experiences. There can be as much difference between two students from the same country as there can be between any international and American student. Also influencing the student's adjustment are environmental factors. It is important for us, then, to consider interpersonal as well as intrapersonal dimensions, when faced with an international student in difficulty. Also helpful is to remember to see adjustment or adaptation as a process. This allows us to look at how we might be able to intervene to facilitate the student's journey in this process.

Pedersen (1991) has many suggestions for improving upon research addressing international students, the adjustment they go through, and the needs they might have, as do other authors reviewed. To summarize some of these suggestions, there are indications that we might do well to implement longitudinal studies of coping behavior in international students and to conduct research aimed at identifying criteria of favorable adjustment, attempting not to polarize adjustment as simply positive (desirable) or negative (undesirable). We need to distinguish, through further research, between the processes that immigrant (long-term) and sojourner (short-term) international students go through as they adjust to being in a culture different from their own, looking at similarities and differences in these processes. It would be helpful for us to define more clearly the concepts we research, and to coordinate research coming from different perspectives and areas, in an attempt to then provide a better sense of coherence to results, which would facilitate the development of, and further research on, theories.

College and university campuses would do well to continue to provide programming geared at this student population, keeping in mind that it might be helpful to target specific cultural groups of international students, as different needs might emerge associated with different geographical regions. Orientation programs would be good avenues for disseminating much information to international students about services provided, how the system works if they need to avail themselves of these services, what to expect from the process they might undergo as they enter the U.S., and to encourage them to become acquainted with Americans. It is important for international students to understand that they may need support from a variety of different people (co-nationals, other international students, and Americans) at different points in time, and to identify and practice skills that are essential in this culture for getting to know each other and communicating more effectively. Interventions could be designed to address feelings of powerlessness, meaninglessness, and social estrangement associated with feeling alienated. There have been some programs developed that address specific points mentioned previously, and it would be helpful to continue sharing these as they are developed. Support groups, classes in English conversation, and the use of peer counselors are other avenues to be considered in programming for this student population. It is essential that support on our campuses for cultural diversity and the valuing of differences come from top administration, as that sets the tone felt by students, faculty and staff, and that we cooperate with each other as we work on our own awareness of and sensitivity to different cultures, as well as on dealing with international students that come to our campuses.

REFERENCES

Allen, F.C.L. & Cole, J.B. (1987). Foreign student syndrome: Fact or fable? *Journal of American College Health, 35,* 182–186.

Boyer, S.P. & Sedlacek, W.E. (1986). Attitudes and perceptions of incoming International students. *Counseling Center Research Report* #4-86. College Park, MD: University of Maryland.

Clark Oropeza, B.A., Fitzgibbon, M., & Baron, A. (1991). Managing mental health crises of foreign college students. *Journal of Counseling and Development, 69,* 280–284.

Dadfar, S. & Friedlander, M.L. (1982). Differential attitudes of International students toward seeking professional psychological help. *Journal of Counseling Psychology, 29*(3), 335–338.

Ebbin, A.J. & Blankenship, E.S. (1986). A longitudinal health care study: International versus domestic students. *Journal of American College Health, 34,* 177–182.

Ebbin, A.J. & Blankenship, E.S. (1988). Stress-related diagnosis and barriers to health care among foreign students: Results of a survey. *Journal of American College Health, 36,* 311–312.

Heikinheimo, P.S. & Shute, J.C.M. (1986). The adaptation of foreign students: Student views and institutional implications. *Journal of College Student Personnel, 27,* 399–406.

Ka-Wai Yuen, R. & Tinsley, H.E.A. (1981). International and American students' expectancies about counseling. *Journal of Counseling Psychology, 28*(1), 66–69.

Mallinckrodt, B. & Leong, F. (1992) International graduate students, stress, and social support. *Journal of College Student Development, 33,* 71–78.

Ogbudimpka, J.E., Creswell, W., Lambert, B., & Kingston, R. (1988). Health needs assessment of International students and their families at the University of Illinois. *Journal of American College Health, 36,* 313–316.

Pedersen, P.B. (1991). Counseling International students. *The Counseling Psychologist, 19*(1), 10–58.

Penn, J.R. & Durham, M.L. (1978). Dimensions of cross-cultural interaction. *Journal of College Student Personnel, 19,* 264–267.

Schram, J.L. & Lauver, P.J. (1988). Alienation in International students. *Journal of College Student Development, 29,* 146–150.

Siegel, C. (1991). Counseling International students: A clinician's comments. *The Counseling Psychologist, 19*(1), 72–75.

Triandis, H.C. (1991). A need for theoretical examination. *The Counseling Psychologist, 19*(1), 59–61.

Vogel, S.H. (1986). Toward understanding the adjustment problems of foreign families in the college community: The case of Japanese wives at the Harvard University Health Services. *Journal of American College Health, 34,* 274–279.

Supplemental Readings

Althen, G. (1991). Some help and some myths. *The Counseling Psychologist, 19*(1), 62–63.

Atkinson, D.R. (1983). Ethnic similarity in Counseling Psychology: A review of research. *The Counseling Psychologist, 11*(3), 79–92.

Atkinson, D.R., Ponterotto, J.G., & Sanchez, A.R. (1984). Attitudes of Vietnamese and Anglo-American students toward counseling. *Journal of College Student Personnel, 25,* 448–452.

Chung, Y.B. (1992). *Training International Counseling Psychology Students.* Paper presented at the 1992 Great Lakes Regional Conference for Counseling Psychology, East Lansing, MI.

DeSouza, E., Prieto, S.L. & Dussair, P. (1993). *A needs assessment of American and International students.* Paper presented at the Southwestern American Psychological Association Convention, Corpus Christi, TX.

Evans, N.J. (1985). Needs assessment methodology: A comparison of the results. *Journal of College Student Personnel, 26*(2), 107–114.

Fouad, N.A. (1991). Counselors to counsel International students: Are we ready? *The Counseling Psychologist, 19*(1), 66–71.

Kuh, G.D. (1982). Purposes and principles for needs assessment in student affairs. *Journal of College Student Personnel, 23,* 202–209.

Leong, F.T.L. & Sedlacek, W.E. (1986). A comparison of International and U.S. students' preferences for help sources. *Journal of College Student Personnel, 27,* 426–430.

Mirsky, J. & Kaushinsky, F. (1988). Psychological processes in immigration and absorption: The case of immigrant students in Israel. *Journal of American College Health, 36,* 329–334.

Ozaki, R. (1988). Special academic counseling for International students. *Journal of College Student Development, 29,* 80–81.

Parr, G., Bradley, L., & Bingi, R. (1992). Concerns and feelings of International students. *Journal of College Student Development, 33,* 20–25.

Report of the National Association for Foreign Student Affairs—American College Health Association Joint Task Force on Foreign Student Health Care (1988).

Strategies for improving health care for foreign students and their dependents. *Journal of American College Health, 36,* 307–310.

Sue, S. & Zane, N.W.S. (1985). Academic achievement and socio-emotional adjustment among Chinese university students. *Journal of Counseling Psychology, 32*(4), 570–579.

Sweeney, M.A. Cottle, W.C., & Kobayashi, M.J. (1980). Nonverbal communication: A cross-cultural comparison of American and Japanese counseling students. *Journal of Counseling Psychology, 27*(2), 150–156.

Valdes, T.M. & Osborne, G.E. (1980). Vocational preferences of Latin-American International students. *Interamerican Journal of Psychology, 14*(1), 57–59.

Chapter 9

CONCLUSIONS AND EPILOGUE

JOSEPH E. TALLEY

Aprincipal conclusion of our work with regard to methodology is that, whenever possible, representatives from the group to be studied should be included in the selection of the questions that will be asked. Further, open-ended questions yielding qualitative and phenomenological data are at least as valuable as quantitative data for an in-depth understanding. Some measure of the respondent's likelihood of using whatever services are being inquired about is also most valuable data. Finally, an approach utilizing two or more methods of data collection offers great benefit. For more specific conclusions with regard to methodology, the reader is referred to the conclusions of the chapters themselves especially as set forth in Chapter Three.

It might be said that one of the primary purposes of conducting a multicultural needs assessment is to promote not simply greater tolerance of differences but rather a true valuing of the diversity among people. Thus, on the one hand there is a goal for our human environment to be changed. Multicultural needs assessments can assist in the process of identifying the specific foci in the human environment in which change is most essential and the specific means with the greatest probability of succeeding in the task. On the other hand, there are specific need-related goals for the constituent cultures that can be made known by way of multicultural needs assessments. One general goal for the multicultural society is for all people to feel more comfortable in both the physical and the human environment. Obviously, a greater valuing of diversity among humans enhances the likelihood of greater comfort for all.

However, these general aspirations must be studied in terms of their specific components and causes. For example, one such general aspiration pertains to the acknowledgement of a culture's heros. In the multicultural society all of our heros cannot be white males of northern

225

European ancestry. We must have heros that are similar in the most salient of ways to those in the constituent cultures in the society. Thus, less salient characteristics such as political affiliation (e.g., the communist party) may be irrelevant to hero status within a constituent group. Heros must emerge from the people and cannot be prescribed by those outside of the group. If the multicultural society does not have heros from all of its constituent groups, how can these constituents identify with that society, value it and work for its good?

On the campus, too, we must have members from the constituent cultures in positions of importance to likewise ensure the investment of people from all groups in the values, purposes and endeavors of the college or university. This is especially true for human service providers such as counseling and mental health professionals. The literature has shown that client-perceived similarity between client and counselor improves the outcome of and satisfaction with counseling and psychotherapy services. The reader is referred to reviews of the literature on this topic for more detail summarized by Talley, Butcher, and Moorman (1992).

At Duke University where most of us began our work with multicultural needs assessments, the results from the data collected were extremely valuable in gaining administrative support for two additional positions in the Counseling and Psychological Services agency. One position was to coordinate and deliver multicultural counseling, psychotherapy and related outreach services. The other position was to coordinate and provide services in the areas of gay, lesbian and bisexual concerns and human sexuality. The multicultural needs assessment was most helpful in presenting the rationale for these additional positions, as it was clear from the study that African-American and gay, lesbian and bisexual students in particular felt that they could not be adequately understood by a counselor or therapist who had not experienced similar dilemmas in life because of race and/or sexual orientation. Data collected from a utilization study (Talley, 1991) demonstrated that the percentage of African-American students from the student body as a whole using counseling services increased to actually exceed the percentage of Caucasian students, using the counseling services once an African-American psychologist was on the staff. Prior to the addition of this staff member, the percentage of African-American students from the student body seeking counseling and psychotherapy services at the agency was less than the percentage of the Caucasian students seeking those same services. This occurred despite the fact that utilization by Caucasian students was already high (over 12 percent of the total student population). Moreover, African-American students reported even greater satisfaction with the services received than did the Caucasian students in a client-satisfaction study conducted after the African-American psychologist was on the staff (Talley, 1992). This satisfaction rating is noteworthy as the satisfaction rating for the Caucasian students was high itself given that the overall mean rating for Caucasian students corresponded to the descriptor "quite satisfied."

Specific changes in favor of valuing the diversity among us have been and will be further identified by multicultural needs assessments as will be the specific interventions needed to actualize these changes. The particular changes and interventions necessary will vary from campus to campus. Nevertheless, it is probable that the major obstacle to implementing these necessary changes will be resistance by those who fear that their particular interests will be compromised with these changes.

In the psychodynamic model of the self a symptom arises when a wish of part of the self conflicts with a fear of another part of the self, and the conflict is not managed by useful defenses. So, too, in the multicultural society a problem (symptom) arises when a need (wish) of one part of the system conflicts with a fear of another part of the system and the conflict is not well regulated by coping mechanisms (defenses). With regard to the multicultural society as an organism, the fears of some constituent parts have heretofore often kept the needs of other constituent parts suppressed. As with the individual human organism, this results in the escalation of tension and the expenditure of a large amount of energy or resources in the defensive process.

In the psychotherapeutic treatment of the multicultural society we must, as in individual psychotherapy, enable those parts harboring unwarranted fears to realize that such fears are outmoded and are no longer, if indeed they ever were, the most productive response. In psychodynamic psychotherapy such realizing may come about by way of a constructive experience in living (Strupp & Binder, 1984). In such an experience, new learning at the emotional level takes place in the context of a relationship. Likewise, it is proposed that constructive experiences in living can be most efficacious inventions in the treatment of the multicultural society. As in the treatment of the individual, the curative component is largely in the relationship. With the society as the intervention target, change will also be a product of relationships with diverse others. However, it may begin with any of us in the therapeutic role offering a constructive experience in living to someone from another segment of the multicultural society.

A crucial component of individual psychodynamic treatment is often an observation/interpretation of the immediate process. That is, a statement responding to the question, "What's going on right now?" The parallel to this process observation in the societal treatment is the multicultural needs assessment. It, too, is a statement with regard to, "What's going on right now?" based on how it has been seen, heard or measured by the assessor/researcher. Further, the function of assessment will generally lead to the function of intervention. The intervener in individual treatment who offers a constructive experience in living may meet resistance in the form of an emotional assault from the client due to the client's accumulated negative feelings (usually anger) often thought of as a negative transference.

In a like manner, the multicultural needs assessor as the one promoting change in the way people relate to one another in the multicultural society may well find that they as the assessor/intervenor become the target of some individuals' accumulated negative feelings of anger and fear. These feelings are for the most part rooted in unawareness fostered by the lack of constructive experiences in living with diverse others. In order for this, now multicultural, society to be functional for anyone we must have relationships among all peoples in which we seek the mutual good, the win/win, rather than the fear driven quest for one up/one down. Our belief that there is not enough to go around for all of that which we all want and need and that there is an abundance of that which no one seems to want or need is perhaps mistaken. Multicultural needs assessment studies will tell us what we each feel that we need to thrive in order to contribute to our society. In so doing the multicultural assessment of needs can be a most potent instrument in the process of change and the transformation of relationships among diverse people.

REFERENCES

Strupp, H. & Binder, J. (1984). *Psychotherapy in a new key: A guide to time-limited dynamic psychotherapy.* Basic Books: New York.

Talley, J. (1991). The annual statistical report of Counseling and Psychological Services. Unpublished manuscript, Duke University, Counseling and Psychological Services, Durham, NC.

Talley, J. (1992). Client satisfaction study results. Unpublished manuscript, Duke University, Counseling and Psychological Services, Durham, NC.

Talley, J., Butcher, T. & Moorman, J. C. (1992). Client satisfaction with very brief psychotherapy. In J. Talley (Ed). *The predictors of successful very brief psychotherapy: A study of differences by gender, age and treatment variables.* Charles C Thomas: Springfield, IL.

APPENDICES

APPENDIX A

SAMPLE GENERAL POPULATION QUESTIONNAIRE

For each of the following, indicate your rating by circling the number that best describes how important this need is to YOU at the PRESENT TIME. We greatly appreciate your participation and effort in enabling us to better serve the students at Duke.

Please circle the letter of the service mode for any topics you are *relatively certain* you would actually use, EVEN if you were moderately busy with other activities.

| | OF WHAT GRADE IMPORTANCE? | | | | | 1 to 1 at CAPS | Group/ Seminar at CAPS | Educational Presentation Elsewhere on Campus |
	none	little	some	very	extremely			
	1	2	3	4	5	A	B	C
1. Choosing my major	1	2	3	4	5	A	B	C
2. Finding written information about careers and educational programs	1	2	3	4	5	A	B	C
3. Understanding my career-related: interests	1	2	3	4	5	A	B	C
skills	1	2	3	4	5	A	B	C
values	1	2	3	4	5	A	B	C
personality	1	2	3	4	5	A	B	C
4. Planning my career or vocation	1	2	3	4	5	A	B	C
5. Improving my study skills	1	2	3	4	5	A	B	C
6. Managing my time effectively	1	2	3	4	5	A	B	C
7. Making decisions & solving problems	1	2	3	4	5	A	B	C
8. Assertively standing up for myself	1	2	3	4	5	A	B	C
9. Communicating more effectively	1	2	3	4	5	A	B	C
10. Developing my leadership skills	1	2	3	4	5	A	B	C
11. Dealing with concerns about sexual identity	1	2	3	4	5	A	B	C
12. Coping with the stresses in my life	1	2	3	4	5	A	B	C
13. Overcoming my fears about taking tests	1	2	3	4	5	A	B	C
14. Dealing with my eating habits	1	2	3	4	5	A	B	C
15. Controlling my smoking	1	2	3	4	5	A	B	C

233

	OF WHAT GRADE IMPORTANCE?					1 to 1 at CAPS	CAPS groups	Educational Presentation
	none	little	some	very	extremely			
16. Resolving disagreements with others	1	2	3	4	5	A	B	C
17. Dealing with obstacles to completing a major project or paper	1	2	3	4	5	A	B	C
18. Understanding and coping with loneliness	1	2	3	4	5	A	B	C
19. Interacting with people of the opposite sex	1	2	3	4	5	A	B	C
20. Developing my helping skills (listening, communicating, caring, etc.)	1	2	3	4	5	A	B	C
21. Dealing with concerns about sexually transmitted diseases	1	2	3	4	5	A	B	C
22. Dealing with AIDS-related issues	1	2	3	4	5	A	B	C
23. Coping with a physical or medical problem	1	2	3	4	5	A	B	C
24. Exploring my marital expectations	1	2	3	4	5	A	B	C
25. Setting reasonable expectations for myself	1	2	3	4	5	A	B	C
26. Improving my relationships with others	1	2	3	4	5	A	B	C
27. Developing self-confidence and self-esteem	1	2	3	4	5	A	B	C
28. Dealing with bulimia (binging/purging)	1	2	3	4	5	A	B	C
29. Getting myself energized to tackle my goals	1	2	3	4	5	A	B	C
30. Dealing with an unwanted pregnancy	1	2	3	4	5	A	B	C
31. Making choices about my sexual behavior	1	2	3	4	5	A	B	C
32. Clarifying my values	1	2	3	4	5	A	B	C
33. Increasing my control of drug usage	1	2	3	4	5	A	B	C
34. Increasing my control of alcohol usage	1	2	3	4	5	A	B	C

	OF WHAT GRADE IMPORTANCE?					1 to 1 at CAPS	CAPS groups	Educational Presentation
	none	little	some	very	extremely			
35. Dealing with friends or family who use/ abuse: a. alcohol	1	2	3	4	5	A	B	C
b. drugs	1	2	3	4	5	A	B	C
36. Coping with sadness or depression	1	2	3	4	5	A	B	C
37. Coping with my separation or divorce	1	2	3	4	5	A	B	C
38. Dealing with a death	1	2	3	4	5	A	B	C
39. Dealing with my parents' divorce or separation	1	2	3	4	5	A	B	C
40. Becoming more independent	1	2	3	4	5	A	B	C
41. Coping with the end of a relationship	1	2	3	4	5	A	B	C
42. Enriching a relationship I have	1	2	3	4	5	A	B	C
43. Dealing with male/female stereotypes	1	2	3	4	5	A	B	C
44. Combining family and school/career	1	2	3	4	5	A	B	C
45. Finding and enjoying leisure time	1	2	3	4	5	A	B	C
46. Making friends	1	2	3	4	5	A	B	C
47. Coping with issues of being in a couple	1	2	3	4	5	A	B	C
48. Coping with being a victim of sexual aggression: a. rape by stranger	1	2	3	4	5	A	B	C
b. acquaintance rape	1	2	3	4	5	A	B	C
c. incest	1	2	3	4	5	A	B	C
49. Dealing with homesickness	1	2	3	4	5	A	B	C
50. Learning to live with roommates	1	2	3	4	5	A	B	C
51. Handling competition	1	2	3	4	5	A	B	C

	OF WHAT GRADE IMPORTANCE?					1 to 1 at CAPS	CAPS groups	Educational Presentation
	none	little	some	very	extremely			
52. Overcoming my fears about speaking in public or in groups	1	2	3	4	5	A	B	C
53. Being part of a two-career couple	1	2	3	4	5	A	B	C
54. Lessening procrastination	1	2	3	4	5	A	B	C
55. Other/Comments/Suggestions								

PLEASE ANSWER THE FOLLOWING:

1. Looking over the list of survey items, are there topics that are so interesting to you that use of the service would be a high priority for you? If so, list *up to three* of these by writing the item number in the space:

_____

2. On which day of the week would you be most likely to attend a program? _____

5. Where on campus would you be most likely to notice a posted flier?

_____

6. We are particularly interested in assessing the needs of special groups of Duke students who may have unique patterns of concerns. Please check if you fall into any of the following groups:

3. When would you be most likely to attend?

_____ beginning of fall semester
_____ middle of fall semester
_____ end of fall semester
_____ summer session
_____ beginning of spring semester
_____ middle of spring semester
_____ end of spring semester
_____ doesn't matter

4. How would you be most likely to hear about a workshop? Please rank in order the top three by marking them, with most important marked #1.

_____ another student
_____ Cable 13
_____ *Chronicle* classified ad
_____ *Chronicle* display ad
_____ *Duke Dialogue* announcement
_____ faculty member
_____ posters or fliers
_____ resident advisor or programmer
_____ special mailing
_____ university official
_____ WXDU

_____ International Student
_____ Student Athlete
_____ Gay or Lesbian Student
_____ Black Student

Sex
_____ Female
_____ Male
Age _____
Year in School
_____ FR
_____ SO
_____ JR
_____ SR
_____ Grad School
_____ Prof School

Marital Status
_____ single
_____ married
_____ divorced
_____ separated
_____ widowed
Residence:
_____ on-campus
_____ off-campus

Ethnicity
_____ Asian
_____ Black
_____ Caucasian
_____ Hispanic
_____ American Indian
_____ Other _____

APPENDIX B

SPECIAL POPULATION SAMPLE SUPPLEMENTARY QUESTIONNAIRE

Additional Questions for Gay and Lesbian Students

OF WHAT GRADE IMPORTANCE? MODE OF SERVICE DELIVERY

	none	little	some	very	extremely	1 to 1 at CAPS	CAPS group	Educational Presentation
1. Knowing of gay/lesbians:								
a. faculty	1	2	3	4	5	A	B	C
b. counselors	1	2	3	4	5	A	B	C
c. medical staff	1	2	3	4	5	A	B	C
who would be especially sensitive to your needs								
2. Acknowledging homosexuality to:								
a. self	1	2	3	4	5	A	B	C
b. parents	1	2	3	4	5	A	B	C
c. siblings	1	2	3	4	5	A	B	C
d. friends	1	2	3	4	5	A	B	C
3. Issues of role conflict and role expectations	1	2	3	4	5	A	B	C

	1	2	3	4	5	A	B	C
4. Issues of parenting	1	2	3	4	5	A	B	C
5. Fear of lifestyle exposure	1	2	3	4	5	A	B	C
6. Assistance in meeting others	1	2	3	4	5	A	B	C
7. Lack of organized social support structures	1	2	3	4	5	A	B	C
8. Special issues in gay or lesbian couples/ relationships	1	2	3	4	5	A	B	C
9. AIDS related issues:								
a. Fear of death and dying	1	2	3	4	5	A	B	C
b. Grieving for other's deaths from AIDS	1	2	3	4	5	A	B	C
c. Fear of isolation and stigmatization	1	2	3	4	5	A	B	C
d. Loss of financial/occupational status	1	2	3	4	5	A	B	C
e. Helplessness	1	2	3	4	5	A	B	C
f. Guilt feelings	1	2	3	4	5	A	B	C
g. Fear of contagion	1	2	3	4	5	A	B	C
i. Loss of self-esteem	1	2	3	4	5	A	B	C
h. Lack of information about AIDS— treatments, transmission, etc.	1	2	3	4	5	A	B	C
10. Other/Comments/Suggestions _____								

APPENDIX C

SPECIAL POPULATION SAMPLE SUPPLEMENTARY QUESTIONNAIRE

Additional Questions for International Students

OF WHAT GRADE IMPORTANCE? MODE OF SERVICE DELIVERY

	none	little	some	very	extremely	1 to 1 at CAPS	CAPS group	Educational Presentation
1. Adjusting to different social customs or ways (e.g., holidays)	1	2	3	4	5	A	B	C
2. Feeling frustrated with studying and communicating in a different language	1	2	3	4	5	A	B	C
3. Getting used to a new lifestyle	1	2	3	4	5	A	B	C
4. Becoming used to the effects of a new climate (weather) on how you feel	1	2	3	4	5	A	B	C
5. Adjusting to different social rules and regulations (e.g., greetings, invitations)	1	2	3	4	5	A	B	C
6. Adjusting to differences in dating and relationship customs	1	2	3	4	5	A	B	C
7. Feeling overwhelmed by the workload at Duke as compared to your home country	1	2	3	4	5	A	B	C

8. Dealing with differences that develop between what you want and what your parents or culture expects   1   2   3   4   5   A   B   C

9. Finding different systems of morals and values in the United States   1   2   3   4   5   A   B   C

10. Worrying about adapting study skills you developed in your home country to academic demands here   1   2   3   4   5   A   B   C

11. Making friends in a new and different culture   1   2   3   4   5   A   B   C

12. Adapting to a different culture   1   2   3   4   5   A   B   C

13. Other/Comments/Suggestions _____

APPENDIX D

SPECIAL POPULATION SAMPLE SUPPLEMENTARY QUESTIONNAIRE

Additional Questions for Duke Student-Athletes

OF WHAT GRADE IMPORTANCE? MODE OF SERVICE DELIVERY

	none	little	some	very	extremely	1 to 1 at CAPS	CAPS group	Educational Presentation
1. The amount of time and effort I must spend practicing my sport	1	2	3	4	5	A	B	C
2. Stress of competition in my sport	1	2	3	4	5	A	B	C
3. Concerns about relationship(s) with my coach(es)	1	2	3	4	5	A	B	C
4. Concerns about relationship(s) with my teammates	1	2	3	4	5	A	B	C
5. Concerns about relationship(s) with non-athlete students	1	2	3	4	5	A	B	C
6. Effects of a sport-related injury	1	2	3	4	5	A	B	C
7. Dealing with my sense of self-esteem as it relates to my academic performance	1	2	3	4	5	A	B	C

242

8. Dealing with my sense of self-esteem as it relates to my athletic performance   1 2 3 4 5 A B C
9. Dealing with athletic burnout   1 2 3 4 5 A B C
10. Learning performance enhancement techniques: relaxation/stress management   1 2 3 4 5 A B C

    imagery/visualization   1 2 3 4 5 A B C

    attention/concentration control   1 2 3 4 5 A B C

11. Wanting to feel more comfortable using:

    a. CAPS services   1 2 3 4 5 A B C

    b. other counseling services   1 2 3 4 5 A B C

12. Other/Comments/Suggestions

If you feel comfortable in indicating which sport(s) you participate in, please circle the number(s) below that correspond:

1. Baseball
2. Basketball—men's
3. Basketball—women's
4. Cross-country—men's
5. Cross-country—women's
6. Fencing—men and women
7. Field hockey
8. Football
9. Golf—men's
10. Golf—women's
11. Lacrosse
12. Soccer
13. Tennis—men's
14. Tennis—women's
15. Swimming—men and women
16. Track—men's
17. Track—women's
18. Volleyball
19. Wrestling
20. Other _____

APPENDIX E

SPECIAL POPULATION SAMPLE SUPPLEMENTARY QUESTIONNAIRE

Additional Questions for Black Students

OF WHAT GRADE IMPORTANCE? MODE OF SERVICE DELIVERY

	none	little	some	very	extremely	1 to 1 at CAPS	CAPS group	Educational Presentation
1. Difficulty developing, establishing or maintaining black identity on campus	1	2	3	4	5	A	B	C
2. Trouble approaching professors	1	2	3	4	5	A	B	C
3. Pressure to associate more than I wish to with: a. other black students	1	2	3	4	5	A	B	C
b. non-black students	1	2	3	4	5	A	B	C
4. Difficulty relating to: a. black students	1	2	3	4	5	A	B	C
b. non-black students	1	2	3	4	5	A	B	C
5. Concerns about: a. dating black students	1	2	3	4	5	A	B	C
b. interracial dating	1	2	3	4	5	A	B	C
6. Dealing with racism a. on the Duke campus	1	2	3	4	5	A	B	C
b. in society at large	1	2	3	4	5	A	B	C
7. Wanting an ongoing small group to discuss common concerns of black students	1	2	3	4	5	A	B	C
8. Wanting a black counselor/therapist to work with me on my concerns	1	2	3	4	5	A	B	C

9. Feeling at a disadvantage in class because of:

a. others' attitudes towards blacks	1	2	3	4	5	A	B	C
b. my academic preparation	1	2	3	4	5	A	B	C
c. my background or life experience	1	2	3	4	5	A	B	C

10. Feeling that my culture is not appreciated or is stereotyped

	1	2	3	4	5	A	B	C

11. Concerns about relating to:

a. my home community	1	2	3	4	5	A	B	C
b. the off-campus social environments	1	2	3	4	5	A	B	C

12. Difficulty discussing my concerns openly with:

a. any students	1	2	3	4	5	A	B	C
b. faculty	1	2	3	4	5	A	B	C
c. professional counselors/therapists	1	2	3	4	5	A	B	C
d. other staff	1	2	3	4	5	A	B	C

13. Difficulty in dealing with the majority culture and understanding how it works

	1	2	3	4	5	A	B	C

14. Other/Comments/Suggestions _____

APPENDIX F

SPECIAL POPULATION COVER LETTER

Duke University

DURHAM
NORTH CAROLINA
27706

COUNSELING AND PSYCHOLOGICAL SERVICES
SUITE 214 OLD CHEMISTRY BUILDING

TELEPHONE (919) 684-5100

January 25, 19 _ _

Dear Student:

Counseling and Psychological Services (CAPS) is interested in
determining the personal/social and career/vocational counseling-
related needs of Duke students. We intend to use the information
to help us offer better programs and services for students.

In order to serve all students in the best way possible, we are
especially interested in hearing from some particular groups of
students. Knowing the psychological and counseling-related needs
of student-athletes is very important to us. Some professionals
who advise and counsel student-athletes have been kind enough to
collaborate with us in formulating some of these questions, and
some questions have been derived from similar studies done at
other universities. Student-athletes have traditionally been
underserved in many environments, and your input could be crucial
in helping us to determine how you could be better served in the
future.

We would like you to complete this brief questionnaire. It will
take only a few minutes. While your participation is strictly
voluntary, we would greatly appreciate it because each person's
responses are highly valuable reflections of the concerns of
students at Duke. Since we are protecting the confidentiality of
your responses through the use of a numerical coding system, do
not write your name on the questionnaire.

As always, all responses will be completely confidential.

Please return the completed questionnaire in the enclosed stamped,
addressed envelope as soon as possible. If we have not heard from
you in three weeks, we will contact you again.

If you have any questions, feel free to contact me at CAPS
(684-5100). Thank you very much for your cooperation.

Sincerely, on behalf of the CAPS staff,

Joseph E. Talley, Ph.D.

Joseph E. Talley, Ph.D.
Coordinator of Research
and Program Evaluation

Jane Doe, Ph.D.
Department of Athletics

JET/s
Enclosures

APPENDIX G

SAMPLE GENERIC FOLLOW-UP LETTER

Duke University

DURHAM
NORTH CAROLINA
27706

COUNSELING AND PSYCHOLOGICAL SERVICES
SUITE 214 OLD CHEMISTRY BUILDING

TELEPHONE (919) 684-5100

February 15, 19_ _

Dear Student:

Approximately three weeks ago we sent you an assessment survey for counseling and psychological service related needs. Since we did not receive all of the completed questionnaires we are sending you a second questionnaire and envelope. Although your participation is voluntary, we would like to note again the great value of your responses. Since we are only sending questionnaires to a select sampling of students, we encourage you to take the few minutes to complete the survey and return it. The information gathered will enable us to offer the best services we can to all Duke students.

If you have already completed and returned the first questionnaire please disregard this letter.

Your responses are completely anonymous.

If I can answer any questions you may have about the project, you may contact me at 684-5100.

We thank you for your contribution to the counseling and psychological services for Duke students.

On behalf of the CAPS Staff,

Joseph E. Talley Ph.D.

Joseph E. Talley, Ph.D.
Coordinator of Research
 and Program Evaluation

JET/s
Enclosures

APPENDIX H

HEREK ET AL. (1991) GUIDELINES FOR AVOIDING HETEROSEXIST BIAS IN RESEARCH

Formulating the Research Question

1. Does the research question ignore or deny the existence of lesbians, gay men, and bisexual people?

2. Does the research question devalue or stigmatize lesbian, gay, and bisexual people?

3. Does the research question reflect cultural stereotypes of lesbians, gay men, and bisexual people?

4. Does the research question implicitly assume that observed characteristics are caused by the subjects' sexual orientation?

Sampling

1. To what degree is the sample representative?

2. If the sample is not a probability sample, does it include sufficient diversity to permit adequate assessment of relevant variables?

3. Is the sample appropriate for the research question?

Research Design and Procedures

1. Is sexual orientation the variable of interest?

2. Is sexual orientation assessed appropriately?

3. Are comparison groups appropriate to the research design?

4. Do questionnaire items or interview protocols assume heterosexuality?

5. Do the researchers' personal attitudes and feelings influence participants' responses?

6. Do experimental manipulations presume that participants are heterosexual?

Protection of Participants

1. Is information obtained about sexual orientation and behavior truly confidential, or what are the limits to confidentiality?

2. Does the research procedure reinforce prejudice or stereotypes among heterosexual respondents?

3. Does the procedure have negative effects on lesbian, gay male, or bisexual participants?

4. Does the recruitment procedure intrude inappropriately on potential participants' privacy?

5. Does the observation procedure intrude inappropriately on participants' privacy?

6. Does the assessment of sexual orientation create stress for participants?

Interpreting and Reporting Results

1. Is an observed difference assumed to reflect a problem or pathology of lesbian, gay, or bisexual participants?

2. Does the language reflect heterosexist bias?

3. Are the limitations of the research findings stated appropriately?

4. Has the researcher attempted to anticipate distortions or misinterpretations of findings by the lay public and in the popular media?

5. Have the results been disseminated to research participants or to the larger gay community?

From: Herek, G. M., Kimmel, D. C., Amaro, H. & Melton, G. B. (1991). Avoiding heterosexist bias in psychological research. *The American Psychologist, 46,* 958–962.

AUTHOR INDEX

SUBJECT INDEX